PRAISE FOR
THE LIVE ENTERPRISE

Value chains must go beyond efficiency and become responsive and resilient. *The Live Enterprise* offers a practical approach to reimagine processes through sentient principles and systems design.

—Scott Vollet, Executive Vice President, Global Operations,
Tempur Sealy International

Flexible architecture and unified platforms are critical to rapidly launch and scale businesses that can ride the wave of disruption. In *The Live Enterprise*, Kavanaugh and Tarafdar share a "design to evolve" mindset and a blueprint for the digital runway that makes it possible.

—Michel Langlois, Chief Development Officer, Calix, Inc.

The triple helix mindset drives toward a more equitable, regenerative, and ultimately prosperous society. *The Live Enterprise* approach offers a practical blueprint to help make this a reality.

—John Elkington, sustainability pioneer,
cofounder at Volans, and author of *Greens Swans:
The Coming Boom in Regenerative Capitalism*

At the SAP Engineering Academy we build around the core idea that people and the right value systems can drive large-scale changes. *The Live Enterprise* lays out these principles plainly and clearly for global business leaders.

—Ferose V.R., Senior Vice President and
Head of the SAP Engineering Academy

Shared digital infrastructure and APIs are essential to scale IoT capabilities in a flexible, cost-efficient manner. *The Live Enterprise* describes a 'digital runway,' a practical platform approach that allows leaders to focus on realizing business opportunities instead of overcoming technology obstacles.

—Prakash Chakravarthi, CEO and Cofounder, Machfu

The only way we'll solve the big structural challenges is to recognize we all live in an interconnected world and have mutual responsibilities. *The Live Enterprise* shares an operating model for firms to prosper in the disruptive digital age, yet also emphasizes the humanity and shared responsibility required to make it happen.

—Jamie Metzl, futurist, global affairs expert, and acclaimed author; founder and chairman of OneShared.World

Nature is the ultimate sustainable economic engine. In *The Live Enterprise*, Kavanaugh and Tarafdar bridge the genius of nature with a blueprint for business to thrive in the digital age, while meeting our environmental and social responsibilities.

—Enric Sala, National Geographic Explorer-in-Residence and author of *The Nature of Nature: Why We Need the Wild*

In *The Live Enterprise*, Kavanaugh and Tarafdar show how every business can complement their drive for intelligent technology with a human-centric mindset. They provide a roadmap to reimagine how we maximize today's economic opportunities while evolving to an equitable, sustainable, and prosperous future.

—Vinay Menon, Senior Client Partner and Global Lead for the AI practice at Korn Ferry

Professionals and students alike are focused on finding work that aligns well with their values. In *The Live Enterprise*, Kavanaugh and Tarafdar provide a guide for next generation business principles, while also aligning to greater social purpose and responsibilities.

—Dr. Christopher Marquis, Professor in Sustainable Enterprise and Management at Cornell University, and author of *Better Business: How the B Corp Movement Is Remaking Capitalism*

THE LIVE ENTERPRISE

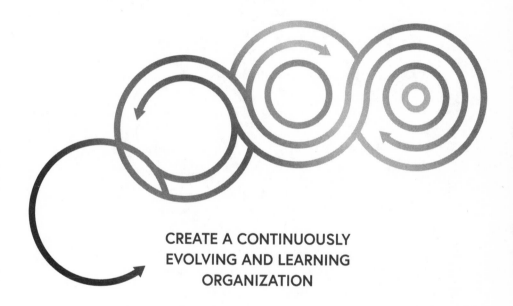

**CREATE A CONTINUOUSLY
EVOLVING AND LEARNING
ORGANIZATION**

JEFF KAVANAUGH

RAFEE TARAFDAR

New York   Chicago   San Francisco   Athens   London   Madrid
Mexico City   Milan   New Delhi   Singapore   Sydney   Toronto

1 2 3 4 5 6 7 8 9   LCR   26 25 24 23 22 21 20

ISBN   978-1-264-26433-9
MHID   1-264-26433-X

e-ISBN   978-1-264-26434-6
e-MHID   1-264-26434-8

Library of Congress Cataloging-in-Publication Data

Names: Kavanaugh, Jeff, author.
Title: The live enterprise : create a continuously evolving and learning organization / Jeff Kavanaugh.
Description: New York : McGraw Hill, [2021] | Includes bibliographical references and index.
Identifiers: LCCN 2020047126 (print) | LCCN 2020047127 (ebook) | ISBN 9781264264339 (hardback) | ISBN 9781264264346 (ebook)
Subjects: LCSH: Big business--Management.
Classification: LCC HD69.P75 K39 2021 (print) | LCC HD69.P75 (ebook) | DDC 658.02/3—dc23
LC record available at https://lccn.loc.gov/2020047126
LC ebook record available at https://lccn.loc.gov/2020047127

McGraw Hill books are available at special quantity discounts to use as premiums and sales promotions or for use in corporate training programs. To contact a representative, please visit the Contact Us pages at www.mhprofessional.com.

For my parents, Lee and Irma, who showed me the path that I follow; for my wife, Melanie, with whom I travel it; and for my children, Katherine and Terri Lynn, whose paths are just beginning.

J.K.

For Shaista, Rehan, and my family.

R.T.

CONTENTS

FOREWORD

Nandan Nilekani

Our understanding of how businesses should operate has evolved over the millennia. From the most basic barter systems to high-frequency stock market trading, the complexity of commerce moves inexorably forward and with increasing speed.

As a result, business leaders must find new ways of thinking, new frameworks just to keep pace, let alone lead our peers. Combined with the COVID-19 pandemic, the accelerated pace of change—technological, social, and political—demands a new mindset.

At Infosys, that new mindset is known as the Live Enterprise, the model through which all our questions, answers, and decisions can be filtered.

The idea is simple but deceptively so. A business should adopt the most advantageous aspects of a living creature, one that senses and responds instantly to external stimuli. If our hands accidentally touch a hot burner on a stove, the body instinctively jerks that hand away in a fraction of a second. We are already safe before we even realized we were in danger.

I got a great deal of experience while leading the Aadhaar initiative in India to provide a unique digital identity to more than 1.25 billion residents, and through the work I did subsequently to help envision UPI, a state of the art payment infrastructure. Both these population-scale platforms are part of the India Stack, that is bringing presence-less, paperless, and cashless service delivery to over a billion people in India. I learnt a great deal about driving transformation at scale, speed and sustainably.

When I came back to Infosys in 2017, I wondered, why not apply these learnings on transformation to global enterprises that are also large and complex and need to reinvent themselves to be like the digital natives? And why not start with Infosys to refine and demonstrate the model to the market?

The world—both its people and organizations—is bombarded with signals. Signals from markets, governments, and areas in which we never think to look. Those who seek to evolve must understand and react more quickly, and accept uncertainty as a constant.

Although this approach seems designed to manage the upheaval created by the current global crisis, Live Enterprise has been a companywide priority even before this disruption. The origins date back several years earlier when we realized our clients and our own company needed to be more resilient.

Organizations that raised their resilience in the years leading up to 2020 were better positioned for this historic period. Change due to COVID-19 was forced on everyone, even those who benefitted most from the status quo. For some companies, survival has been a day-to-day, moment-to-moment effort—no strategy, just hard work. However, most of us realize that work ethic is important but not enough.

Disrupting yourself makes you stronger and better prepared for the disruptions you can't control. In a sense, that's what our company did, not knowing the dangers ahead except for the dangers of standing still. Learning and innovation go hand in hand. The arrogance of success is to think that what you did yesterday will be sufficient for tomorrow.

Still, knowing you need to disrupt or be disrupted is easy; we've heard that advice and warning for years. That refrain is now louder than ever. Even the first small step toward self-disruption isn't that hard. It's the first great leap, the all-in commitment that gives organizational leadership a pause.

Infosys was a successful Indian firm for its first decade. Starting with economic liberalization in the early 1990s, we purposefully decided to transform into a global company. The alternative was to fade into the background or fade away entirely. A critical component of success is knowing when to challenge yourself and go all out, whether it's as an individual employee or the entire organization.

It's especially difficult for established institutions to respond decisively to change. New organizational structures and models provide an opportunity to build these ways of thinking directly into a company's DNA. This approach pushes us to more closely examine important issues, such as stakeholder capitalism and the skills gap. Otherwise, it would be human nature to fall back on approaches that served us well to date, but not necessarily in the future.

The human element can hold us back or propel us forward. The most advanced, innovative, and respected companies often have the most impressive digital tools. However, adoption of that technology and decisions about how best to use it flow from people and their mindsets. When we talk about disruptions and swoon over the latest advances, it's easy to lose sight of the fact that humans are at the core of all innovation and are the beating heart of a Live Enterprise.

When used for its highest purpose, technology amplifies and empowers humans rather than replaces them. Imagine an organization where the creativity of a workforce is fully unleashed in the service to achieve audacious goals.

Such personal realization requires continuous learning. An organization can't advance if its workforce is standing still. We must be both employer and educator, sharing a parallel journey that isn't always well illuminated.

A Live Enterprise—no matter the size—must also learn from potential competitors and adopt the best practices and features we see in Silicon Valley and other high-tech centers of influence. Infosys and its more than 240,000 employees strive to match the speed and agility of startups, which have set the pace for business and innovation.

When these efforts succeed, the result is a networked, collaborative organization with seamless teamwork as a crucial attribute. Then the best of the organization can be brought to every internal and external interaction.

Ideas are a fuel that can be found throughout a Live Enterprise. True leaders are able to harness the collective ideas, insights, experience, and knowledge found in almost any organization. Those ideas, however, offer little value if they are trapped in bureaucracy and can't reach escape velocity.

Established industry giants can no longer afford to take months to make decisions and years to execute them. Companies must rapidly respond to the stimuli around them. If they don't, competitors will.

At Infosys, we created this idea of the Live Enterprise and applied it to ourselves first. Our clients need to know that we believe in what we advocate. Who wants a meal prepared by a chef who wouldn't eat his own cooking? Or seek treatment from a doctor who wouldn't follow her own advice?

We created a system where repetitive operations are streamlined and automated so our people can focus on the customers, their own teams, and investment in their own learning.

We have accelerated our efforts to become a Live Enterprise but aren't ready to congratulate ourselves just yet. Live Enterprise is a path to travel, not a destination to reach. There is no endpoint where we become completely resilient, 100 percent agile, and perfectly intuitive. If we implement this strategy thoroughly, we will always be evolving into a new, better version of ourselves.

ACKNOWLEDGMENTS

To Infosys

We thank the following people at Infosys for their encouragement and support:

Nandan Nilekani, for defining the vision of Live Enterprise and guiding, mentoring, and supporting us through the journey and without whom this would not have been possible.

Pramod Varma and Sanjay Purohit, as partners to Infosys for mentoring, guiding, asking the right questions, and ensuring that we are thinking big and doing the right things.

Salil Parekh, UB Pravin Rao, Ravi Kumar S., Mohit Joshi, Binod H. R., Deepak Padaki, Krish Shankar, Jasmeet Singh, Karmesh Vaswani, Anand Swaminathan, Ashish Kumar Dash, Richard Lobo, Nandini S., and Sushanth Tharappan, for their sponsorship and support.

Narendra Sonawane, Thirumala Aarohi, Nabarun Roy, Purohit V.S., Rajkumar R., Harish Gudi, Rajesh Thampy, Priyapravas Avasthi, Ramkumar "Dargha", Allahbaksh, Peeyush Agarwal—the core team of Infosys Live Enterprise to bring this to life.

Delivery leadership: Satish H. C., Dinesh Rao, Shaji Mathew, Srikantan Moorthy, Narisimha Kopparapu, Balakrishna D. R., Rajeev Ranjan, Rajesh Varrier, Srini Kamadi, Shishank Gupta, Rajneesh Malviya, Indranil Mukherjee, Vibhuti Kumar Dubey, Prasad Joshi, Nitesh Bansal, Ravi Kiran Kuchibhotla, Ramesh Amancharla, and all delivery leaders.

The Infosys Knowledge Institute Team—especially Kerry Taylor, whose creativity, energy, and blood-and-guts passion was truly inspirational.

Also, IKI's Nikki Seifert, Jeff Mosier, Ramesh Narayan, and others, for their contribution and support.

For reviewing and providing inputs—Nandini S., Anoop Kumar, Shan Latheef, Rajeev Nayar, Sebastian Lewis, Ben Wiener, Prasad Joshi, John Gikopoulos, Anand Santhanam, Jonquil Hackenberg, Alok Uniyal, Skyler Mattson, Rajesh Ahuja, and Naresh Chaudhary.

Information Services team—Amit Gupta, Ganapathi Raman Balasubramanian, Gaurav Kumar, Himanshu Arora, Kiran Gole, Ramesh G., Shilpa Aphale, Sunil Thakur, Vadiraj Adiga, Vinod Sai, Babuji Rajendra, Priya Jacob, Muthukrishnan Sankaraiah, Ashvini Upadhyay, SenthilKumar C., Anil Yadav and the extended IS team.

Education, Training, and Assessment team—Shyamprasad K. R., Prajith Nair, Kiran N. G., Padma Bhamidipati, Rajeev Vutthharahalli, Jayan Sen, and the extended ETA team.

Quality team—Anoop Kumar, Alok Uniyal, Ganesh Subramanian, Srinivas S., Gaurav Agarwal, and the extended quality team.

Computers & Communications Division team—Prasad, Praveen, Ashok, Shivabasu, Yogi, and extended CCD team.

Business Enabling Function teams—Sharmistha Adhya, Deepa Premkumar, Saraswathi C., and extended HR team..

Strategic Technology team—Allahbaksh Asadullah, Sreeram V, Dhoomil Sheta, Jaskirat Sodhi, Vidya Lakshmi, Lakshmi Indraganti, Joe Walter, Vikash Kumar, Vishwanath Taware, Sridhar Murty, Sesha Sai Koduri, Subramanian Radhakrishna, Rakesh Pissay, Sachin Agarwal, William Barry and Ashim Bhuyan.

Experience Design Team: Manoj Neelakanthan, John Philip R., Senthil Kumar Subbayya, Tanvi Padmanabh Kelkar, Sreyashi Dastidar, Ajai Raghav P.C., Ralf Gehrig, Thomas Blackburn, and more.

Infosys Consulting team—Jayalakshmi Subramanian, Soumya Bhattacharya, Diana Salomi, Amit Munshi, Tarkeshwar Kumar Singh, Vaibhav Khandelwal, Vipin Gopan, Rohan Agrawal, Srishti Sharma, and Leston Dsouza

Global Delivery—Shyam Kumar Dodduvala, Sudhanshu Hate, Shashidara B. R., Ramaswami Mohandoss, Manesh Sadasivan, Koshy Varghese, Binooj Purayath, Ashok Panda, Syed Ahmed, Manas Sarkar, Hasit Trivedi, and extended team. Also, Vivek Raghavan for guiding on AI services.

Information Security Group team—Vishal Salvi and extended team.

Data Privacy Office team—Srinivas P.

Legal and Intellectual Property cell—Jyoti Pawar, Faiz, and extended team.

Marketing team—Sumit Virmani, Balaji Sampath, Suyog, Harini Babu, and Ajai Raghav P.C.

Live Enterprise Go To Market team—Mitrankur Majumdar, Navin Rammohan, Kshitij Shah, Venugopal Nair, Rajiv Puri, Ravi Taire, Uday Kotla, Henry Johnston, and Santosh K.C.

Jeff Kavanaugh

No book is possible without the help of many generous contributors. I thank the many people across Infosys, mentioned in our nearby Infosys acknowledgement. Also, my thanks to the business leaders and subject matter experts whose work is cited in the book and who shared their experiences with me through Infosys Knowledge Institute research, as a client, in the classroom, or beyond.

This book would not have happened without my agent, Jim Levine, and my publisher team at McGraw-Hill, especially Cheryl Segura, championing the project at the very start, and Stephen Isaacs for continuity across development and launch. Also, heartfelt thanks to Mark Fortier, Norbert Beatty, and the team at Fortier PR.

Thanks to Infosys for allowing me to guide and grow the Infosys Knowledge Institute, which provided support for research and interviews for the book. Another round of thanks to the Knowledge Institute team, especially Kerry Taylor, who poured his blood, sweat, toil, and tears into the development of this book. Last, I thank my wife, Melanie, and daughters, Katherine and Terri Lynn.

Rafee Tarafdar

Live Enterprise is the collective journey of every Infoscion, and without their collaboration, contribution, and encouragement this would not have been possible. I thank all the named and unnamed Infoscions who are working on our transformation to be a Live Enterprise and are now partnering with our clients in their own transformations.

This book would not have happened without Jim Levine, Cheryl Segura, Stephen Isaacs, Mark Fortier, Norbert Beatty, and the team at Fortier PR to help get the word out and amplify the message.

I thank my wife, Shaista, and son, Rehan, for encouraging and supporting in writing this book. Without their support and patience, this would not have been possible.

1

THE LIVE
ENTERPRISE MODEL

Ten Digits

On September 29, 2010, 10 people met in Tembhli, a village in the Indian state of Maharashtra, to receive their Aadhaar numbers, the very first in India, perhaps even in the world. Aadhaar is a 12-digit unique number based on an individual's unique biometric details such as fingerprints and iris scans, plus demographic data such as date of birth and address. Named after the Hindi word for "foundation," Aadhaar is managed by the Unique Identification Authority of India (UIDAI),[1] with each user issued a card cross-referenced with their biometric data held in a database. Infosys cofounder Nandan Nilekani stepped away from his highly successful tenure as CEO to launch this audacious Indian moonshot. The original idea behind Aadhaar was simple—"better inclusion"—to create a centralized system based on a single recognizable ID to replace the former decentralized system, which often left marginalized people struggling to obtain state services and was prey to corruption.

Since those first 10 people in Tembhli, Aadhaar has become the world's largest biometric ID system, with World Bank Chief Economist Paul Romer calling it the most sophisticated ID program in the world.[2] Aadhaar now has over 1.2 billion enrolled members and has seeded over 250 additional

1

programs, delivering high-velocity access to government and private sector services. In effect, Aadhaar has become a digital network shifting the equilibrium of citizen and state, at scale. The initiative took only six years to reach a billion people—from 10 *digits* (fingers on two hands) to *10* digits (a billion). This is all the more remarkable because the experts at the Bank for International Settlements concluded that based on current state in 2008, India was predicted to take a full 46 years to get from 20 percent banking inclusion to 80 percent.

Aadhaar was the first move in the India Stack,[3] the project creating a unified software platform to bring India's population into the digital age. India Stack is a set of application programming interfaces (APIs) that allows governments, businesses, startups, and developers to use a unique digital infrastructure to solve India's hard problems toward presence-less, paperless, and cashless service delivery.

These APIs have brought millions of Indians into the formal economy by reducing friction, plus fostered innovation to build products for financial inclusion, healthcare, and educational services at scale. At the same time, Aadhaar costs only $1.16 for each enrollment,[4] the lowest of any ID program in the world. From the government's perspective, they drove a paradigm shift in the way government services are delivered in a transparent, accountable, and leakage-free model—saving the Indian government as much as $12.4 billion in costs annually.[5]

How were Aadhaar and India Stack able to make this moonshot leap in enrollment and financial impact in under a decade? The answer is deceptively simple—*it was designed to evolve from inception.* In essence, it was an exponential decade of progress. Nandan and the other architects of Aadhaar were justifiably proud. Yet as he stepped away from government service, he wondered, "Why can't we apply the India Stack learnings in enterprises that are also large, complex, and struggle to make nonlinear moves in their systems?"

That question was very much on Nandan's mind when he came back to Infosys in 2017 as chairman of the board. That is how the India Stack principles mutated from a societal platform and were reapplied in the corporate world as the genesis of Live Enterprise. Many of the principles proved to be applicable in a commercial enterprise, shifting the landscape equilibrium to higher purpose and higher performance.

The Next Big Leap

When Nandan returned to Infosys in 2017, it was a similar but different company. While the campuses were still pristine and the staff completed projects with professionalism and energy, the previous innovative high-growth trajectory had become operationally, asymptotically stale. The employee experience was desktop centric, enterprise processes had not leveraged the power of digital native technologies, and open-source adoption was limited. Putting it politely, there were ample opportunities across Infosys to be more agile, responsive, and networked, and to increase the velocity of ideas and innovation.

We took a hard look at our own organization, as what had served us phenomenally well for over three decades had reached the limits of its effectiveness. Innovation had become more an exercise in optimization and efficiency, not creativity and brand value. After a succession of founder CEOs, it took an external CEO and then return of a charismatic founder to find the courage to change the strategy and enterprise operating model. This change was difficult because the executive team was justifiably proud of their legacy and the economic miracle that propelled Infosys to that point. For the subsequent transformation, senior leadership commitment was critical to be sure, but there are also specific practices highlighted in this book that actually made it happen and became part of the company culture.

This agile startup resilience imperative was not unique to Infosys. As a technology consulting and services firm, Infosys has a firsthand view to the digital transformation journeys of over 1,400 of the largest, most complex enterprises on the planet. These are not trivial commercial arrangements—often strategic, decades-long relationships with multiple active programs at each client. This responsibility requires us to be practical and deliver results in the tight space of moving requirements, shrinking budgets, and a dynamic set of stakeholders. This perspective also provides many data points, as we observe, assist, and colead in the digital journeys of our clients.

Recognizing the need for change, our senior executives tasked a small group of Infosys leaders and external visionaries to brainstorm as to the next potential, exponential leap. That spawned more research and experimentation, specifically on the future of experience, cloud, data, artificial intelligence (AI), edge computing, cybersecurity, organizational model, and potential conceptual constructs to aid in the journey. Through that process the idea emerged that *while the industrial economy was shaped by Adam Smith's invisible hand, we hypothesized that the digital age is constructed by the invisible brain.* We then deconstructed what that meant and how to do it.

We developed principles that could sit on top of such a brain—how to create zero proximity and conduct simulations—and we drew parallels from the biological brain and how the enterprise can replicate it. We imagined how to leverage the potential of 240,000 people as if they were all connected together as one, and how such an enterprise would be sentient because that's how human brains function. However, sentience is a state, so we chose "Live" as the theme because it conveys motion and embodies evolution—a journey, not a destination.

The India Stack success with identity, electronic credential, and unified payments gave our team the confidence this can be applied within enterprises at scale, and let us reimagine what the next couple of decades would look like for Infosys and industry overall. Traditionally, companies find a solution and then immediately move to replication. They find a problem, pilot in some areas to prove that it works, and then say, "now let's replicate." At Infosys we think differently. We also conduct that experimental pilot, we find it works, and then we *don't* replicate it—we unbundle it. What works in Dallas may not work in Frankfurt. The solution is unbundled in Dallas—say, we find there's one policy, one process, and three skills required. Something is moved to the enterprise learning platform, something goes into the policy framework, and so on. Then it can be rebundled for Frankfurt and see how it works there. This unbundle, rebundle, unbundle, rebundle is like the natural world. We call it dolphining, for how dolphins swim in the ocean. Like dolphins, the model keeps going up and down, and up and down, in cycles. Over time the frequency becomes faster and more efficient, because an organization gets better at the "unbundle—rebundle—apply" approach to improvement and adoption.

All of this thinking, principles, and ideas went into conceptualizing the Live Enterprise. We reimagined Infosys to be an ecosystem of humans and things that are connected with each other through a network that is continuously emitting signals and is observed, processed, and acted upon by a digital brain. This brain manages the connective knowledge and ecosystem, learns from each interaction, and drives value exchange in each interaction. This is all designed with a platform mindset, a digital runway for the company.

Before developing market offerings, and consequently platform services around these offers, we applied the ideas and technology at Infosys to prove the concept, refine the approach, and show evidence of success. We and our Infosys colleagues experienced all this firsthand during the transformation at Infosys, and through working with clients on their journeys as well. This experience led us to envision and develop a new, nontraditional operating model for the modern era.

The Case for Live Enterprise

As we undertook our journey at Infosys, we stayed focused on the fundamental question: *How can large complex enterprises behave like startups with nonlinear moves while maintaining resilience?*

The research for this book shares the learnings from putting these ideas into practice at Infosys. It also highlights feedback from clients facing similar challenges and extends earlier Infosys research tracking the progress of digital transformation globally. In each of the last few years, the Infosys Knowledge Institute surveyed more than 1,000 respondents from large companies globally about the digital initiatives they adopted. Based on their responses, we categorized companies into low, medium, and high-performance categories. Across the multiple studies, we found that organizations readily moved from the low to medium category, but making the leap to the highest level was far less frequent. Despite investment and management support, these companies reached a digital ceiling (see Figure 1.1).

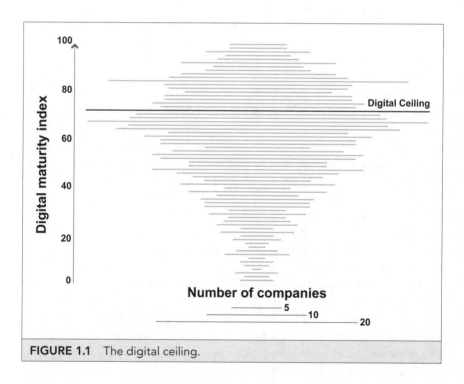

FIGURE 1.1 The digital ceiling.

What held these companies back, and what was special about firms that did reach the next level? What did they do differently? We used our own company as the ultimate laboratory to experiment aggressively, scale efficiently, and adopt with empathy.

Our Infosys experience, complemented by client services and our research, has provided an abundance of data points as to what works and what does not. How do we know the Live Enterprise model works? This approach helped Infosys increase its market valuation from $33 billion to $69 billion (over 100 percent) in three years. Importantly, it provided enterprise resilience during the COVID-19 pandemic, moving 240,000 workers from office to remote work in a matter of days, and actually surpassing previous year financial results in the quarter ending June 2020, in the heart of the global lockdown. Infosys has also helped numerous companies make the transition to digital technologies and resilient, sustained performance. However, this book is not about Infosys—it shares insights and practical recommendations for leaders to improve their own operating model and performance. It also celebrates the emerging stars of the post-COVID digital age, business leaders who evolve their legacy business, as well as visionary stakeholder capitalists who are blazing a trail for environmental and social impact.

The promise and peril of the digital future has been forecast for years, from turn-of-the-century dotcom boom and bust, through the rise of mobile applications and social media, and more recently through Industry 4.0. What's changed is that exponential technologies like cloud, mobile, AI, open source, and Internet of things have matured and converged. We are seeing the results of this converged life-cycle maturity at the same time that stakeholder capitalism has come of age: the next generation of customers and employees is more than simply aware of sustainability and equality—they demand action from enterprises. Globalism has spurred the rise of the corporate city-state, where large enterprises have additional societal responsibilities in addition to, or perhaps even because of, their role as generators of financial returns. And of course, the COVID-19 pandemic was the match that lit the tinderbox and dramatically accelerated change. We see this manifested in seven areas or domains, and traditional and Live Enterprise perspectives for each are illustrated in Table 1.1.

The very nature of **organizations** has come under pressure. Hierarchical and even matrix models are simply too static in a world where, much like water follows lower-lying land, real authority and influence cut across traditional silos and evolve frequently based on customer and project needs. Organizations must be able to address many initiatives simultaneously and update structures quickly based on market needs.

The way we think about **experience** has changed. In their lives outside work, employees can ask Alexa for anything, enjoy the conveniences of smart homes, and use a variety of communication apps without having to type emails. Then they come to work and deal with a torrent of emails, struggle with archaic processes and tools, while creating cumbersome manual workarounds. Employees, especially digital natives, count on anytime, anywhere, personalized, and predictive experience, whether work occurs in an office building or from home.

TABLE 1.1 Evolution of operating model elements.

Operating Model Element	Traditional (from)	Live Enterprise model (to)
Organization	• Command and control • Functional, line-of-business-based large teams • Physical workplace • Waterfall processes • Technology as enabler	• Self-organizing work teams • Cross-functional and platform-mindset-based small teams • Anytime, anywhere workplace • Distributed agile processes • Technology as strategic differentiator
Experience	• Efficiency • Usability • Limited personalization • One size fits all • Qualitative	• Effectiveness • Delight • Predictive • Inclusive design • Measurable
Value Chain	• Distant from input • High latency • Offline, periodic analysis • Periodic surveys • Complex process	• Proximity to source • Zero latency • Instant simulation • Instant micro-feedback • Guided practice
Decisions	• Deterministic • Manual • What-if analysis • Distributed organizational knowledge • Insights for review	• Stochastic • Semi-automated • Predictive and prescriptive • Connected and curated organizational knowledge • Insights to actions
Talent	• Cost center • Retention • Problem-solving • Instructor-led training • Uniskilled	• Competitive advantage • Employee engagement • Problem-finding • Anytime, anywhere, any topic learning • Multiskilled
IT Systems	• Features and functionality mindset • Designed for known requirements • Monolithic systems • Moderate automation • Limited telemetry	• Platform mindset • Designed for evolvability • Unbundled services • Extreme automation • Observable
Change	• Program-driven large change • Program level • Top down • Existing routines • Unidirectional	• Sigma of micro-changes • Significant change level • Bottom up • Building new routines • Bidirectional

Source: Infosys

Value chains have changed. For decades value chains focused on process effectiveness and product and service delivery, fulfilling value propositions to customers and other beneficiaries. Supply chains delivered goods from source of supply to the end consumer in a high-quality, timely manner. But now enterprises must consider responsive value chains that can be reconfigured quickly for changing business needs, have zero latency, are circular in nature, and are part of an ecosystem. Further, they must address labor practices, worker health, and alternatives in case of sudden supply disruption. While the concepts are not new, the detailed data enable rapid response times that were simply not possible before.

Decisions are the triggers of the digital economy, the actions that initiate response and provide it shape and direction. Deterministic rules engines have accelerated decision making, but more is needed. Like the human mind, which is wired to see patterns, the explosion of data requires new ways to process real-time information in conjunction with insights from past experiences to create machine-based intuition and action.

Talent has progressed from a cost to be minimized to source of competitive advantage. The so-called war for talent is actually a talent famine, as broad swathes of in-demand skills are greatly underserved. This also applies to talent sources, which are no longer a small batch of traditional business schools but entire new talent pools and learning pathways to groom the workforce of tomorrow.

IT systems are evolving from static processing engines to agents of change. However, many of them are designed for specific features and functionality and therefore struggle to evolve as newer features, functions, and experiments have to be rolled out. There is a need to develop using a platform mindset that enables continuous unbundling and rebundling, increasing the velocity of new ideas and innovation, and is designed for change and evolvability.

Change management is changing as well. Gone are the days of rigid, top-down, novel-length communication plans and forms-driven change. When program operations are driven by daily scrum stand-up meetings, much smaller increments are needed to keep change initiatives in synch with the rapidly evolving world around it. The sigma of these micro-changes helps bring about larger change during a transformation. Change interventions are instituted bottom-up in a micro-change—aided by changing routines in the current process (routine +1) and by providing the right cues, nudges, rewards, and recognition, leading to the ultimate behavioral shift and the desired outcomes. As users are empowered to drive change, then convenience, adoption, behavior, and value realization replace system go-live as the metric for success.

The Live Enterprise Model

There is perhaps no more powerful nor less understood tool than the humble operating model. They visually represent how organizations deliver value to internal and external customers and influence the entire organization. Unfortunately, they simply can't keep up with rapid market changes, and that's why executives struggle to apply existing frameworks. As Infosys developed the Live Enterprise model, we found that the traditional operating model framework does not meet the requirements of a modern large, complex organization. To seek nonlinear change, we dismantled old operating models rather than supplemented them. We took a page from the agile playbook and focused on guiding principles over rigid structure.

We started with six strategic objectives:

- Agility of a startup
- Responsive to customer needs
- Networked and connected ecosystem
- Velocity of ideas and innovations
- Competitive advantage through platforms
- Extreme automation in everything we do

These objectives are strategies. The organization is agile enough not to be constrained by specific models and metrics, and is constantly evolving to better itself. In the true sense, it behaves like all living beings, which continually evolve in response to the world around them.

These objectives work in concert to accomplish four outcomes:

- **Quantum organization.** Agile organizational structure that drives collaboration, innovation, strategic alignment, and new culture across distributed interconnected teams.
- **Perceptive experiences.** Respond quickly, yet thoughtfully and scientifically, to opportunities to create valuable new employee and customer experiences.
- **Responsive value chains.** Repurpose, reimagine, and reengineer the value chain to see what is not there, can be improved, or can be eliminated.
- **Intuitive decisions.** Automate systems and activate intelligence so that routine decisions and responses can be acted upon with maximum human intuition and minimum human intervention, so that humans can focus on higher order analysis and decisions not suited for machines.

These outcomes are made possible through four ingredients:

- ► Hybrid talent
- ► Design to evolve
- ► Digital runway
- ► Micro is the new mega

Given the pressures leaders face to survive, they need new models to address the challenges. Taken together, the eight elements—the four outcomes and four ingredients—described previously can be seen as the leverage points in the enterprise operating model. Each of the operating model elements has a core theme: quantum organization, perceptive experience, responsive value chain, intuitive decisions, hybrid talent, design to evolve, digital runway, and micro is the new mega (see Figure 1.2).

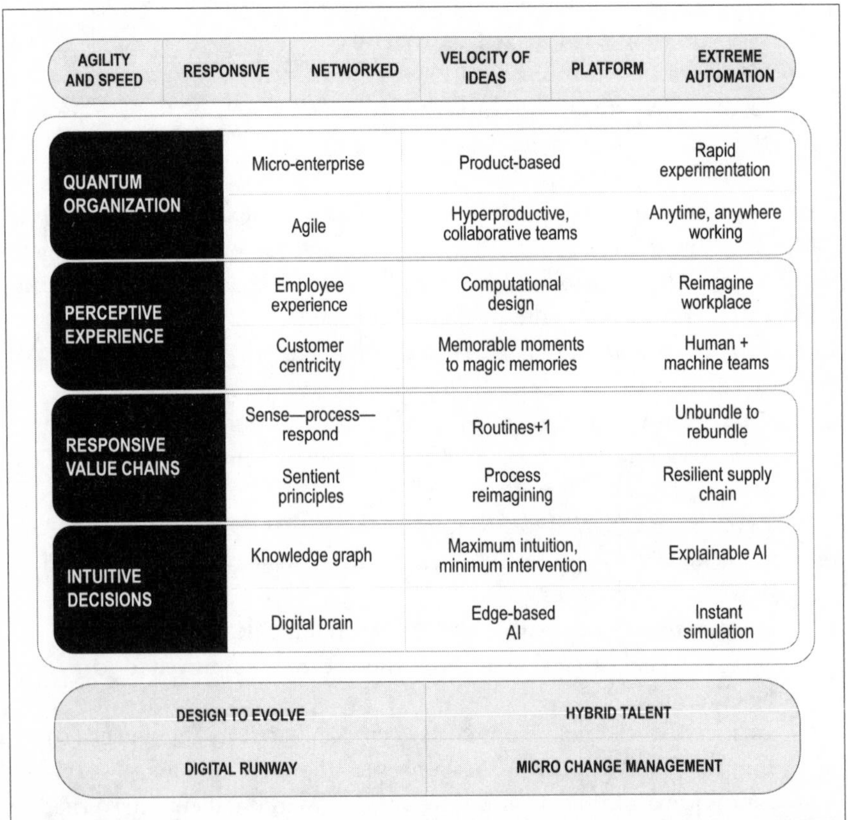

AGILITY AND SPEED	RESPONSIVE	NETWORKED	VELOCITY OF IDEAS	PLATFORM	EXTREME AUTOMATION
QUANTUM ORGANIZATION	Micro-enterprise		Product-based		Rapid experimentation
	Agile		Hyperproductive, collaborative teams		Anytime, anywhere working
PERCEPTIVE EXPERIENCE	Employee experience		Computational design		Reimagine workplace
	Customer centricity		Memorable moments to magic memories		Human + machine teams
RESPONSIVE VALUE CHAINS	Sense—process—respond		Routines+1		Unbundle to rebundle
	Sentient principles		Process reimagining		Resilient supply chain
INTUITIVE DECISIONS	Knowledge graph		Maximum intuition, minimum intervention		Explainable AI
	Digital brain		Edge-based AI		Instant simulation

DESIGN TO EVOLVE	HYBRID TALENT
DIGITAL RUNWAY	MICRO CHANGE MANAGEMENT

FIGURE 1.2 The Live Enterprise model.

These eight themes offer guidance on how to change perspective and view the enterprise as a living organism, enabled by technology. Table 1.2 shows a summary of the Live Enterprise model themes, along with the key ideas for each theme. Let's review each of the eight themes in more detail.

TABLE 1.2 The Live Enterprise model.

Model Element	Operating Theme	Key Ideas
Organization	Quantum organization	• Product-centric organization • Agile development at scale • Hyper-productive teams • Workplace collaboration
Experience	Perceptive experience	• Interactions over transactions • Adaptable design • Inclusive design • Measurable design
Value chain	Responsive value chain	• Proximity to source • Zero latency • Instant simulation • Micro-feedback • Guided practice
Decisions	Intuitive decisions	• Digital brain • Knowledge graph • AI services • Explainable and ethical AI
Talent	Hybrid talent	• Problem-finding • Learnability • Creativity • Alternate talent pools
IT Systems	Design to evolve	• Architect for evolvability • Layered architecture and services • Augmented existing core systems • Micro-releases
IT Systems	Digital runway	• Enterprise shared digital infrastructure • Unbundling and rebundling • Open source as a strategy • Everything as code
Change	Micro is the new mega	• Move enterprise equilibrium • Small, irreversible changes • Sigma of micro-changes • Nudges and new routines

Source: Infosys

Quantum Organization

The first theme is the **quantum organization**. Traditionally, an organization was a static set of containers in which operational targets were assigned and head count placed. Even as old-school command-and-control organizations are transitioning to distributed, leaner organizational models, the venerable organizational chart and command-and-control leadership persists. It was slow to change, but economies of scale and influence still enabled success, with skunk works teams for new initiatives and sufficient numbers of risk-taking intrapreneurs.

Yet today the organization is under pressure like never before, and traditional models are challenged for effectiveness, agility, and even fairness. Developing a sustainable, resilient organization requires a fresh look at the design, funding models, team collaboration, and ultimately a culture shift throughout the enterprise. We refer to this as the quantum organization, and similar to a multistate particle, a modern enterprise must successfully manage many initiatives simultaneously in multiple changing states. A quantum organization provides the tools and playbooks required to help distributed teams solve their own problems, based on their context and needs using the unbundling and rebundling strategy.

It is not enough to have a few groups innovating outside the core business, because scale is necessary for sustained impact. Incumbents have tried to emulate the nimbleness of startups by refining their long-standing models, and they have turned to agile software development for answers.

Agile has grown from a niche methodology to drive tech products at the edge to a mainstream management philosophy. But companies struggle to take it beyond the project team level and achieve more than superficial results. Agile has also given rise to the product-centric organization, where pods of workers organize around a "product" to be delivered, not a function to be supported. In the old organizational model, a person's function, title, and span of control were important, and now priority has evolved to what they know, their expertise, and how fast they get things done.

Perceptive Experience

The experience landscape looks markedly different today than it did a decade ago. Design thinking has been a tremendous success, enabling the creation of products and services that better serve both customer expectations and business needs.

At the same time, design thinking has reached the point of diminishing returns as more companies adopt it and new challenges emerge. This and other traditional methods of designing digital experiences, which rely exclusively on the creative and analytical abilities of designers, are limited in their ability to solve design challenges to their full potential. Designers need a new approach to maintain current momentum and meet growing expectations and responsibilities.

Today we are moving to a world of computational power of technology, which augments and amplifies designer problem-solving abilities, breaking through current limitations. The goal is not to replace people with technology, but to use technology where it outperforms humans (data processing and algorithmic calculations) and allow designers to focus on what they are best at (creative thinking and emotional intelligence). These changes can be understood in terms of three macro-level challenges: *design adaptable* for change, *design inclusive* for evolving consumers, and *design measurable* for evidence in design.

These challenges have enlarged the locus of experience from customer to employee, and from transactions to interactions. Interactions happen in three distinct categories: human to human, human to platform, and platform to platform. The objective is how value can be created in each interaction. This includes responding quickly yet thoughtfully and scientifically to opportunities to create valuable new employee and customer experiences. Learnings are incorporated to spot emerging and unmet needs.

Perceptive experiences also require reimagining underlying processes using the five sentient routines to provide all the information to users at the point they make decisions (*proximity to source*), enable their needs to be met without multiple steps and approvals (*zero latency*), and enable users to evaluate alternatives at the point of decision making (*instant simulation*). Perceptive experiences also recommend routine decisions and actions, seek feedback at the end of each interaction (*micro-feedback*), and help users navigate on their own through *guided practice*. The telemetry captured across each of these interactions measures and continuously improves the experience and underlying processes.

This represents a major shift in how experiences will be designed. The success of design as a discipline has driven a profound change in the operational landscape: design excellence matters, to customers, employees, and even shareholders. While design thinking is part of the toolkit, especially in the early "art of the possible" phase, a more quantitative approach is required.

Responsive Value Chains

Traditionally value chains were viewed as "delivering the goods," literally for product companies and through cavernous call centers and distributed depots for services firms. There was intelligence on the front end to design product and service offerings, but the bulk of the chain was seen as a one-way exercise in efficiency, to fulfill the product or service at the lowest price point to meet service level requirements. Logistics and trade regulations made life interesting, but were relatively static, as was the supplier base, which often took a long time to certify and establish and therefore only changed when absolutely necessary.

Stakeholder capitalism in the form of environment, social, and governance (ESG) requirements has turned this model on its head in multiple dimensions. Two-way communication is required up and down the network. Provenance or place of origin has become a traceable requirement. Consumers are concerned about labor practices for lower-tier suppliers to the brands they purchase. After the COVID pandemic burst onto the world scene, worker health and safety instantly became top priorities even as they created numerous challenges to operate, while following rapidly evolving and often confusing government policies. All the while, operations leaders have had to be vigilant and ready to quickly alter supply networks or trading partners in the case of sudden disruption.

Taken together, this has forced enterprises to take a fresh look at what they offer and how they fulfill their value proposition. They must think ecosystem, not chain, as everything is becoming integrated across many nodes. The ecosystem view encourages a repurpose, reimagine, and reengineer mindset to see what is not there, what can be improved, how it can be made sentient, and what can be eliminated to deliver more value.

Businesses now need much more information about their raw material inputs and the suppliers who extract, modify, and transport them. Businesses shoulder a greater responsibility for what happens beyond their corporate borders. From supplier to consumer-facing firm, this is both a challenge and opportunity to remake a long-standing chain of supplier relationships into a web of ecosystem relationships.

Solely focusing on customer-facing value chains will not be enough. Internal organizational processes and policies also need to be reimagined to ensure that they establish the foundation to drive internal agility, cross-collaboration, and speed to bring responsive value chains to life.

Intuitive Decisions

The human mind is wired to see patterns. It processes information in conjunction with insights from past experiences to create intuition, and intuition guides much of our decisions. Today leading organizations are developing a similar intuition to drive decisions swiftly and accurately, and to act with resilience in the face of disruption. AI and automation lie at the core of this endeavor to automate systems and develop sentient principles so that decisions and responses to data-led insights are acted upon with maximum human intuition and minimum human intervention.

This manifests in an ecosystem of tools that captures and maps complex and vast process environments. Businesses will rely on historical data, both qualitative and quantitative, to learn from and then guide the formation of patterns that automatically detect, classify, and resolve problems. These patterns also help companies see opportunities to get better at the things they already do.

For existing IT systems and core systems, tools like robotic process automation have created a cyber worker that takes on much of the deterministic decision load. Organizations now have the potential to drive intuitive decisions swiftly and accurately and to operate with resilience. Artificial intelligence, with machine learning and related tools, lies at the core of this capability and should be weaved into all new organizational initiatives.

This allows businesses to automate routine and deterministic decisions while providing instant simulation capabilities for users to experiment and test, before making more complex decisions about what and how to adapt in response to disruption that emanates after a crisis situation. In the stark COVID example, businesses have had to make many significant decisions quickly, and businesses running on the cloud with AI-enabled intuitive decisions gained a distinct edge.

Hybrid Talent

Employees have always been an important capital resource, but in the digital age the emphasis has evolved from labor costs to knowledge work productivity. With automation taking over repetitive known tasks, the challenge is to attract and nurture a pool of problem-finders to find the right problems that need solved. Hybrid talent is the future of the workforce. Beyond "full-stack" workers who possess both STEM (science, technology, engineering, and math) skills and empathetic creativity, hybrid talent will be a seamless mix of humans, machines, and the gig economy to bring the right talent at the right time for the task at hand.

Hybrid talent is at the forefront of the so-called war for talent. However, for the digital jobs of today and the future, there is actually a talent famine. Millions of positions remain unfilled, despite the many job losses associated with the COVID pandemic and its economic aftermath, which disproportionally affected lower-skilled workers. This epic demand–supply mismatch for digital skills has become the human capital challenge of the decade.

To fill this gap, a variety of new models have entered the market to provide alternatives to traditional pools like the major universities. Liberal arts colleges, community colleges, private certifications, and even online learning platforms have become providers of digital talent at all levels and provide better access to underserved populations. Some large enterprises and regional economic development groups also provide their own professional training programs to bridge students from educational institutions to true job readiness.

This new approach to professional education focuses on practical learning, where foundational professional skills are complemented by specific technology skills. For experienced employees, lifelong learning and access to anytime, anywhere learning platforms enable reskilling and a workforce that adapts to whatever business or technology requirements arise. The "anywhere" aspect is important, because COVID-19 drove home the point that a high percentage of work—and learning—can be done remotely from home. With the world of work permanently changed, a resilient, reskilled workforce is required to keep up with the evolving work roles and locations.

Design to Evolve

Most enterprises deal with the duality of accelerating their cloud and digital initiatives while maintaining business operations in their new normal. While enterprises continue to leverage technology to improve productivity, the most successful businesses also transform to improve customer experience and employee engagement. The enterprises that survive will be those that navigate this duality and become resilient. In human terms, when one arm gets injured, the rest of the body makes up for that injured arm and copes until it gets healed. Business resilience means ability to respond to market disruptions with another capability compensating for the area under duress, while still meeting continually rising expectations.

This duality means defining and developing an evolutionary architectural approach using the Live Enterprise thinking that makes the existing IT landscape robust and resilient, hides the complexity, and lays down a strong foundation for the digital runway. Given the complexity and scale of existing IT core systems, a rip-and-replace approach is too disruptive, and a more evolutionary approach to continuously unbundle and rebundle critical processes and functionality is required. These changes are accomplished over a period of time using agile methodology and six-week sprints. These sprints are crucial to transformation and enable the evolution one change at a time, happening continuously and at scale.

As enterprise architecture evolves, three underlying themes stand out. First, architecture is unified, but not uniform. Second, the model shares the ability to solve, so the entire organization learns and is able to solve its own problems. Third, micro-change leads to progress at scale, every six weeks across the organization. These three important elements of the evolution can be easily overlooked because people tend to only see things on the surface and can forget the underlying building blocks of architecture, learning, and micro-change at scale.

Digital Runway

In large global organizations, we have seen that unfortunately the best ideas and innovation happen in pockets, local occurrences without scale. It may be straightforward to rapidly experiment, innovate, and develop point solutions, but it is a real challenge to unbundle them into shared digital infrastructure services. Further, few companies can then scale, productize, and deploy across the organization so that global users can unbundle these services and then rebundle to solve problems specific to their lines of business and geographies. Those able to do this successfully have built a digital runway for their company, increasing the velocity of new ideas and innovations across their user community in a short span of time.

Digital runway provides a shared digital infrastructure for the company. It curates and organizes knowledge, platforms, processes, and other resources required to deliver initiatives in an accelerated manner. The idea is to bring all these elements together in a cohesive manner and drive velocity of new innovations by aggressively using the shared digital infrastructure. This also enables proven ideas from one area to be unbundled and scaled to the rest of the organization at an accelerated pace, since they are based on the same digital infrastructure.

Digital runways use unbundled functionality across services—a powerful approach to building software architectures. Traditional service-oriented architectures integrate business applications; microservices architectures are built from small, independent processes that communicate with each other using language-agnostic APIs. This provides a solid current foundation with maximum future flexibility. The digital runway also enables development of a partner ecosystem, where partner solutions are quickly integrated to deliver new features and innovations.

Micro Is the New Mega

Large-scale enterprise transformations take time, and value realization typically takes even longer. However, by thinking micro, the larger transformation is deconstructed into a number of smaller initiatives. These are delivered by micro-teams composed of hybrid talent that reimagine micro-processes, unbundle them into micro-front-ends and micro-services, with micro-releases done in sprints of six weeks, and manage the change for each release.

The Live Enterprise model uses frequent releases at scale in continuous short sprints, which renders traditional organizational change management ineffective. This required us to develop micro-change management as a new approach to drive adoption, convenience, change in behavior, and ongoing value realization.

The entire sprinting cycle to make a change at scale every six weeks is an amazing discipline. If the equilibrium of the company moves by an inch or even a millimeter every six weeks, the collective effect over a year moves the organization to a completely different place, because it creates a compounding and not linear effect.

Journey to Live Enterprise

The operating themes indicate where to focus and what do differently. The question then becomes, how do you get there? This section provides an overview on the journey to become a Live Enterprise—continuously evolving and learning (see Figure 1.3).

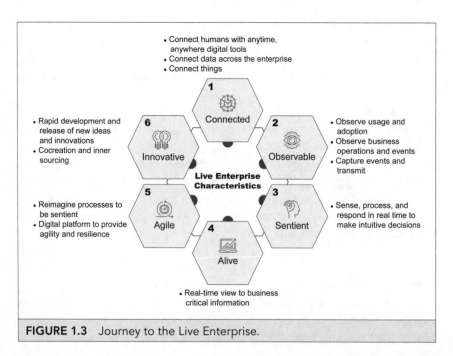

FIGURE 1.3   Journey to the Live Enterprise.

The first characteristic is **connected**, across three aspects: humans, data, and things. *Human* connectedness means organizations put digital tools in the hands of each of their human users so that they can access information and services wherever they are, anytime, anywhere, using any mechanism they want, and perform these actions by themselves. For example, Infosys converted dozens of separate systems to power the employee life cycle through three key mobile-first interfaces: LaunchPad to onboard new employees, and once they become an employee, they use InfyMe for personal productivity and Lex for learning. The second aspect of connected is *data*. Across the hundreds of client organizations we reviewed, we found that unlocking value from data is a significant challenge, especially factoring the need to develop data into insights and then convert insights into actions. To overcome these challenges, tools like knowledge graphs link all this data together in useful form. The third part of connectedness is *things*. As more and more things (hardware) become driven by software, it has become easier to connect, operate, and monitor through APIs. This is showing up everywhere: corporate campus entry doors, employee ID cards, and building controls, as examples. API-driven means easier integration, and they can be instantiated at the click of a button, enabling any physical device.

The next characteristic is **observable**. Once an organization has connected humans, connected data, and connected things, each of these emits telemetry data, signals streaming from each of these connections. This is similar to the human central nervous system, where we have five senses that capture external signals as input and send to the brain. In this case, humans, data, and things capture these signals, and observability enables it to be sensed and processed. There are three aspects to this observability. The first part is simply analyzing the data itself, to understand what's going on across the connected ecosystem and where to improve. The second is how well the most important features delivered through these connected tools are being used, what is working, and what is not working that requires reimagining. The third part of observability is the capability to capture data across all architectural layers in a coherent manner to enable sense, process, and respond through the relationships between data.

Once organizations start observing, then they can also sense, process, and respond—become **sentient**. If all these signals are in place, they can be acted upon. Decision making is typically deterministic, based on predefined rules. While good for individual decisions, these quickly run into problems at complexity and scale. Slowly, companies are moving to make more decisions through predictive models and using machine learning, deep learning, differential programming, and other probabilistic methods. An individual or organization becomes autonomous as more decisions are made in this way.

Once the organization develops the ability to make decisions in an automated manner and has real-time visibility to everything, it becomes **alive**.

To bring sentience to everything within a Live Enterprise, **agility** is required in the business processes, operating model, and underlying infrastructure. Existing processes and experience are reimagined to create sentient routines, then designed and implemented by distributed agile teams, and rolled out through micro-releases and change management. Modern agile redefines value delivery in an AI-first way, beyond development operations and security. This also requires a digital runway that provides shared digital infrastructure, with the ability to provision hardware and software at the click of a button or through APIs.

This is the point at which it is possible to quickly unbundle and rebundle at enterprise scale to drive **innovation** and increase the velocity of ideas and solutions. This innovation also includes distributing intellectual property quickly to capture new market opportunities. This capability is also enabled by the digital runway that is essential to link competencies with execution at the edge.

Guide to the Rest of the Book

The next eight chapters explore each of the eight Live Enterprise model themes. The chapters also cover how to apply them. We share a rich mix of examples from companies that get it right, as well as cautionary tales. We highlight experiences from our own transformation at Infosys and weave in findings from our primary research conducted over the last few years.

In the following chapter we cover how organizations can be structured to reflect multistate quantum principles and how automation accelerates change, even for large enterprises. Next, we explore how experience can become more perceptive. Then we look at value chains, how to reimagine processes and make them more responsive. We then cover how decision making becomes more intuitive and evolves knowledge management to sentience.

Chapter 6 explains how talent is now a hybrid combination of humans, machines, and the gig economy, and the critical role of learning. Then the next chapter, "Design to Evolve," addresses the design, architecture, and deployment of the Live Enterprise operating themes. The following chapter establishes the digital runway needed to enable the organization to do so many things, so quickly, at scale. The best ideas are not valuable unless they see the light of day, and the subsequent chapter on micro-change management addresses how small changes can drive big results.

Chapter 10 brings all these ideas together in the context of stakeholder capitalism and the complex set of constituents that businesses must now serve. In addition to generating returns for shareholders, leaders must also operate with heightened focus on environment, society, and governance. This includes employees, activist consumers, and responsibilities on broad societal topics like diversity and inclusion. We show how just as in nature, the Live Enterprise model provides guidance to a more sustainable, learning, and evolving organization.

The epilogue brings the book full circle, recapping the Live Enterprise model, macro lessons from the Infosys journey, and an aspirational message for the future.

While flashy success is highlighted where relevant, the emphasis of this book is on the practical reality of building long-term success in a short-term, whipsawed world. As the lessons of COVID-19 have taught us, resilience comes not from marginal improvements when times are good, but from flexible foundational capabilities that hold true even in highly adverse conditions.

The focus for leaders is still employees, customers, and the value propositions they represent. But if Live Enterprise appears to be a tech-heavy construct, that's because it is. The famous words of Marc Andreesen ring true: Software is indeed eating the world, and this model makes full use of the tech phenomenon while keeping customers, employees, and societal interests top of mind.

RECAP: The Live Enterprise Model

- The Live Enterprise is a journey, not an event. The model enables the organization to rapidly experiment, learn, and scale—the strategy of "micro is the new mega" being critical to demonstrating early and continuous wins to build momentum and turn naysayers into believers.
- The digital runway is shared infrastructure upon which platforms and solutions can be developed to increase the velocity of new ideas and innovations. Sentience is at the core of this, providing the ability to sense, process, and respond.
- While the vision and plans can be big, the journey must be broken into manageable, smaller chunks that can then be executed in short sprints for quick, iterative improvements. This creates an operating environment where new platforms and initiatives can be launched at rapid scale.
- Resilience is effective response to disruptions, without stepping off the treadmill of delivering core business expectations. In the new normal, this requires an anytime, anywhere operating model, where users are empowered and enabled with digital tools and self-service capabilities, consumed synchronously or asynchronously.

(2)

QUANTUM ORGANIZATION

Organizational Structure and Design

Gretna Green is a small village in Scotland, just north of the border with England. In 1754, the Marriage Act prevented couples under the age of 21 marrying in England—causing star-crossed lovers to elope north of the border. Once a Scottish Las Vegas without Elvis, Gretna Green remains forever associated with hope, love, and romance.

This little village also bears witness to one of nature's marvels—the murmuration of birds. On winter evenings you can scan the sky for flocks of starlings pulsing and twisting in synchrony, hundreds of thousands acting in unison as if a single organism. Folklore said it was a psychic link. Science, however, believes it's about information flow, the "information center hypothesis,"[1] or collective resilience from the mutual sharing of information.

In 2013, researchers discovered each starling's movement affects its seven closest neighbors, with each of these affecting their nearest seven, and so on.[2] Why seven? To optimize the trade-off between group cohesion and individual effort. In effect, each bird acts as a quantum of information, with the flock an open architecture that can sense, respond, and more easily adapt to change.

These murmurations echo across nature—monarch butterflies on pilgrimage from the Great Plains to Mexico's mountains, or silver schools of Atlantic herring a billion strong. They share properties of emergent behavior based on rules that accelerate group decision making and resilience, all without the need for central coordination. The skies at Gretna Green reveal something fundamental—an operating model based on simple rules, no center or leader, resilience via small units that sense and respond with agility at scale—a quantum organization tested, perfected, and hard-coded into nature via 480 million years of evolution.

A quantum organization operates in multiple states simultaneously and is highly adaptable. It is not tied down by hierarchy or rigid process, and even its organization chart is fluid. Our experience and research have shown that a quantum organization approach to enterprise operating models is not only valid, but essential to improve speed, adaptability, and resilience.

The Culture Shift

The 2020 pandemic not only redefined how we live but also how we think and perceive time. COVID-19 caused companies around the world to change the clock speed of work, going into overdrive to enable many millions of employees to work from home with secure access to corporate resources and to each other. This need for speed and connection represented a long-term, perhaps permanent behavioral shift. Quarantines, lockdowns, and social distancing drove seismic shifts in business and consumer behavior, increasing pressure to accelerate digital transformation and maximize technology use.

Uncertainty about the future is a particularly unnerving aspect of the new normal. To mitigate, the entire enterprise needs to move quickly together and evolve. Large enterprise response to the pandemic demonstrated that companies can be lifelike, responsive, evolving entities at enterprise scale—and any company, however large and complex, can transform to be adaptive and resilient. In fact, they may have no alternative in order to survive.

The combination of market competition, ESG requirements, and health concerns have placed organizations under unprecedented pressure, with traditional models challenged for effectiveness and agility, and judged on diversity and fairness. Developing a sustainable, resilient organization requires a fresh look at the design, team collaboration, and ultimately culture throughout the organization.

In this chapter we explore organization design and model implications. We also take a fresh look at agile and its movement from the margin to the mainstream. Then we focus on product-based thinking and close with an examination of DevOps as a tool to free up creativity and reduce risk.

Intelligent Design

In a post-COVID-19 culture, distributed teams are a fact of life. Although colocation is the ideal, it isn't necessary for successful agile adoption. A more important consideration is whether the underlying culture facilitates agile behaviors and whether the team is proficient in operating agile methods.

In the wake of the greatest business disruption in living memory, agile organizations are the most adaptable to change, the best equipped to survive. This was certainly evident within our company, Infosys. In 2018–2019 we were deep into our own transformation, simplifying employee experience and underlying processes in the pursuit of anytime, anywhere working. Instead of employees coming to our physical premises to use information, services, and training, these services were provisioned to employees on their devices to perform most of their day-to-day operations. Pre-pandemic, nearly 80 percent of our application development work for clients was already delivered using distributed agile methodology. Post-COVID-19, all our agile teams went remote and had to quickly adapt to the new normal. When the outbreak occurred, our existing distributed agile capability enabled Infosys employees to quickly move to a remote-working model, where 93 percent of the 240,000-person workforce started working remotely with minimal disruptions to the business. Six weeks into remote working, we surveyed nearly 150 of our scrum teams across 50 of our key client accounts to understand how the teams were coping. The results were remarkable, reflecting the impact of agile maturity:

▶ Most of the teams had quickly self-organized and adapted their daily work routines, activities, and schedule without waiting for instructions from someone up the hierarchy.

▶ Using existing collaboration and tooling infrastructure, the teams quickly got back to their pre-COVID-19 work cadence and continued delivery without issues.
  - For a global auto manufacturer, based on sentiment analysis on end user feedback, a scrum team ideated and implemented a feature in just two weeks, with quick client acceptance.
  - For a leading bank, another team transitioned from a colocated agile model to a distributed remote agile model and deployed its global transformation program on schedule with zero impact on business commitments, and with sustained feature velocity.

▶ Recognizing that physical distancing impacts social bonding within the scrum team, we found that teams quickly and proactively introduced virtual connects, using virtual cafés and social lounges as well as frequent surveys to check team pulse.

All this was possible primarily because a scrum team (smallest unit of an agile organization) by its very nature is a self-organizing, self-directed, and autonomous team—best suited to sense changes in its environment and respond rapidly, dramatically reducing the long cycle times typically seen in a traditional enterprise. In many ways a scrum team is a microcosm of an agile organization.

In another example, 9,000 recent college hire employees were in training at the Infosys corporate campus, and due to the COVID-19 outbreak, they relocated back to their homes. However, their learning continued digitally using the company's Lex learning platform, which included extensive instructor and administrator feedback, which provided whole student engagement beyond the content instruction itself.

These seemingly basic operational processes improved enterprise resilience, and having these capabilities in place made a significant impact on Infosys's ability to adapt and even excel in spite of the sudden disruption caused by the pandemic.

According to multiple studies, over the last two decades median CEO tenure at the world's largest public companies has been only about five years. As a result, senior executives effectively have one chance to deliver major organizational change, one chance to get it right. From our own recent experience at Infosys and across our client base, an intriguing question emerged: *Within the limited tenure of modern executives, how does a company adapt its organizational design to create lasting change?* We used that question to guide our approach to agile as we scaled from teams to programs to the enterprise level.

Continuously Evolving Organizational Models

An organizational model defines the relationships, team development, and consumer's role in how a business operates. Relationship has replaced hierarchy as disruptive technologies and market forces have flattened layers of management. Regardless of these forces, large organizations still need to function, serving customers with many offerings through thousands of distributed employees globally. The solution is a micro-enterprise model, where elements of an enterprise serve business needs, while drawing on (and sharing with) the shared resources of the larger company. Live Enterprise is essentially the "no operating model" option, and the organization model also focuses on principles and guidelines over rigid structure and command-and-control.

Much like quantum physics supplemented classic Newtonian physics, the quantum organization in the Live Enterprise model expands the traditional definition of organization structure and operating model. Operating models deliver value propositions to customers using levers of organization, information, location, and suppliers, and are enabled by management systems. Traditionally, a target model showed a future state for an enterprise to deliver on its strategy. However, the rate of market change has greatly outstripped the rate at which a business can change, which leaves the traditional operating model permanently misaligned. As executives have come to grips with this stark reality, they have realized that a new approach is needed.

Intelligence is more than knowledge and even more than sophisticated strategies. As Charles Darwin noted, it is based on how efficient a species became at doing the things they need to survive. Speed, adaptability, and resilience become valuable assets in the quantum organization model. The quantum organization has a strong foundation and playbook, from which a number of strategic initiatives, experiments, and innovations can be launched. Not all of them will succeed, but when the new idea launch velocity is high, the organization is set up to operate in multiple states simultaneously.

Amazon is arguably the best-known example of a quantum organization. In the words of noted tech analyst Benedict Evans, "Amazon is a machine to make a machine—it is a machine to make more Amazon."[3] In other words, the business model itself creates more effective businesses. A quantum organization is not linear like traditional models, but drives nonlinearity by enabling multiple organizational initiatives at any given point in time. These initiatives run in parallel and at scale to drive results that show up in operations, not just project readouts. Shared digital infrastructure enables ideas to become teams, and experiments to become offerings, following an organic, market-driven drumbeat (see Figure 2.1, next page).

Figure 2.1 illustrates the quantum organization. It is built around micro-teams, guided by user centricity, and supported by a digital runway of shared technology infrastructure. The framework is covered in this chapter through the following sections: "From Margins to Mainstream" (micro-releases and user centric), "The Product-Based Organization" (micro-teams and networked ecosystem), and "DevOps and Security" (part of digital runway).

The key characteristics of the quantum organization are as follows:

- ▶ **User at the heart of all initiatives.** Fundamental questions are asked at the beginning of each project. Why are we doing this, and how will this help the user (who could be a customer, employee, or partner)? Will this add a new routine that is value additive or remove non-value-adding tasks? Will it save time for the user or provide a better, frictionless experience?
- ▶ **Hyper-productive collaborative teams.** Connects the silos that exist in any organization, guided by value stream and user journey. This requires formation of agile cross-functional teams that take an

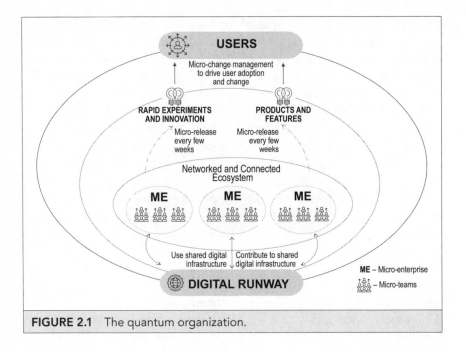

FIGURE 2.1   The quantum organization.

end-to-end view of the value stream, business metrics, KPIs, and user experience. Composed of smaller product teams that use distributed agile engineering models to rapidly build and deliver end products.

▶ **Rapid experimentation and innovation.** Instead of long delivery times and quest for perfection, teams rapidly experiment with new ideas and roll them out to users quickly. They introduce new features every few weeks with rapid releases and then mature and scale over a period of time. Hyper-productive teams use this mindset to conceptualize and deliver innovations to users, local initially and then at scale.

▶ **Shared digital infrastructure.** For rapid innovation and velocity, open architecture is needed to build on the organizational assets developed as part of the shared digital infrastructure. We address this in the DevOps section later in this chapter, and then in more architectural detail in Chapter 8, "Digital Runway." Shared digital infrastructure connects humans, data, and things across the ecosystem and makes this available to the team to build contextual and intelligent products for its users. It also jump-starts the entire product to be delivered in weeks, rather than months or years.

▶ **Micro-change management.** In a quantum organization with high innovation velocity and frequent feature release, adoption must also occur rapidly. This change is fundamentally different than the traditional new product or program rollout, where a single large campaign is expected to drive change. Instead, a frequent series of small interventions is needed to drive adoption, and this is called microchange management. Like murmuration, this agile approach to change is both simple and profound, accommodating pace of change and accepting the inherent uncertainty of future requirements. Our experience at Infosys and with hundreds of clients has shown this micro-approach is required to drive change in user behavior and culture, and to introduce a venture capital mindset to prioritize product backlogs based on what gains adoption with users.

From Margins to Mainstream

Snowbird

In February 2001, 17 "organizational anarchists" met at the Snowbird ski resort in the Wasatch Mountains of Utah.[4] Calling themselves The Agile Alliance,[5] the 17 wrestled with a problem nature had already solved 480 million years before. The 17 agreed on the Manifesto for Agile Software Development, and the meeting's most visionary statements focused on the mission of the enterprise itself: "Our highest priority is to satisfy the customer . . . Agile processes harness change for the customer's competitive advantage."

In effect, almost 20 years before the Davos Manifesto[6] and The Great Reset,[7] the Agile Alliance authored a manifesto for the pre-pandemic world. They not only looked to the core concepts of stakeholder capitalism and sustainability but in a two-for-one deal, inspired world (r)evolution in agile management and organizational design.

In his seminal book *The Meaning of Evolution*, legendary paleontologist George Gaylord Simpson noted, "There is in evolution a continual balancing of the two advantages: the advantage of increasing specialization in sufficiently stable conditions, and the advantage of versatility in changing conditions."[8] This duality applies beautifully to enterprises as well. Specialize for advantage when business is stable, and be flexible for times of uncertainty.

The Agile Manifesto fulfilled two evolutionary advantages by identifying four key areas of value:

1. Individuals and interactions over processes and tools
2. Working software over comprehensive documentation
3. Customer collaboration over contract negotiation
4. Responding to change over following a plan

The four areas of value pointed the way to increased software specialization in stable conditions. However, they also opened the way to wider versatility in changing conditions. In less than 20 years, these four areas of value have helped agile evolve and transcend the software space. By being adapted across organizations and industries, agile is now about more than management practices focused on clean code and software.

Agile has grown from a niche methodology to drive tech products at the margins to a mainstream management philosophy. Two decades on, the challenge is enterprise agile—delivering agile at global scale. In the era of The Great Reset, the World Economic Forum's call to action for "the management of a global commons" demands nothing less.

The Five Agile Attributes

The authors have studied, experimented with, and delivered in agile methods during our 15-plus years at Infosys. After adopting it ourselves across the entire 240,000-employee base, working with hundreds of clients on agile programs, and conducting several studies through our research institute, we have identified five essential elements of agile organizations (see Figure 2.2).

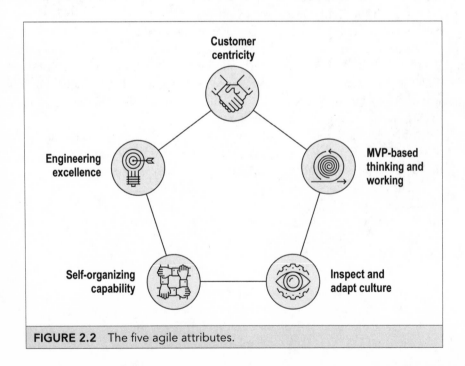

FIGURE 2.2 The five agile attributes.

1. **Customer centricity.** The voice of the customer always remains central to teams, thanks to the close working relationship with the product owner. This also develops end user empathy and provides teams a sense of shared purpose, which otherwise are distanced from the end user.
2. **MVP-based thinking and working.** Rapid creation of working product results in frequent value realization, incrementally over short iterations. The frequent show-and-tell nature enables rapid feedback loops that keep teams authentic to the end goal, and allows for quick course-correction or pivot, if needed.
3. **Inspect and adapt culture.** The teams frequently reflect, adapt, and improve their working practices. This also helps quick adjustment to changes in the internal and external environment.
4. **Self-organizing capability.** The teams are self-empowered and foster a culture of open communication, which allows them to organize and manage their work effectively, resolving team-level impediments smoothly. Information radiators enable teams to self-govern. Servant leadership enables this capability.
5. **Engineering excellence.** Teams constantly explore the latest tools and engineering practices that allow them to innovate and drive technical agility—use of microservices, extreme automation, cloud, DevSecOps, or low code platforms. Highly automated delivery pipelines allow teams to develop, test, and deploy software rapidly.

Combined, these five attributes help the enterprise become a learning organization that sustains continuous improvement. Fundamentally, agile is about culture—an organization's core assumptions, drivers, and mental models that drive behaviors. While few formally hierarchical organizations still exist, the shadow of centralized command-and-control hangs over initiatives and everyday operations. Agile teams work best when they are autonomous and self-organizing, and that is disruptive to traditional top-down, centralized control. This is why agile began in the margins and slowly and methodically made its way into more functions and greater programs. The pandemic, however, accelerated this adoption and created a hybrid world of teams working remotely from home and physically in the office. In effect, COVID-19 launched the biggest work-from-home experiment in history.

The Virtual and the Physical
Agile traditionally seemed unsuited for remote teams, because agile approaches typically emphasized the need for teams to be in constant

communication with one another, preferably in a single physical location where collaboration unfolds naturally and organically. COVID-19, however, turned that conventional wisdom on its head, with Gartner research revealing 91 percent of organizations implemented work from home arrangements.[9]

We saw firsthand during COVID-19 the challenge to move the entire Infosys organization to a remote-working model. Collaboration and business operations had to be conducted in a remote-first way, yet with excellent digital experience. We had more than 10 categories of tools that users needed to collaborate with their customers, partners, and colleagues. Honestly, the experience was initially broken, because users had to switch across multiple tools to accomplish their work. After identifying specific needs, we formed a small, hyper-productive team within our Wingspan learning platform. This team experimented with new ideas and built a digital workplace platform from the ground up and rolled it out across the organization in 45 days. The first big test was our annual sales event with 2,500 employees, where the platform became an online conference, complete with interactive breakout rooms and even a technology showcase in virtual reality exhibit halls. The point is that a quantum organization is resilient and agile because it is set up for speed and uncertainty, to take ideas from concept to rollout across an organization in a short span of time and adapt to change and even disruption like working from home.

The hybrid virtual-physical work model marks the beginning of a permanent trend, with Generation Z's entrance to the workforce predicted to increase demand for remote working by 30 percent by 2030.[10] A quantum organization addresses the challenges raised by the generational shift and rise of remote work:

- ▶ **Unclear roles and responsibilities**, especially in middle management.
- ▶ **Staff selection not based on agile needs,** because organizations don't understand agile role requirements, they are not committed to agile methods, or leaders don't understand how it benefits them.
- ▶ **Broader organizational policies not aligned to agile ways of working,** like performance plans and incentives, budgeting, and planning practices.
- ▶ **Inability to integrate or operate an agile team within traditional organizational structures,** coordinating agile and non-agile teams and other internal project teams, as well as interfacing with traditional customers (internal) and clients (external stakeholders).
- ▶ **Inability to shift control or governance mechanisms** to create space for self-organizing, autonomous, collaborative agile teams, and failing to understand or integrate a constant "adjust and adapt" cycle.

▶ **Difficulty to transition conventional short-term, project-based team structures to long-term, product-based agile structures.** If business leaders, the architects of organizational structure, continue to drive project-based cultures, agile's benefits will underachieve.

▶ **Innovation not valued or understood as essential.** Companies with this mindset risk becoming obsolete but often do not yet realize it, due to legacy thinking or lack of exposure to innovative forms of agile such as lean startup.[11]

A learning organization mindset and continuous improvement drive successful agile transformation. This requires leaders to be visible and active to facilitate the cultural change needed.

The Product-Based Organization

Products over Projects

Agile has given rise to the product organization. This new organizational construct creates value by creating autonomous, cross-functional, and self-directed teams. This is not to emphasize products over customers, but a focus on product outcomes over functional activities that are disconnected from customer deliverables. These teams organize around a "product" to be delivered, not a function to be supported, and these teams persist for the duration of the *product* roadmap. In the old organizational model, teams were stood up to deliver a *project*, only to be dissolved once the project was over. A product-based team construct is actually more customer-centric, with greater accountability for product outcomes.

There are four characteristics of product-based organization (see Figure 2.3).

| Customer and user-centric approach to value | Product teams are persistent teams | Fund value streams, not products | Collaboration as way of life |

FIGURE 2.3   Product-based organization.

1. **Customer- and user-centric approach to identify, organize, and deliver value.** To aid in this approach, there are six fundamental

practices for teams to understand the problem to be solved and the underlying solution: persona development, minimum viable product (MVP), user experience, customer journey mapping, story mapping, and feature workshop.

2. **Product teams are persistent teams.** They are designed to be self-sufficient with the ability to deliver features that deliver business value. The product teams are autonomous and define their own back-logs and strategies, keeping in mind customer and business needs. They work closely with cross-functional value streams to ensure that individual product teams are collaborating to deliver value and make the customer journey seamless.

3. **Fund value streams, not projects.** Shift from funding projects to funding value streams and associated product teams, with the MVP approach guiding funding decisions. Funding cycles become shorter and more frequent, allowing business the flexibility to recalibrate its investments based on the value realized as well as changes in the external environment.

4. **Collaboration.** Product-based organizations have a significantly higher level of collaboration between business and technology teams, compared to the traditional model.

The Product-Based Journey

The journey to a product-based organization has six steps (see Figure 2.4).

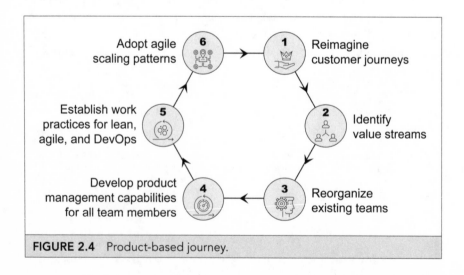

FIGURE 2.4   Product-based journey.

1. Reimagine customer journeys for significant products and services.
2. Identify the value streams that orchestrate those journeys, including the technology, products, and teams.
3. Reorganize existing teams into product teams that support the value streams identified earlier.
4. Develop product management capabilities for all team members, and develop competency in roles for business owner, product manager and product owner.
5. Establish work practices for lean, agile, and DevOps, with related tooling.
6. Adopt agile scaling patterns to adopt the product-based organization model across the enterprise. Popular scaling patterns include Scaled Agile Framework (SAFe), Spotify, Scrum@Scale, Large-Scale Scrum (LeSS), Nexus, and Disciplined Agile.

A leading Australian telco client struggled with time to value and customer satisfaction. To address it, they accelerated releases and incorporated market feedback more readily, and to do so they implemented a product-based operating model. Over an 18-month period, they stood up over 130 product (feature) teams called pods. These small teams were aligned to business value streams and helped the client significantly accelerate its digital journey. Their deployment cycle accelerated from three months to three weeks, and their overall cycle time of user story design to go-live decreased from 100 to 20 days. As part of this transformation, they established agile and DevOps ways of working, building strong alignment and dissolving the boundary between the IT and line of business organization.

Mindset and Structure

Many organizations have adopted the so-called Spotify model to bring about the structural changes required to be an agile enterprise and move to a product-based operating construct. The central premise is that teams are autonomous and self-sufficient, and this improves business agility. However, this amount of structural modification often requires dismantling functional boundaries, can be quite disruptive, and requires significant organizational change management to get it right.

The Tribe-Squads-Chapters-Guild construct from the Spotify model can be a powerful way to reimagine organizational design to make it nimble, responsive, and product-centric, which also fosters an agile mindset. The model is built on autonomy and trust, because when there is trust, there can be ownership and accountability. Trust creates an environment where failure is taken not as negative but as a rapid opportunity to learn, innovate, and change.

During the Infosys transformation journey to adopt Live Enterprise concepts, we formed multiple hyper-productive cross-functional teams. These teams took end-to-end ownership of a specific micro-platform. With focused scope, the teams use the enterprise shared digital infrastructure to quickly turn ideas into micro-platforms that are then rolled out to the users.

When Infosys developed a platform for experience configuration, we assembled a cross-functional team of experience designers, behavioral experts, software engineers, and process owners. This was a global team from England, the United States, and India, and they collaboratively developed the product backlog with release milestones to be delivered every six weeks. They also set up engineering and testing to be automated, and designed it to be remote-first. The experience configurator micro-platform quickly went from internal usage to also become a valuable tool for clients. The hyper-productive team approach changes the mindset from a onetime herculean effort to a repeatable, self-organizing process. Revisiting our overall resilience theme, it accepts both the pace and uncertainty inherent in the market, and works within constraints to evolve quickly and accurately.

Like nature herself, a quantum organization has a product focus, based on simple rules and small groups that sense and respond with agility at scale. Getting there depends on establishing clear strategy, understanding customer needs, creating a prioritized product roadmap, and delivering superior customer experience.

After 480 million years of evolution, nature gave starlings, monarch butterflies, and herring the perfect operating model for their environment. By the same token, an agile product focus must be human-centric, a diverse stakeholder ecosystem that includes development team, product owner, scrum master, and customer.

DevOps and Security

Velocity 2009

DevOps was born at the Velocity Web Performance and Operations Conference in 2009, in reaction to the siloed waterfall IT in existence for decades.[12] DevOps joins development and operations to redefine organizational structure and culture to enable rapid, agile software development and scalable, always-on operations. This optimizes the customer experience via high-quality code deployed in rapid increments, with additional benefits including optimized customer experience, shorter development cycles, increased software deployment frequency, reduced failure rate, and faster time to market.

Why a section on DevOps in a chapter on organization? Software has permeated business to the core, and even the most physical of activities is augmented and amplified through technology. The care and feeding of that technology occurs through software development operations, or DevOps. As machines become teammates to human workers, it is a natural evolution to consider robots as part of the organization, not the capital asset base. DevOps is the pursuit of efficient technology performance in enterprise operations, and this area is rapidly expanding in influence and impact across companies, across industries. Our experience has found that far too many organizations have a technology-centric view of DevOps—that it's just about tooling. However, DevOps has much more to do with having the right set of processes and policies in place that lead teams to collaborate with each other. It's about the people model, processes, and policies to get a larger set of people working together.

DevOps implementation is an organizational catalyst for cultural change, fostering increased communication, collaboration, and innovation. In effect, it's a human-centric and technology-enabled way to release code faster, better, and cheaper. This goal hinges again on adopting the right mindset, which is to be collaborative and guided by leader expertise and involvement, valuing individual contribution via small, agile units. These units (pods) respond faster to business requirements and ensure innovation is balanced with security and operational needs. The stakeholder ecosystem plays a central role, with individuals in development, testing, operations, and software architecture each having a seat at the table. Workflow and communication are more transparent, which deepens group understanding of the service or product being developed and attenuates the risk from incremental software releases.

What does this mean in the real world? Infosys research found that DevOps for many companies improves service quality and reliability by 25 percent, and reduces the software release cycle by 75 percent. A leading bank in South America faced the disruptive competitive challenges of online payment providers, peer-to-peer lending, and explosive growth from the fintech industry overall. Also an Infosys client, this bank's leadership established a clear goal to make their technology simpler, better, and faster, taking advantage of their highly valuable service inventory and increasing speed to market for some of its game-changing applications. The DevOps program took 13 months to complete and achieved dramatic results: software deployment time was reduced from two weeks to two days, 70 percent reduction in manual testing, $7 million in annual cost savings, and thousands of service hours saved.

The Human-Technology Frontier

Despite DevOps being more than technology, tech certainly plays an important role in its effectiveness. Automated regression testing provided early benefits by rapidly testing the myriad of potential combinations without the burden and variability of human involvement. The amount of intelligence in this automation has steadily increased to complex-rules-based algorithms and pattern recognition to harden code for potential future scenarios. With the hype and promise surrounding AI, it is tempting to view AI as the de facto answer. However, that may lead to the proverbial hammer treating everything as if it were a nail. For AI to serve the organization and not vice versa, focus on the business problem, not the technology:

- ▶ Don't build it unless the customer needs it.
- ▶ Identify business cases for AI solutions to drive impactful business change.
- ▶ Build the relevant organizational structure and roles—data scientists, data engineers, business analysts.
- ▶ Embed into AI–human intelligence feedback loops that foster learning.

Security: A Shark Net with Holes

Organizations that leverage DevOps for enterprise agility often struggle with software and application security. Like a shark net with holes, application security is often left to separate teams in separate testing phases. As the DevSecOps trend gathers momentum, organizations must encode security within the code—and the mindset with enterprise DNA—to ensure clean code, protect application data, and fortify infrastructure.

A winning DevSecOps strategy leverages people, process, and technology to enhance software security in an automated, integrated, and transparent manner. On a tactical level DevOps programs should follow six rules (see Figure 2.5).

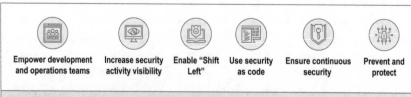

| Empower development and operations teams | Increase security activity visibility | Enable "Shift Left" | Use security as code | Ensure continuous security | Prevent and protect |

FIGURE 2.5   DevOps principles.

1. **Empower development and operations teams** to deliver secure applications.
2. **Increase security activity visibility** so they can be tracked, tasked, and measured.
3. **Enable "Shift Left."** Adopt security measures early, from the design phase through the software delivery cycle, and test continuously.
4. **Use security as code**, automating security actions into actionable test cases and tools that can be continuously verified.
5. **Ensure continuous security** via the ability to respond effectively to threats as they emerge. Integrate security with the threat landscape and intelligence.
6. **Prevent and protect** by finding the balance between prevention (SecOps) and protection (DevOps) to minimize security issues.

At Infosys, as part of our own transformation to the Live Enterprise model, we embraced extreme automation in everything we do as one of our major objectives. We developed the company digital platform and started building micro-platforms on it to deliver new features and functionality like InfyMe for employee apps and Lex for anytime learning. We used our own Infosys DevOps platform as the backbone for all our engineering and operations effort. Fully automated DevSecOps enabled new releases and features on demand and across the cloud environment to meet business needs. The "Shift Left" mindset adopted with DevSecOps ensured that security, compliance, and functionality checks were performed upfront and this improved software release quality. This backbone enabled us to build new ideas from concept to pilot in six to eight weeks.

Agile needs a different culture, and the literature is full of stories of early failures linked to lack of culture change over all other causes. Given its importance, here are three themes that we found valuable on our Infosys agile journey and consistently heard in my work with several clients on theirs:

1. **Set the tone from the top.** The active leadership from Infosys chairman Nandan Nilekani made agile—and Live Enterprise—a reality at Infosys.
2. **Dismantle, not supplement.** Purposefully dismantle the old operating models, rather than supplement them. For nonlinear results, design for change, else you are destined for incremental gains at best.
3. **Establish common purpose.** While every company seems to talk about customer centricity, it is just as important to remove internal friction and competition so employees are actually able to focus on customers.

While agile has become a household word in the enterprise lexicon, there is a difference between awareness and impact. According to Knowledge Institute research, fewer than 20 percent of enterprises consider themselves mature adopters in the use of agile across units. Most are doing agile in name only, following the rituals, yet not the actual practices. This reinforces the point that agile frameworks and activities that lack the core values and practices are not agile—they're just another process. However, by adopting the mindset and ideas described previously, companies can make real progress toward the organization ideal.

RECAP: Quantum Organization

- Quantum organizations provide tools for rapid experimentation through the digital runway, innovation at the edges by distributed micro-teams, and extreme automation at scale for repeatable processes and functions. They are designed to deliver continuous incremental value every few weeks to progress the organizational equilibrium.
- The digital runway enables product-based teams to rebundle and build solutions specific to market, country, or region and use modern DevOps to drive speed and scale. Platforms build platforms, creating a vibrant partner and client ecosystem.
- Quantum organizations promote interactions between users, user to platform, and platform to platform to drive value exchange in each interaction, thereby delivering more cumulative value. They build and nurture communities composed of talent, knowledge, playbooks, learning assets, and platforms to drive adoption and continuous enrichment.
- Quantum organization culture uses smaller, hyper-productive, and cross-functional agile teams as their "special forces." This creates faster, increased innovation velocity and takes a value stream view, embedding collaboration into the DNA of every business process.

3

PERCEPTIVE EXPERIENCE

Perception

Three Hearts, Nine Brains, and a Head with Eight Arms

Octopuses have blue blood, no bones, three hearts, nine brains, and eight arms joined to the head. Two hearts send blood to the gills, while the third pumps it around the body. A central brain sits in the head, with one at the base of each arm to control movement. The majority of neurons are found in the arms, which can independently touch, taste, and control basic motion without input from the main brain.

As a result, an octopus can "see" photons with its skin and change color without inputs from the eyes or brain. Despite being color-blind via a lack of cones in their eyes, 400 million years of evolution allows octopuses to be nature's ninjas, to hide from prey via camouflage among the most dynamic in nature. How they process visual information, and then send out the correct commands to their skin, is something we don't yet understand.

Octopuses also change color to communicate, their skin a visual grammar of its own. They do this with the aid of specialized cells called chromatophores containing color-producing pigment, and light reflectors called iridophores and leucophores. Combined, these produce the uncanny changes in skin color and texture that reflect evolutionary design thinking at its finest.

In effect, the octopus' perception is an external, mostly accurate version of reality. They draw the map and merge it with the landscape.

Innovation, Creativity, Emotional Intelligence

Compared to just a decade ago, today's corporate experience landscape is radically different, with COVID-19 pressing the button on even faster, more fundamental changes. The field of experience design has been reshaped by the tremendous success of design thinking, enabling the creation of products and services that better serve both customer expectations and employee needs. However, to continue to meet these rising requirements, a new approach is needed.

In the Live Enterprise model, perceptive experiences are delivered by blending the capabilities of heart, brain, and machine together in an integrated way. Every user is a unique cosmos, with its emotion, ambitions, and potential. At the core, there is an inherent human nature, surrounded by the wider environment and the context in which they operate. To significantly enhance user experience, we need to understand their emotional state and contextualize the experience to make it personalized and useful for their needs. The enterprise digital brain constantly senses the signals emitted by users as part of their experiential actions and events to anticipate their needs and recommend actions that optimize their productivity.

The computational power of technology and telemetry is used continuously to understand experience design effectiveness and user challenges. The telemetry learns from user actions, understands relevance of the predictive suggestions or recommendations, and identifies points of friction in the user journey. Combining these aspects through computational design allows designers to focus on what they do best—innovation, creative thinking, and emotional intelligence.

It's a long and winding road, and we're still playing catch-up. Then again, when it comes to experience, nature did have a 3.8-billion-year head start.

A New Model of Experience

The success of design thinking has coincided with significant change to the operational landscape marked by an unprecedented change of pace, evolving consumers and employees, plus a growing appetite for evidence. Design thinking enabled profound and transformational change for business by reframing problems to focus on users and their needs. It emphasizes problem finding before problem solving, what should be done before diving into how to do it. The problem space is explored to go beyond requirements definition (what a user needs) to uncover motivations (why they want it) and understand what is really going on. This establishes a problem worth solving, and then traditional brainstorming can open up the solution space, identify ideas, and rapidly experiment with prototypes and quick feedback through iterations to converge on solutions that are personally desirable, technically feasible, and economically viable. We call this flare–focus, flare–focus: broaden the problem space, then identify a specific problem, then explore multiple possibilities, and finally converge on a solution.

A beneficial by-product is getting to the tangible more quickly, like a prototype or user journey. Design thinking demands evidence. The past decade has witnessed the transformative power of design thinking, as design-led organizations outperformed their peers. Apple, Microsoft, and Nike are well-known examples of firms that have used design thinking effectively to drive bottom-up innovation, and we have used it extensively at Infosys as well. This success has driven a profound change in the operational landscape—widespread acceptance that design excellence matters, to customers, employees, and even shareholders. At the same time, design thinking has shown limits to move from single initiatives to enterprise effectiveness. It is reaching the point of parity as more companies adopt it and new challenges emerge. Design thinking needs to be complemented by a new model to maintain current momentum, and to meet growing stakeholder expectations and company responsibilities. The required changes can be understood in terms of three macro-level challenges, each of which will affect all organizations in the decade ahead: change is the only constant, evolving expectations and a growing appetite for evidence. (See Figure 3.1.)

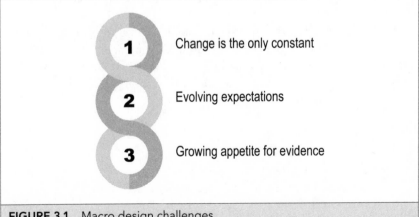

FIGURE 3.1 Macro design challenges.

Change Is the Only Constant

The accelerating pace of innovation is disrupting established business models. Technology already changes faster than humans or organizations can process, and yet the pace of change is only getting faster. In an environment where change is the only constant, organizations require an unprecedented level of business agility to operate successfully. Our own experience, as well as working with the world's largest companies, has shown that the traditional linear approach to developing products and services is no longer fit for purpose. Even with agile delivery methods, projects take too long to progress between iterations and cannot keep pace with changing requirements. A new approach is required—one that embraces the new reality and shapes experiences that, like evolution itself, continuously adapt to change.

Evolving Expectations

The relentless uptick in customer and employee expectations from digital services challenges organizations to deliver increasingly better experiences. A person has fluid expectations for customer experience because any one experience they have permeates every other experience they will have in the future, regardless of industry or context. No longer is your customer or employee experience (EX) measured exclusively against your industry competitors, but also against technology pioneers like Apple, Airbnb, Uber, and so on.

This challenge transcends the traditional barrier between the consumer and enterprise markets. We no longer accept experiences in our working lives that are significantly worse than the experiences we receive as consumers. To add complexity, as our society undergoes a cultural drive toward an individualism that celebrates diversity, traditional methodologies that assign people to broad demographic groupings don't provide the level of detail needed to address this adequately.

While organizations that sell to consumers attempt to address this diversity by targeting ever-more specific customer segments, companies in the enterprise market cannot. New methods are needed that allow organizations to understand a more diverse range of distinct user needs with the same depth of understanding.

Growing Appetite for Evidence

As experience becomes the differentiating factor for service-oriented organizations, it has also become a driving force for value creation. Our experience working with the Infosys executive team and many large client organizations has shown that they are no longer willing to make decisions based on consultant opinions or industry best practices. Instead, leaders demand hard evidence of the value that a given design decision delivers against their business objectives.

The user research methodologies that served us well until now need to be supercharged to respond to the increased demands placed on them. At the same time, we must ensure that this desire for evidence does not impede creative thinking and innovation. Designing effective products and services in this context is a challenge that is complex and multidimensional, and demands bold, innovative answers that often break new ground.

The New Paradigm

Current methods to design digital experiences rely primarily on the creative and analytical abilities of designers and are limited in their ability to solve design challenges to their full potential. The computational power of technology augments and amplifies designer problem-solving abilities, overcoming these limitations. Computational design addresses the macro-level design challenges of change as the only constant, evolving expectations and the growing appetite for evidence. This represents a pivotal change in the way products and services are designed, and the approach is based on three principles: *design adaptable, design inclusive,* and *design measurable.* When adopted together, these principles provide designers and businesses an approach to address the challenges. (See Figure 3.2.)

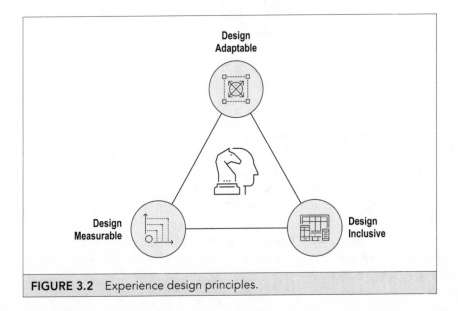

FIGURE 3.2 Experience design principles.

Design Adaptable

To address the challenge of a changing landscape, common perspectives toward change must also evolve. The current view that change is a risk to be mitigated gives way to a new paradigm that sees change as an opportunity to embrace. Design solutions need to be adaptable so organizations react to change in a fast, frictionless, and cost-effective way.

Design Inclusive

To address the complexities of evolving customer and EX, businesses must evolve the way they understand, segment, and target users. The current belief that sees a single-best design solution yields to a new paradigm that sees design manifest itself in a thousand variants, customized to the user on the basis of a deep understanding of who they are. Computational design serves each user with a tailored experience that matches their needs and expectations.

Design Measurable

To address the growing importance of evidence-based decision making, approaches to measurement must also evolve. The current view that sees measurement as an activity undertaken after release gives way to a new approach that sees measurement as core to design, built into its DNA from inception. Define what success looks like through unambiguous KPIs, as one of the first activities designers undertake. These KPIs enable continuous measurement of design effectiveness, leading to a shift in decision making from opinion to tangible, objective evidence.

Experience is the new frontier of value creation, a frontier that continually expands. In this landscape, organizations create value by adopting principles of computational design—adaptive, inclusive, measurable—and deliver experiences that meet growing customer and employee expectations and lead to better business outcomes.

Organizations that embrace this new reality will receive an abundance of valuable data points for customers, employees, and users overall. To ignore this quantitative approach will trap companies into projects that may be anecdotally accurate pilots, but fail to deliver value when fully deployed.

Computational design has applicability in wider areas like architecture as well; however, here we are referring to computational design in the context of experience design.

Computational Design

Transcending Design Limits in Form and Function

Designing successful digital experiences requires understanding people using qualitative and quantitative methods, using insights developed from the data to create a number of different creative approaches, and assessing the success of these approaches. These activities are currently limited by designer capacity for computation, but technology can overcome these limits.

Take modern architecture, for example, where computational and generative design technologies model and shape some of the world's most impressive buildings—masterpieces of form and function impossible to conceive and build before these capabilities were developed. Computational capabilities have dramatically disrupted the architectural market, changing not only the final, designed product but also the ways of working to achieve it. The result has not been a replacement of the human component but rather an augmentation, helping architects and engineers reach new levels of creativity and delivery.

Computational design has only begun to realize its potential in the field of experience design. Introducing a computational dimension in the design process will catalyze a new generation of experiences—*computational experiences*—and a new approach to solve business problems. This new design model is driven by four principles—sentience indicators, codified design language, continuous measurement, and an integration-first approach.

Understanding Through Sentience Indicators

In traditional design methodologies, experience designers use personas to understand users. This technique creates an imaginary avatar as a surrogate for humans, to assess the effectiveness of design ideas. Despite designer best efforts to base personas on reality, the technique is deeply flawed. Personas encourage designers to see users as a homogenous cohort, rather than a diverse population of individuals—and anyone who doesn't fit the cohort is ignored. The best design processes incorporate actual people into the process to correct for the limitations of personas or user journeys that may miss the way real people actually interact with the experience.

Computational design keeps the focus on humans rather than personas by interpreting, codifying, and measuring the behavior of a diverse group of real users in real time at a detailed level. It eliminates the need to rely on personas as a proxy for users. Instead, products can be designed using data from real users, opening the path to individual needs, motivations, aspirations, and concerns. This process is continuous and fully automated. It computes, analyzes, and unlocks correlations between psychometric data and telemetry data, plus defines behavioral indicators of user characteristics. Because the process moves designers closer to true awareness, these metrics are called key sentience indicators (KSIs). (See Figure 3.3.)

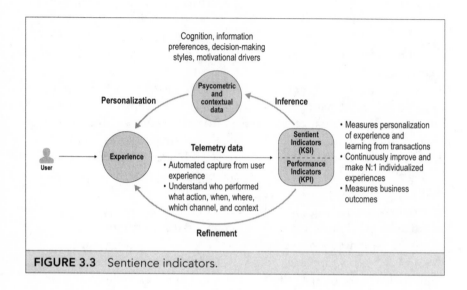

FIGURE 3.3   Sentience indicators.

Codified Design Language over Aesthetics

To apply the power of computation to the design of products and services, designers define experiences in a way that computers understand—codified as *information*, rather than aesthetics. The computational design schema is a structured model of information that defines the structure, style, and content of the interface with KSIs. Experiences defined in this way can be manipulated by algorithms that generate multiple variants in response to data inputs.

Many subtly different variants are generated without the need to produce endless design visuals. This automatic generation marks a shift from the creation of a single monolithic experience dictated entirely by a designer, to a continuously evolving, live experience *directed* by a designer and *amplified* through technology.

Measurability Coded into DNA

To meet the demand for evidence-based design, solutions must have a codified measurability element embedded into their DNA from the beginning. This measurability assesses design efficacy in a tangible, live context. Analysis and testing become part of the design process itself, with designers enhancing their assessment of design ideas with data and relying less on intuition, or on imperfect prototypes tested in artificial situations. Computational design shifts to data-driven decision making, where solutions are objectively assessed and unconscious bias minimized.

An Integration-First Approach

Computational design turns traditional workflow on its head. Instead of integrating design solutions into technical architecture after all design decisions have been made and an experience created, the solution is integrated at the start. Developers work out how a product interacts with supporting systems before the experience has been designed. This upfront integration step renders design ideas directly into the product, with connections to back-end systems already established.

This shift from a linear, sequential development process to a continuous deployment capability means there is almost no latency to propose a design idea and assess its success. Designers no longer manually and loosely estimate costs and benefits to implement design ideas, given their new freedom to propose any number of design ideas and test them directly in the product.

The Case for Adoption

Computational design delivers a tailored experience to every user, so products and services better meet evolving end user expectations. In addition, computational design capabilities increase efficiency by optimizing operational processes. In a transactional journey, this efficiency includes effort reduction, self-serve adoption, and drop-off reduction. As a revenue driver, computational design drives engagement and conversions. Transactional journey metrics include conversion ratio and increased engagement.

Figure 3.4 (see next page) represents how the experience is configured and tailored to each user based on their personality and behavioral traits.

The value of computational design is unlocked progressively, on a compounding basis, as it is deployed in a growing number of scenarios and capabilities within the adopting organization's landscape. Although individual gains might be relative and tactical in isolation, the aggregated gains become a strategically important matter and influence decision making.

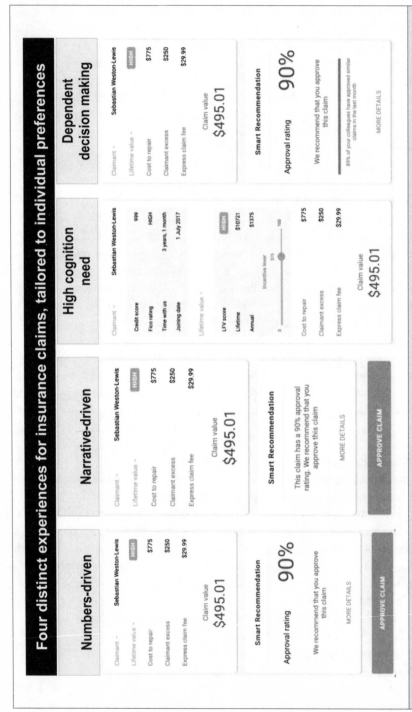

FIGURE 3.4 Customized experience design.

We recommend applying computational design to experiences involving the following criteria:

▶ **Decisions.** Based on role, information preferences, mandate, previous decision-making patterns, or need for cognition.

▶ **Navigation.** How people navigate through an application, similar to Netflix (search, browse by genre, browse by actor, trending [adding peer pressure]). This affects the amount of content choices presented initially and recommendation intensity.

▶ **Support required.** Dynamically increase level of support to complete a transaction. Examples include login, shopping cart checkout, or mortgage application.

▶ **Transactional opportunity.** Dynamically display upsell/cross-sell opportunity in the form of content or service premium, depending on purchaser type. Applies to any transactional site.

▶ **Information and insight.** Applies to dashboards, landing pages, and product listing pages. Based on information preferences, role, decision-making style, and need for cognition.

A Cultural Catalyst for Change

As experience continues to differentiate, design will continue its rise in organizational importance. Gone are the days where a design department engaged mostly in the production of internal marketing material. Design professionals moved up the value chain from visual communications to become designers of the business. As organizations embed design into enterprise architecture and culture, their designers need a diverse set of skills, experiences, and perspectives. Computational design requires a cultural transition within the design function itself, bringing together the worlds of design, technology, and business.

As computational design demonstrates the value of design through a KPI lens, it minimizes one of the primary causes of friction in traditional design—lack of a quantified business case. The appetite and openness to undertake innovation will grow, as computational design continues to deliver compounding value.

Reimagine Employee Experience

EX as Priority

While there are plenty of definitions for employee experience (EX), the key concept is employees at the center, aligned with enterprise. We define EX as organizations and their employees collaborating to create personalized, motivating experiences across work, workforce, and workplace to improve performance and alignment to purpose. Employee experience traditionally played second fiddle to customer experience, but no longer, as organizations understand EX drives business success.

Gallup demonstrates through their research surveys that employee engagement and satisfaction have a direct impact on company performance. Companies with highly engaged workforces outperform their peers by over 100 percent in earnings per share.[1] Happy employees are more productive at work and more likely to recommend the organization to others when they leave. According to Gallup, highly engaged business units reflect lower absences and employee turnover, higher productivity, and even increased sales and profitability. Our own experience bears this out as well. As Live Enterprise principles were adopted across Infosys, employee turnover declined and sales increased.

While savvy companies have always valued employees, three trends elevated the prioritization of employee experience for other firms. First, the talent shortage demonstrated the stakes involved, to get and keep the talent needed to run the business. Stakeholder capitalism highlighted the need to see beyond profitability as corporate goals, and employees took note of their employer's stance on environmental and social issues. Of course, the pandemic also drove home the point that EX includes well-being as well as sentiment and productivity. Tying this all together is trust, that invisible yet deep-seated feeling that is also influenced by how companies address privacy concerns and personal data. Companies must create compelling experiences that win trust so that employees are willing to share that data.

These experiences need to meet employee needs across the life cycle from hire to retire, and reimagined in the context of an anytime, anywhere operating model, where work gets done by employees from anywhere using the connected digital tools provided to them. This is not just about experience, but also requires reimagining existing operational processes, organizational policies, employee engagement, and health and wellness. Increasingly, enterprises need the flexibility to let employees work anytime, anywhere (remotely, at office, at remote site) across a broad spectrum of options: from 100 percent at physical premises to 0 percent at physical premises and all work performed remotely. Reimagining of experiences and processes is done in collaboration to ensure that sentient and computational design elements are weaved in across the entire process.

Go to Win

General Peter Pace (USMC-Ret.), former chair of the US Joint Chiefs of Staff, commented that to succeed, a leader must deliver across three dimensions: "Give very clear guidance, resource it appropriately and go to win."[2]

That guidance shapes employee experience, but the more empowered and self-directed teams are, the harder it becomes to do.

Managers are responsible for 70 percent of the variance in employee engagement,[3] and it's no surprise EX and state of mind rank high on the chief human resource officer (CHRO) agenda. In the pandemic's switch to mass working from home, EX became central to the C-suite agenda too. However, given workforce diversity and variance across industries, there is no one-size-fits-all approach to EX. A good experience for one employee may not be so for another. To deliver on the individual needs of their people, companies must understand expectations, design to deliver that experience, and measure how the solution impacts experience.

Experience-Centric Process Design

Traditionally, process design looked at compliance and efficiency as primary parameters, with experience an afterthought at best. Processes were not designed to deliver a certain experience. That school of thought has now been turned on its head with experience-centric process design. What does that mean to design for EX? Put the employee at the center of the design process, considering their needs and behaviors; consider the functional requirements of the company; consider the culture within which the process exists; then use those inputs to determine the optimal processes and the best digital tools to enable those processes and experiences.

Employee expectations are simple to document, but difficult to make a reality:

- ▶ Employees expect the tools to do their job effectively, like data access at the point decisions are made.
- ▶ Employees expect to use their preferred channels and devices. This could be access to apps and data on smartphones, or the option to connect with the helpdesk via email, phone, chat, or self-service.
- ▶ Employees expect to be empowered to resolve issues quickly. Provide self- service capabilities and minimize the touch points to resolve an issue.

Employee interactions should be fast, accurate, and successful; then deliver them in a manner that exceeds expectations. For example, employees engage with HR frequently on a variety of issues during their tenure at an organization. Their expectation with HR is to receive a one-stop, stress-free experience. HR's priority is to ensure the resolution is completed and recorded, in compliance with policies and regulations. To deliver this successfully they need to understand and align with the employee's frame of mind.

Employee interactions are increasingly digital, and technology plays a significant role to determine satisfaction. The company should provide digital systems that are simple for employees to use, base them on processes designed for experience and performance, and strengthen these systems via continuous cycles of user feedback.

Experience Measurement

Only dissatisfied or extremely delighted employees tend to provide feedback on satisfaction surveys, and measuring employee satisfaction can be difficult, with responses from these groups around only 4 to 5 percent of total participants. A better way to measure experience is to distinguish EX from the desired outcome.

EX is not an outcome in itself. However, it can help predict outcomes of interest, such as engagement or satisfaction. For example, the goal may be increased customer engagement, supported by sentiment analysis at the help desk level, by text analysis of tickets raised. These measurements create a broad, encompassing index of employee happiness that can be benchmarked and tracked over time.

A leading Australia-based telecom company (and Infosys client) deployed an employee sentiment analysis and monitoring tool. Conversation between employees and agents was extracted from the ticketing platform, and a text-mining model was developed and applied on each incoming conversation. From this, every conversation was assigned a sentiment score, which identified trigger points that could potentially lead to escalation or employee dissatisfaction. Based on real-time sentiment scores, each query was flagged and color-coded. The outcome? Timely identification of issues and effective query resolution significantly improved employee satisfaction, and poor sentiments were shared with advocates on the HR team for proactive, affirmative steps to address employee happiness.

The Workplace Reimagined

Moments, Memories, and Magic

Rapidly evolving circumstances require that organizations create employee-centered business environments. Although this represents a cultural shift for traditionalists who just got used to the idea of being customer-centric, our Infosys EX and research indicates employee-centricity does more than improve operational metrics. It also builds resilience through longer employee tenure and develops stronger collaboration and reputation networks.

Every employee is on their own journey, one with a series of moments, memories, and magic—to them, as well as the firm. The business world became familiar with the power of moments that matter through the book of similar name by Chip and Dan Heath. The Live Enterprise principle of micro-change management is based on defining small changes based on noteworthy moments, then reinforcing these interactions so they become memories. These memories are certainly employee memories, but they also become memories in the enterprise knowledge graph and input into the digital brain. Then the best of these memories are combined, enhanced, and amplified to become magical—"wow factors," in the old vernacular.

This concept is loosely aligned to the work of Abraham Maslow, the legendary twentieth-century psychologist, whose 1943 paper "A Theory of Human Motivation"[4] described humans as a perpetually wanting animal and introduced his famous hierarchy of human needs. This is a critical point in 2020, because the pandemic challenged the previously sacrosanct hierarchy of needs and forced us to look at it with fresh eyes. While safety and security were still basic needs, our employees also simultaneously cared about belonging and self-esteem. Some employees even used the pandemic lockdowns as serendipitous opportunities to achieve their full potential, including creative activities—which happens to be the definition of self-actualization. Again, while this reaffirms the needs that Maslow identified, our findings also suggest a transition from a hierarchy to a holistic simultaneous set of needs when people are under stress. This provides information to designers to design experiences that support employees even when working in stressful environments.

Psychology shows that when remembering our experiences, we forget the minute-by-minute and instead focus on certain moments of high intensity or emotion—first day at school, first kiss, birth of a child, or taste of an orange. In the corporate world, leaders are traditionally not equipped to create the flow from moments to memories to magic, because each of these involve distinctly different capabilities of empathy, change management, and sentience. The Live Enterprise model relates each of these experience capabilities in logical progression, aided by flexible architecture and shared digital infrastructure.

Reimagining the Employee Journey

Times have changed, perhaps the understatement of the century. The traditional office workweek has gone, so too the old concept of the "office" itself, as the pace of change has accelerated and people no longer expect to stay 35 years at one company before collecting the gold watch. Consumers switch brands in a heartbeat if their expectations are not met, and employees do too—particularly millennials and generation X. Employees want a career in work environments that share their values and support their journey, a place where they can learn, be challenged, and make a difference in their field or the wider world.

For years, organizations strived to provide good customer experiences, create sensible user journeys, predict customer behavior, and deliver what they want, when and where they want it. Turns out, employees are no different. As Richard Branson said, "Look after your staff, they'll look after your customers. It's that simple." Yet for years employees received the poorest experience of any company stakeholder: with green screens and slow networks, help(less) desks, and sterile cubicles, employees looked with envy as customer and partners received priority and consideration for experience and funding. Exceptions occurred at high-flying tech firms and some other notable companies, but employees typically did not receive high-quality experience and internal systems even at high-performing firms. As the talent war broke out and the talent famine emerged for desirable jobs, companies began to change their priorities, and the COVID-19 outbreak accelerated the shift to valuing employees and their experience.

This is reinforced by Skyler Mattson, president of WONGDOODY, Infosys's global design and experience studio: "The future of work cannot just be the CHRO's job, it must be on the rest of the C-Suite agenda. What we did for consumer experience has to happen for employees—not just a cost-saving exercise, but also a revenue and margin generation opportunity."

To give employees the best experience, the first step is to listen to what they need to determine what they value, no matter how or where they're working—in the office, at home, on the road, or on Teams or Zoom. A useful approach is to apply customer experience principles to employee experience. (See Figure 3.5.)

Mapping the Journey

When they join a company, every employee embarks on a unique journey with many average days but also significant moments, memories, and magic, which are personal to them. These include moving to another role or location, being promoted, or surviving redundancy.

While traditionally the EX covers every employee interaction, special attention should be given to the most significant ones and leaving nothing to chance:

▶ Transitions, like first day on a job, promotion, or leaving the organization.

Customer experience component	How it can be translated in employee experience	Benefits
Personalized experience	Create memorable experiences, reduce friction, identify insightful use case understanding, apply checklist to drive user action	Engaged and operational employee from Day 1
Empathy	Provide a safe and collaborative environment where employees can try, fail, learn	Resilient organization that is truly customer-centric
Encourage involvement	Include call to action such as experimenting with content and peer interactions	Foster adoption through guided learning and support
Integrated and multichannel	Make all touch points lead to a centralized hub	Consistent and adaptable, evolving employee experience across any channel or device
Follow-up	Monitor employee satisfaction and engagement	Provide coaching and continuously optimize the experience

FIGURE 3.5 Replicating customer experience in EX.

Source: Infosys, "The Changing Workplace: Changing Tactics to Craft a Best in Class Employee Experience."

▶ Milestones, such as one-year employment anniversary or achieving a significant sales target.
▶ Pits, such as a critical tool or process not working properly, personal tough times, or even lockdown at home for health reasons.
▶ System interactions on the tools we use to do our basic job function (employee personal productivity app, learning app, onboarding app). While transactions are not memorable individually, over time they inform employee opinion on whether the company values their experience.

To map EX, identify these moments in your organization by talking to employees, and interview a representative sample to discover strengths and pain points in the employee community. (See Figure 3.6.)

Contactless Contact (Center)

The customer service function is undergoing transformation. This manifests as traditional contact centers operating as remote ready centers, traditional voice interactions moving to contactless self-service channels, siloed channels

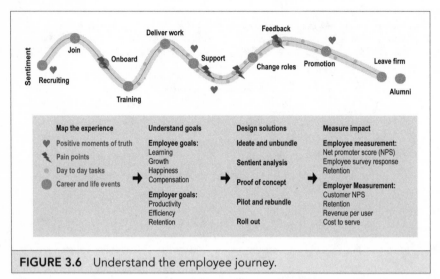

FIGURE 3.6 Understand the employee journey.

Source: Infosys, "The Changing Workplace: Changing Tactics to Craft a Best in Class Employee Experience."

merging to provide an omnichannel experience, and high-touch experiences becoming self-service driven. After the COVID-19 outbreak, these existing trends accelerated, with all companies moving toward the anytime, anywhere model.

At Infosys, a lot of operations that were traditionally done through the contact center have now been made available through our InfyMe personal productivity app, and it has reduced the volume of calls and made it easier for our employees to access these services anytime, anywhere.

Beyond convenience, the experience is also becoming sentient with AI services used to perform deep analytics and deliver real-time guidance to agents so that they are better prepared to handle customer interactions. This improves both customer satisfaction and agent performance. AI predictions, learning, and next best actions empower both new and experienced agents. These capabilities help reimagine entire customer care operations by providing intelligence to aid better communication, smarter and faster decision making, and delivering value at scale.

Carbon + Silicon: The Human-AI Dynamic

As consumers, AI is an increasingly common component of our digital journeys, guiding us with recommendation engines and chatbots that are available 24/7 to answer questions and provide support. AI tools are designed to make things simpler and more efficient, and in a world of information and system overload, they also support and improve the EX.

Too often, when employees think of internal systems, they think of complex web portals and navigation paths. At Infosys, employee applications were a long list of individually functional, but collectively confusing applications. Our internal information systems team converted dozens of separate applications into three employee mobile apps: InfyMe for internal processes, Lex for learning, and LaunchPad for new hire onboarding. The app simplification significantly improved the EX by integrating mobile, chatbot, voice, widgets, and messenger functionality. These stories and their benefits are true across the employee life cycle, but AI assistants are especially helpful in the areas of professional and personal development. Assistants improve professional development by learning about the employee's preferences and interests, and making personalized recommendations that align employee and organization goals. Personal development is aided through analysis of all available employee data and interactions to improve their soft skills and develop their own self-coaching approach.

For human resource leaders, EX unlocks new opportunities to engage employees, in addition to enabling operational efficiency. By bringing all of a team's calendars and relationships together, intelligent applications can suggest time slots when managers should check in with each team member and gently reinforce policy, helping keep companies on the right side of employment law and what's right for their people. Also, employee engagement is dynamic and can now be monitored in real time, on an ongoing basis, with feedback and recommended intervention as relevant.

RECAP: Perceptive Experience

- User centricity is key to everything in the Live Enterprise, with a laser focus on delivering better experience and user hyper-productivity.
- Three ingredients are required to make this work—*heart*, focused on better experience; *brain*, focused on efficiency and continuous learning; and *machine*, focused on measuring, learning, and continuous improvement.
- Heart, brain, and machine create an intelligent, personalized experience that understands the user's context and intent, is predictive, and adapts based on their usage patterns.
- Computational design is a new approach to solve business problems. This new design model is driven by four principles—sentience indicators, codified design language, continuous measurement, and an integration-first approach.
- The platform brings understanding to the user experience, using telemetry to understand usage patterns and frictions in a process of continuous improvement. Data is captured only once—if the information already exists in the enterprise, then users should not be asked to it enter again.

(4)

RESPONSIVE VALUE CHAINS

Hidden Wiring

Yellowstone Lupus

Spanning Wyoming, Montana, and Idaho, Yellowstone National Park was created on March 1, 1872, after being signed into law by US President Ulysses S. Grant. By 1926, Yellowstone's last wolf pack had been hunted to elimination, relieving pressure on the elk population, the wolf's main prey. This caused the elk to stay sedentary and overgraze on willow trees, which beavers needed to survive the winter.

On January 12, 1995, eight *lupus* (gray) wolves were reintroduced to Yellowstone, with an additional 23 reintroduced by the end of the following year, and they galvanized the park's ecosystem.[1] The sole beaver colony in 1995 grew to nine by 2020, thanks to predatory wolves keeping elk on the move, halting the overgrazing and granting beavers an abundant source of food.

It didn't end there. More beavers meant more dams and ponds, meaning a recharged water table in streams, and shaded water for fish. Elk populations avoided the cycle of boom and bust, with more willow creating homes for songbirds. Eagles, ravens, coyotes, and bears benefited too, free to scavenge the elk carcasses in winter helpfully left by wolves.

Lupus restored balance to Yellowstone's habitat and serves as an example of the invisible secondary and tertiary impacts and unintended consequences of actions within a value chain. It also provides a constructive lesson from nature for enterprise value chains.

Keystone Species

Nature is the ultimate value chain, the product of 3.8 billion years of evolutionary experimentation, of regenerative trial and error.

Around 90 percent of wild plant species and 75 percent of crops we use for food rely on pollination by bees, butterflies, and other animals. If bees were a corporation, Forbes estimates their market cap would be $20 billion,[2] with a honeybee colony 100 times more valuable to the community than to its beekeeper (not surprising, given a hive of 50,000 honeybees pollinates half a million plants a day[3]). Insect pollination is worth over $200 billion a year—larger than all but 30 public companies globally—about 10 percent of the total value of annual global agricultural production, and worth over $25 for every man, woman, and child on the planet.[4]

In human terms, bees are part of a value chain not only crucial to our economy, but to our very survival. Value chains are the hidden wiring in our lean, cross-border world of just-in-time. Since China joined the World Trade Organization in December 2001, the global trade in intermediate goods—goods and services used in the eventual production of a final good or finished product—tripled to $10 trillion a year. At the same time, supply chains have grown in scale and complexity, with the likes of Procter & Gamble having over 75,000 suppliers,[5] Walmart 100,000,[6] and Total more than 150,000.[7]

In Yellowstone, the gray wolf acts as a "keystone" species, critical to health of the wider ecosystem. Keystone species come in three types—predators (like the gray wolf), ecosystem engineers (the beaver), and mutualists (like bees and plants). In this chapter we ask, *who are the keystone species in your enterprise value chain, and what types are they?* We also explore how to reimagine with sentient processes to improve performance and resilience.

Value Chains and Zen

In the mid-1700s, Francois Quesnay was the leading thinker among the *physiocrats*—from the Greek for "nature" (*physis*) and "power" (*kratos*)—the earliest school of economic thought. As well as applying the term "*laissez-faire*" (let be), Quesnay published a circular flow diagram of the economy to explain the causes of growth. It was perhaps the first description of a value chain and, along with Joseph Schumpeter, Quesnay is considered one of the great early economists (ironic, given he was originally one of Louis XV's four doctors).

In Michael Porter's seminal 1985 work on value chain analysis,[8] he deconstructed value chains into five primary activities—inbound logistics, operations, outbound logistics, marketing and sales, and service. These are supported by four secondary activities—procurement, human resource management, infrastructure, and technological development. Essentially, the value chain comprises all business activities that create the value of a product or service in the eyes of the customer. While the original language implies supply chains and products, in the digital age, people and bits matter as much as physical product, and modern value chains represent an untapped opportunity in the form of gig economy and marketplaces.

Much like the Yellowstone lupus, responsive value chains are the keystone species that provide stability directly and through their beneficial secondary and tertiary impacts. The value chain across the enterprise ecosystem depends upon change and stability, reimagining and resilience.

Like the best Zen *koan* statement of nonduality, reimagining and resilience are both different and the same. After Wuhan went into COVID-19 lockdown on January 23, 2020, companies scrambled to find both resilience against disruption and reimagining for a changed world.

Sentient Principles

The Cambridge Declaration

On July 7, 2012, the planet's top neuroscientists met at Cambridge University's Churchill College, alma mater to 32 Nobel Laureates, to hold the inaugural Francis Crick Memorial Conference. They released the Cambridge Declaration on Consciousness,[9] signaling perhaps one of history's greatest shifts in human thought. The declaration formally acknowledged that "non-human animals have the capacity to exhibit intentional behaviors." They said that humans are not unique in possessing the "neurological substrates" that generate consciousness. Non-human animals also possess them, including all mammals and birds, and many other creatures, including octopuses.

In simple terms, we are not alone. Other animals are sentient too, which raises the question, why can't machines or even enterprises be sentient as well?

Sentience in the Enterprise

Sentience has several definitions, an ability to sense and perceive, a state of awareness and also responsive to sense impressions. Simplistically, sentience is a state of awareness with perception. To deliver the outcomes of the Live Enterprise model, the architectural layers should have a state of awareness that provides them the ability to sense, process, and respond to changes in state.

In the traditional systems, only the user state is maintained and managed and only for a specific interaction channel; however, to be sentient, state awareness at multiple levels is required as depicted in Figure 4.1.

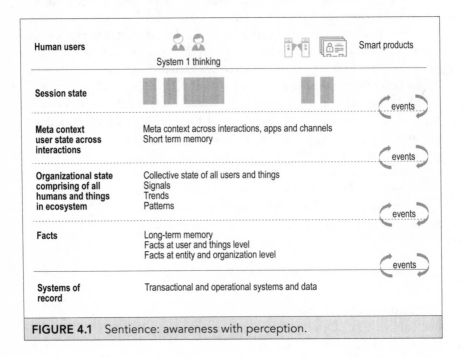

FIGURE 4.1 Sentience: awareness with perception.

User state is managed as part of the session state for the interactions executed within each channel, but there is also a need to manage meta context across each interaction so that state can be carried from one interaction channel to other. An example is the handoff between devices from Apple, one could start an activity like reading an article on one device and then continue reading on another device in the same place, if it meets their continuity requirements.

The collective state of all users and things across the enterprise should be managed, to start curating the organizational state. The organizational state can then be used to understand the collective state of the enterprise at any point of time, trending signals (user mood after a significant event, highly used feature, or most searched information) and trending patterns. Organizational state awareness helps the enterprise understand and react to these signals or patterns in a deterministic or exploratory manner. The state can then be referenced against the organizational body of knowledge to look for anomalies and correlations.

Combined, these layers these create organizational sentience that seeks to make every interaction value-adding, predictive, autonomous, and evolving by continuously learning. Processes are reimagined using organizational sentience and the five sentient principles.

The Five Sentient Principles

Live Enterprise process analysis and reimagining is accomplished through five sentient principles. (See Figure 4.2.)

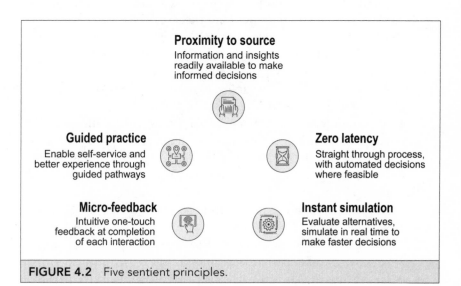

Proximity to source
Information and insights readily available to make informed decisions

Guided practice
Enable self-service and better experience through guided pathways

Zero latency
Straight through process, with automated decisions where feasible

Micro-feedback
Intuitive one-touch feedback at completion of each interaction

Instant simulation
Evaluate alternatives, simulate in real time to make faster decisions

FIGURE 4.2 Five sentient principles.

1. **Proximity to source.** Users should be provided with all the information and insights required for them to make a decision, at the interaction point where a decision needs to be made. This should happen within the same flow of the same user journey and interactions, so that users don't have to go to different screens and applications to find additional information.

   Let's look at the approval flow for travel, a common (pre-COVID-19, anyway) process experienced by many employees. Most routine travel requests should follow a single streamlined approval without requiring additional levels; however, for special situations or exceptions it may have to be referred for escalated approvals. When the travel request goes for approval, the approver should have visibility to the budget available for travel, the number of travel requests in the pipeline, criticality of travel, and the implications of approving this travel on future travels. If the approver has visibility to all the information, then a data-based decision can be made immediately.

2. **Zero latency.** Zero latency identifies how a company arrives at straight through processing across the value chain with the minimal number of steps and approvals required to complete the interaction. Put simply, zero latency is response following input, without delay. Traditionally this has been measured using the turn-around time (TAT) metric for business processes.

   In the insurance industry, claims is a typical business process that has a lengthy turnaround time, and we have observed that work goes through several layers and approvals for a claim to be processed and approved. Our clients are reimagining their claims process using AI to make it straight through for certain types of low-value claims, and to use proactive monitoring and automation to also enable straight through processing in their core claims systems.

3. **Instant simulation.** Instant simulation provides the ability to not only conduct traditional what-if analysis, but also explore alternatives and simulate to make the correct decision. It requires running simulations, practicing the process and predicting potential futures. Users evaluate alternatives at the point of decision making.

   If there is a supply chain disruption due to a route network going down, then the platform should provide the ability to evaluate several alternatives to fulfill the order and simulate the impact of fulfillment time across the alternative routes all in the same user flow.

4. **Micro-feedback.** Micro-feedback is user feedback gathered in the workflow. At the end of each user interaction, ask a simple question to understand their overall experience for this interaction. Increasingly we are seeing usage of visuals to gather feedback, as it is quick and more user friendly.

   As value chains are reimagined by deconstructing them into sets of interactions, use the micro-feedback gathered for each interaction to understand friction points in the overall value chain and to evolve through continuous micro feedback.

5. **Guided practice.** Guided practice provides a well-defined user pathway to complete a specific task or activity. The best practices get codified into the interaction flow itself. This is essential to develop new routines and drive behavior change.

In the learning area, if the user wants to build expertise in a specific technology stack, then the learning platform analyzes their current goals, skills, and expertise, then develops a guided learning path for them to build expertise over time to become an expert. The platform recommends the courses, certifications, and communities to accomplish the objectives.

Sentient Processes

In any large enterprise there are dozens of business processes supporting value chains and business enabling functions. For any process-reimagining exercise, the initial questions that come to mind are, where do you start, and why reimagine a process that works today?

Senior business leaders and process owners often have an intuition of which processes have problems based on customer issues, system issues, and the turnaround times for the processes. However, it is a hunch at best and requires a deeper, more scientific analysis to understand the issues, variations in processes, and improvement opportunities.

Once an initial list of processes is identified based on perceived issues and benefits, they should be classified into two broad categories. One group are processes that are largely manual, and the second are those that are already digitized at some level. For the manual processes, process discovery tools should be used to understand current process performance and user operation.

For the processes that are partially or fully digitized, the mission critical ones will either be running on ERP systems, legacy mainframes, niche so-called best-of-breed products, a bespoke system, or a combination of them. Using existing logs and events generated by these systems, it is now possible to process mine to uncover useful metrics to identify the right candidates for process reimagining.

Process Discovery

Process discovery tools are used to record and capture all the actions performed by knowledge workers in their day-to-day business operations. This information is captured and used to digitize existing manual or semimanual processes, and process maps are generated from this data. Digitized process maps are used as an input to identify high-value processes that can be reimagined to provide exponential value using the Live Enterprise approach. Additional incremental benefits can be realized through deterministic methods like robotic process automation and digitization.

Process Mining

Process mining tools are used to discover, monitor, and analyze runtime processes, identify process variations, and provide real-time performance data. Leading process mining tools are designed to work well with ERP, SAAS platforms, and modern bespoke applications. For mainframe and legacy applications, custom tools may be required to perform process mining.

Process Reimagining Prioritization

Once the data from the actual process execution is gathered using process discovery and process mining, the processes are prioritized for reimagining using the following criteria:

- ▶ **Business criticality and value.** The importance of the process to the overall business, and its impact on revenue, margin, net promoter score, and customer experience. Essential, high-impact processes should be prioritized.
- ▶ **Repetitiveness.** The frequency with which processes are repeated. Less frequently executed processes or one-off processes should be avoided, unless required to meet regulatory or compliance requirements. These could be good candidates for automation and intuitive decisions.
- ▶ **Volume.** The concurrent and total number of transactions and operations performed as part of the process. This helps understand the criticality and complexity involved in reimagining.
- ▶ **Variance.** The variations in the runtime execution of the same process. More variations mean more complexity, with high time to change.
- ▶ **Latency (turnaround time).** Total time to complete the process end to end versus the aspirational turnaround time expected by the business and the customers. This information is useful for progress on zero latency processes.
- ▶ **Touchpoints (human and machine).** The number of handoffs between users, systems, and offline processes like emails to complete an end-to-end process. More touchpoints mean more friction and impact the zero latency and experience objectives.
- ▶ **User experience.** User ability to accomplish an operation through self-service and a unified anytime, anywhere experience versus multiple steps, approvals, and software applications.
- ▶ **Complexity.** Implementation complexity based on the number of touchpoints, variance, integration points, and user experience. If these are business critical, then they are good candidates for process reimagining.

▶ **Intelligence.** Decisions that can be deterministically codified versus ones that require higher order thinking that require AI services or human intelligence. Where possible, consider AI-first processes and introduce instant simulation capabilities.

Based on the previous criteria, a prioritized list of process areas can be identified. This list should then be analyzed through the process reimagining and sentient analysis framework to develop the future processes.

Sentient Analysis Framework

The sentience analysis framework provides a structure for process analysis and "busting," deconstruction and reimagining. Prioritized business processes are classified as manual, semidigitized, or fully digitized. These processes can be either reimagined from the ground up to deliver exponential value or reengineered to drive significant incremental value through these five steps. (See Figure 4.3.)

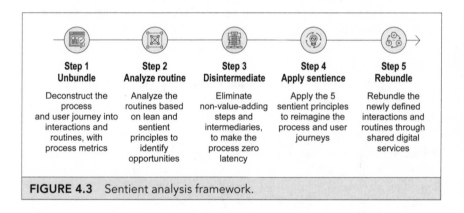

Step 1 Unbundle	Step 2 Analyze routine	Step 3 Disintermediate	Step 4 Apply sentience	Step 5 Rebundle
Deconstruct the process and user journey into interactions and routines, with process metrics	Analyze the routines based on lean and sentient principles to identify opportunities	Eliminate non-value-adding steps and intermediaries, to make the process zero latency	Apply the 5 sentient principles to reimagine the process and user journeys	Rebundle the newly defined interactions and routines through shared digital services

FIGURE 4.3 Sentient analysis framework.

▶ **Unbundle.** Deconstruct the entire business process and the user interactions into a set of user journey and routines, with the breakdown of process metrics at each routine level.

▶ **Analyze routines.** Analyze the routines to determine which of these should be eliminated, changed and new routines created to drive change in the behavior.

▶ **Disintermediate.** Eliminate all the steps and routines that add to latency, add no value, or impact experience, and also remove intermediaries in the process.

▶ **Apply sentience.** Consistently apply sentient principles to the user journeys and interactions so that sentience is designed into the entire reimagined process.

▶ **Rebundle.** Use the shared digital infrastructure services to accelerate benefits realization by rebundling the newly defined interactions and routines.

Let us take an example to illustrate these in action. The typical recruitment process is composed of several steps. A hiring manager develops a job description document defining the role, responsibilities, and skills required and shares it with the recruiter. The recruiter goes over the job sites to search for skills matching the requirements and then downloads the candidate profiles and performs background checks as mandated by the organization. Once the background checks are done, the shortlisted profiles are shared with the hiring manager, who goes over the profiles and then shortlists the candidates. The candidate details are then shared with the recruiter to set up interviews.

Now consider this reimagined process. All the candidate profiles available on accessible job sites are downloaded automatically, and the talent AI service reviews the profiles and extracts all the relevant information like candidate personally identifiable information details (provided in résumé), skills, employers, nature of work, availability, and so on, and loads them into the talent graph. Whenever the hiring manager has an open position, they launch a query against the talent graph, and the talent AI service can find the best matches against the requirements defined by the hiring manager and even search based on existing employee profiles to find the best fit match. What used to take several days and weeks can now be done in real time. The talent AI service must be trained with unbiased data to ensure the matches don't have any biases.

Once designed and implemented, reimagined processes are then delivered using the "micro is mega" thinking by breaking it down into a number of micro-releases and sprints. We cover this concept in Chapter 9.

Structured, Sentient Sprints

In another real-world example, COVID-19 had a crucial impact on real estate, with companies the world over facing the challenge of matching office space with space optimization. The numbers were stark—with lockdowns and travel restrictions forcing employees to work from home, the first half of 2020 saw global commercial real estate occupancy plummet, and investment fell by nearly 30 percent to $321 billion.[10] Infosys operates over 45 million square feet of real estate, and office occupancy and worker safety were real issues.

How did Infosys deal with this dynamic? We'd already created a live occupancy dashboard for each of our buildings in our Bangalore campus, which gave us a rough understanding of occupancy. Then we went deeper, cross-referencing this information with employee travel arrangements, meetings, and vacations to arrive at the real, hour-by-hour occupancy rate. At any point in time, we know how many people are seated in a particular building, in a particular floor, in a particular wing—and for how many hours a day.

The result? We were able to release 2,000 seats in Bangalore alone, freeing up capacity, positively impacting capex, and when the pandemic did strike, equipping the C-suite with the tools to make the right decisions at speed and scale.

Another example, this time of staffing. At Infosys, we use many subcontractors, some for internal work but also thousands for the many client projects we perform. While estimating and approving contractors, it required multiple steps to understand profitability—billing rates, number of hours worked, taxation details, and margin thresholds. Applying the five principles of sentient analysis and framework, we reimagined each stage of the subcontractor process and designed a simple calculator based on the same logic used by the finance team. Rather than depend on someone in finance thousands of miles away, managers globally can now make decisions on the spot and do so within their own approval levels.

Proximity to source, zero latency, instant simulation, micro-feedback, and guided practice—interrelated elements delivered in structured, sentient sprints. It's a powerful combination, where reimagined routines and process allowed us to improve the day-to-day work lives of Infosys employees and elevate EX as an enterprise-level function.

However, a process reimagined is only effective if it's a process adopted. The challenge lies in changing behavior.

Behavioral Change

Mind Tricks and Mentalists

Erik Weisz was born in Budapest in 1874, the son of a rabbi with seven children. Erik eventually moved to New York and at age 20 became a professional magician, renaming himself "Harry Houdini" in homage to the French magician Jean Eugène Robert-Houdin. Almost inevitably, the great Houdini was a household name when he passed away on Halloween at the age of 52.

Great magicians and mentalists understood human psychology better than most, whether amazing audiences or debunking spiritualist charlatans. As director of the MAGIC Lab at Goldsmiths, University of London, Gustav Kuhn leads a team exploring the role of magic in free will, perception, and psychology. Magicians create a cognitive conflict between what we believe and what we experience. Converting that conflict to confirmation is the key to behavior change, including adopting new ways of working in business transformation.

Perception is plastic and malleable. We make "reality" with our own minds, and the magician is a metaphor for the mental complexities shaping our perception—the real trick is to realize the magic happens in our minds, not out there on stage. For external business benefit, seek internal behavior change.

Changing Routines, Changing Behavior

When organizations develop a new routine or process, or reengineer an existing one, their efforts are often based on certain suggestion, cues, and triggers. For maximum effectiveness and employee adoption of new routines, companies typically define and deliver distinctive employee rewards, incentives, and disincentives. However, despite these rewards, adoption rates of new routines are often low, due to apprehension—a natural human reaction to change. As a result, the business impact of these incentives and disincentives is also low and impedes ability to meet program and company objectives.

The challenge is how to ensure that new routines are adopted with minimal reservations by the intended recipients and ultimately achieve the desired results? Put simply, how does a reimagined process become efficient and effective?

Behavioral studies have demonstrated that much of everyday human behavior is performed frequently and automatically—in other words, habitually with people developing habits based on their beliefs.[11] As a result, if a new habit is to be inculcated in a person, it should appeal to their belief system. Based on these findings, it is important that a reimagined process or routine should appeal to employee beliefs, that the individual genuinely believes this new routine is designed for their benefit. Only then will their behavior change and the enterprise realize significant improvement in efficiency, effectiveness, and innovation aptitude.

For routines and process to appeal to employee belief systems, they should be rooted in customer experience and reimagined from the perspective of the people who will actually use them. These human-centered reimaginings are called a "sentient process." As Shakespeare's Henry V warned his troops on the eve of Agincourt, "All things are ready if our minds be so."

Evolving CX to EX

The sentient process and principles are integral to the way experience is designed and delivered to the users. Sentient user experience improves collaboration with customers and partners. It is demonstrated through reimagined processes and routines that are empathetic to user needs. This empathy needs an advocate, and employees fulfill this critical role. As a result, companies build resilience and reimagine process by being inclusive and keeping in mind both customer experience (CX) and employee experience (EX).

Companies increasingly recognize the value of EX to attract and recruit talent and to increase employee productivity. Research from MIT[12] reveals that companies with great EX also outperform competitors on innovation, customer satisfaction, and profitability, delivering:

- ▶ Over half of revenues from new products and services in top quartile companies, compared to less than one fourth in the bottom quartile
- ▶ Over twice the customer satisfaction in the top quartile, compared to the bottom
- ▶ 25 percent greater profitability in top quartile companies than their bottom quartile peers

Just as CX encompasses every interaction across the customer journey, EX encompasses each interaction an employee has with their employer, from job application and initial recruitment, to everyday work experiences and post-employment activities like referrals.

EX advocates stress that it is more than simply employee engagement, and that every aspect of an organization must be involved. However, many companies and consultants take a siloed approach to EX, treating it as part of the HR function—and fail to recognize the value of a human-focused, employee-centric operating model.

EX, Ecosystems, and Archetypes

EX excellence at enterprise scale releases the full potential of the enterprise's greatest asset—its people—and this mass-localized response capability improves market response speed and accuracy. Computational design customizes EX, even at the platform level, transcending HR's exclusive domain so it can reach every facet of a company. The result is a personalized experience for the employee in their collaboration with others internal and external to the enterprise.

Just as in computational design of biological systems, EX design considers the people context in a digital ecosystem. It accomplishes this through the use of archetypes, or behavioral profiles, an assumed ideal pattern based on supporting data. A salesperson archetype, for instance, is assertive, has dense social and business networks, and may make emotion-based decisions. An operations archetype is cautious, has less dense networks, and seeks information to help them make decisions. This is a starting point from which further personalization occurs.

The principle behind EX computational design is that AI works as a digital brain, using data to deliver the right information to users (i.e., employees) with zero latency, at the point they are making their decision. At the same time, it keeps archetypes from lapsing into stereotypes, which are preconceived and oversimplified characteristics.

Corporate Sentience Is Human-Centered

Companies should expand their approach to EX so that it includes the day-to-day work lives of employees and treats EX as an enterprise-level function, not just an HR one. Computational design has the potential to benefit companies to become more customer-centric via informed, empowered employees. It levels the playing field, placing all employees on equal footing as contributors to and recipients of the intellectual capital of the company—as the MIT research demonstrates, ultimately empowering companies to innovate and outperform, powered by automation and AI services.

However, COVID-19 shed light on the inconvenient truth that, when it comes to digitalization, humans still matter—silicon still needs carbon. While automation delivers in terms of cost, speed, and accuracy, lockdowns and quarantines proved that when supply chains stop supplying, value chains lose value, and these ambiguous challenges required the human touch. If proof were ever necessary, the global pandemic demonstrated that people remain a crucial component of the global value chain. We remain a keystone species in this value chain—mutualists like bees and plants—people and technology working together in the physical-digital (the "phygital") to operate and reimagine the enterprise process map.

Problem Children

A fully automated, homogenous process is often inadequate for a successful value stream, with automation appropriate for only a percentage of business scenarios. In a heterogeneous organization like Infosys, with people coming from multiple contexts and units in the organization, standards cannot accommodate all processes. We have found that around 5 percent of transactions fall beyond the bounds of what's normal and can be served with formal documents already in place. The rest of these "problem children" need attention because they can cause a poor user experience, due to the people processing these transactions not being fully equipped to make decisions, and possibly due to inadequate understanding of all the business rules. Some of these scenarios remain undefined, with every problem child transaction having to go through the same painful, manual process. This creates latency, waiting time, frustration, and inefficiency—the very antithesis to the five dimensions of sentient analysis (proximity to source, zero latency, instant simulation, micro-feedback, and guided practice).

Empowered Teams

To deal with these problem children, we experimented by creating an empowered, cross-functional team drawn from key functions across the company—selecting representatives from units like HR, IT, taxation, finance, and global immigration. This team meets daily to look at the backlog of problem children transactions that failed to be resolved in reasonable time. (See Figure 4.4.)

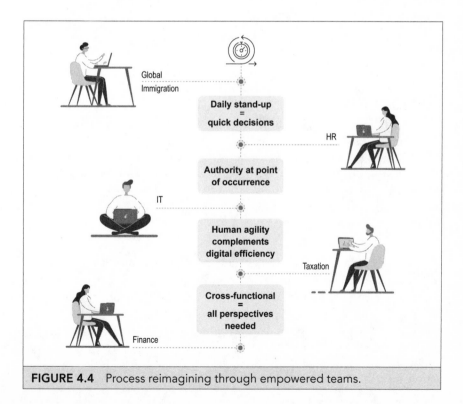

FIGURE 4.4   Process reimagining through empowered teams.

Crucially, this team is empowered to take decisions, to say yes or no. The team is supported by each member's manager, avoiding the need to refer back to their boss and the bosses' bosses. This empowerment and shift to EX have increased agility and speed of responsiveness in making quicker decisions as part of the daily stand-ups.

Process reimagining is not a monolithic approach, and one size does not fit all. In the quest for automation, also understand there are exceptions, and they can be stratified, and embrace the fact that the Live Enterprise model is a human-centric endeavor, while taking full advantage of technology's promise.

Yin and Yang

Like nature itself, self-interest is self-organizing, with evolution driven by many micro-changes that produce large changes in outcome.[13] In the Live Enterprise model, the people closest to the 5 percent of non-normal transactions are the people empowered to address them—and they work in concert with the AI and automation addressing the remaining 95 percent.

Strategically, this allows enterprises to deliver on the following:

▶ Increased velocity of reaction and response to a rapidly changing external environment
▶ Increased velocity of ideas to apply collective insights, experience and knowledge we already possess
▶ Collaborate as a networked organization and prioritize teamwork as the most important goal, with the organization's strengths brought to bear in every customer interaction
▶ Streamline and automate all repetitive operations so people focus on the customer, their own teams, and invest in their own learning
▶ "Walk the talk" of the message to customers and provide them a glimpse of their possible future

The learning here is that even as leaders aspire to be tech companies that fully embrace the benefits of extreme automation, at the same time, they must recognize the yin and yang of human-digital symbiosis. Once again, humans remain a keystone species in the value chain—mutualist carbon and silicon: people and technology working better together than either on their own.

It was only after Wuhan that we realized how important this really is.

Supply Chains

Triple Symbiosis

The value chain examples covered in the chapter thus far focused mostly on people and services. Supply chains add special considerations due to the physical nature of products and the logistical constraints of bringing raw materials to a manufacturing location, conversion to a more valuable product, and then the considerations of storage and distribution to the end consumer.

Given supply chains comprise a system of organizations, people, process, and data to move a product from supplier to customer, they require unique considerations beyond people and technology. Supply chains require a triple symbiosis, an integrated human-digital-physical response. Only then can enterprises achieve supply sentience via reimagined processes and routines that track real-time movement across land, sea, and air. While awareness is a valuable step, resilience requires ecosystem-wide adoption of responses to signal changes, from routine demand-supply fluctuations to unforeseen disruption. While natural disasters and political events occur, COVID-19 has been the most recent, dramatic, and globally pervasive disruption and a test of resilience. Beyond the normal issues of supply and demand, worker health and safety became mission-critical variables as well.

Seeing Beyond

In the end, supply chain resilience is about asking the right questions and having right model to provide the answers you need. What can make what we offer more valuable to our customers? What else can we do that more accurately captures the exact things our customers want, especially right now? And how do we nurture the flexibility to repurpose saved people productivity into reimagining our customer value chains?

While enterprise reports are readily available on traditional performance metrics, risks loom upstream and downstream, outside of the direct line of sight for immediate customers and suppliers. Once again, it's about reimagining any process in the value chain, using the five sentient principles—proximity to source, zero latency, instant simulation, micro-feedback and guided practice.

These principles provide guidance to repurpose people productivity into reimagining and reengineering the company's value chain—see what is not there, what needs to be made better, and what can be eliminated to deliver more value. This drives continuous, agile cycles of rapid adaptation.

RECAP: Responsive Value Chains

- Sentience drives complete reimagination of the value chain through five sentient principles: proximity to source, zero latency, instant simulation, micro-feedback, and guided practice.
- Prioritize business processes for re-imagining through discovery for manual processes and mining for digitized ones. Business value increases when value chains are more responsive and intuitive.
- Unbundle the business process and capabilities into a set of foundational services that are loosely coupled, modular and layered to build value-added features and functions on them. These foundational services can be rebundled in multiple ways to solve different problems or build new products and services.
- For real adoption to occur, employees must develop habits based on beliefs that align to the new process and enterprise overall, and to believe the new routine is designed for their benefit.

(5)

INTUITIVE DECISIONS

From Knowledge to Intuition

Plastic Brains and Neuron Forests

It takes 302 neurons to keep a worm's nervous system ticking, while the capuchin monkey has around 3.7 billion neurons.[1,2] For us humans, the magic number is 100 billion neurons—about the same number of stars in the Milky Way. Those 100 billion neurons spark more than 100 trillion connections, called a "neuron forest" by the experts, where information runs at up to 250 miles an hour inside our skulls. Literally, we are a mass of neural networks that guide our cognition and reasoning, as well as more subtle qualities such as hunches, gut feelings, intuition, and love.

Based on measurements across over a hundred populations,[3] all this happens within an average brain volume of 1,350 cubic centimeters—about the same as four cans of Coke. Running a neuron forest, however, doesn't come cheap. Although only 2 percent of our body weight, the brain consumes almost 25 percent of our energy,[4] using a fifth of the body's blood and oxygen to pump up to a liter of blood through the brain *every single minute*.[5] It's a similar story in the digital world, with digital communication estimated to use a fifth of all electricity on earth by 2025,[6] and data centers alone are estimated to produce over 3 percent of the global carbon emissions in the same period.

One hundred billion neurons generating more than 100 trillion connections gives us an edge—brain plasticity—the ability to rewire neuronal pathways and information flows, create new connections, and adapt to experience.[7] This neuroplasticity comes in two flavors:

▶ **Functional plasticity.** The brain's ability to move functions from a damaged area of the brain to other undamaged areas, often found in stroke victims.

▶ **Structural plasticity.** The brain's ability to actually change its physical structure as a result of learning. London cab drivers, for example, have to pass the world's most stringent test ("The Knowledge"[8]) before earning a cab license. They must commit over 60,000 London streets and 320 routes to memory over the course of four years. London taxi drivers have more gray matter in their posterior hippocampi.[9] In effect, they pump their memory centers like Arnold Schwarzenegger pumped his biceps.

Maximum Intuition, Minimum Intervention

Thanks to those 100 billion neurons, the human mind is wired to see patterns, an essential aspect of intelligence. The mind processes information in conjunction with insights from past experiences to create intuition, and intuition guides much of our decisions.

Leading organizations are developing a similar intuition to drive decisions swiftly and accurately, and to act with resilience in the face of disruption. Sentience enabled by AI and automation are fundamental to this capability so that decisions and responses to data-led insights are acted upon with maximum human intuition and minimum human intervention.

This manifests in an ecosystem of tools that captures and maps complex and vast process environments. Businesses rely on historical and live data, both qualitative and quantitative, to learn from and then guide the formation of patterns that automatically detect, classify, and resolve problems. These patterns also help companies see opportunities to improve the things they already do.

Organizations use process and mining tools to digitize existing manual and semiautomated processes, and also capture variants and flow. Robotic process automation and similar tools have created digital workers, worker bots, and micro-bots that automate, optimize, and take on much of the deterministic decision load. While this rules-based automation has had enormous impact, organizations now have the potential to develop a similar intuitive approach to make decisions swiftly, accurately, and even with self-healing resilience in the face of disruption. AI and related tools of machine learning (ML), deep learning (DL), and natural language understanding (NLU) make this possible.

These tools allow businesses to automate routine and deterministic decisions, while at the same time provide instant simulation capabilities for users to experiment and test. Then users can make more complex decisions about what and how to adapt, like in response to disruption that emanates after a crisis situation.

Context with Data at the Center

COVID-19 pushed millions of companies into uncharted territory. Conferences turned virtual, Zoom replaced air travel, and work routines changed. The work paradigm shifted, and companies rapidly evolved to support remote collaboration at scale.

These changes also increased use of data to make informed and critical business decisions. As data moves from independent data centers to a centralized cloud and to the edge, AI algorithms will mature and optimally plan operations and infrastructure. Enterprises will transform their process-based ecosystem into an intelligence-driven ecosystem. This shift will be orchestrated through algorithms with data at the center. As this shift occurs, experience will be delivered through the context captured across digital touchpoints—and it will be delivered quickly, with feedback and knowledge provided instantly at the point of question. This requires enterprises to move from managing data to becoming intelligent with AI at its core.

We see this happening in the conversational commerce market. The user can start a conversation through one of the channels they are already using like WhatsApp or a WeChat, and take a picture of the product that they liked and are keen to buy; then the platform automatically does a visual search and finds the best fit matches and recommends to the user in the same interface. The customer can get more details about the product over the same conversation in the same channel (Q&A chat), with the platform providing the ability to check out and close the transaction at that point. If the user decides to not act and after few days gets into a conversation through another channel (perhaps contact center), then the platform carries the context and helps the customer associate drive closure of the product sale.

From Managing Data to AI at Its Core

It seems every business is in the midst of a digital transformation journey and accelerating cloud adoption to operate in a remote-working model. This provides a unique opportunity to modernize, remove boundaries, and increase intelligence in enterprise systems.

The Three Horizons

AI has evolved rapidly in recent years, with companies progressing through distinct stages of adoption and AI usage. This evolution can be explained by examining AI maturity across three horizons—past, present, and future:

Horizon 1 (H1) systems are characterized by fragmented data and intelligence within existing systems, with capabilities like recommendation and fault prediction, implemented using classical AI algorithms like Naive Bayes,[10] support vector machines,[11] and Random Forest.[12] Today most of the enterprise data sits within these systems and is being used to deliver the basic predictive and recommendation services.

Horizon 2 (H2) systems are characterized by centralizing data into data warehouses and data platforms and using data intelligently to drive better insights. Data from H1 is modernized and moved to newer architectures to enable better visibility and data-driven decisions. These datasets are also used for AI techniques like deep learning that are very data hungry.

Horizon 3 (H3) is distinguished from H1 and H2 through connected data across the company and external sources. Data is combined physically in the knowledge graph or virtually curated, cleansed, and connected in an automated manner. Connected data across and beyond the enterprise derives insights from these connections. Usage of AI services is starting to become core to business processes, which is driving the need for explainable and ethical AI practices.

These horizons are depicted in Figure 5.1.

As enterprises move toward an AI-driven core, the usage of algorithms, models, and services also becomes increasingly sophisticated. Figure 5.2 shows the evolution of algorithms required to deliver AI capabilities across the three horizons.

The field of AI has made rapid progress over the last decade, and enterprises are starting to move from point AI services and solutions to large-scale deployment and adoption, though they are still at nascent stages. We studied the maturity and trends in AI adoption across our more than 1,400 clients and the industry overall, and found 11 macro-trends across seven AI subdomains. (See Figure 5.3.)

1. AI algorithms and architectures
2. Computer vision
3. Speech

H3
DATA ECONOMY AND LIVE ENTERPRISE
Data the New Capital, AI Transforms Life, Economy

Enterprises have data connected across the ecosystem
Intelligent and connected data systems become the
digital brain

H2
DATA AND DIGITAL NATIVE ENTERPRISE
Innovate, Transform, Reimagine Business

Organizations undergoing digital transformation
Use innovation and reimagining to leverage digital
technology strategically

H1
DATA-DRIVEN ENTERPRISE
Better Decisions

FIGURE 5.1   Connected data across the three horizons.

Source: Infosys, "Connected Data: Powering the Live Enterprise."

	Horizon 1 (Mainstream)	Horizon 2 (Adopt, Scale)	Horizon 3 (Envision, Invent, Disrupt)
Algorithms	• Logistic Regression • Naive Bayes • Random Forest • Support Vector Machines (SVM) • Collaborative Filtering • n-grams	• Convolution Neural Networks (CNN) • Long Short-Term Memory (LSTM) • Recurrent Neural Networks (RNN) • Word2Vec • GloVe • Transfer Learning (Vision)	• Explainable AI • Generative Networks • Fine Grained Classification • Capsule Networks • Meta Learning • Transfer Tearning (Text) • Single Shot Learning • Reinforcement Learning • Auto ML • Neural ArchitectureSearch (NAS)
Use Cases	• Recommendations • Prediction • Document, Image Classification • Sentiment Analysis • Named Entity Recognition (NER) • Keyword Extractions	• Object Detection • Face Recognition • Product Brand Recognition, Classification • Speech Recognition • Sentence Completion • Speech Transcriptions • Topic Classification • Topic Extraction • Intent Mining • Question Extraction	• Scene Captioning • Scene Detection • Store Footfall Counts • Specific Object Class Detection • Video Scene Prediction • Auto Learning • Fake Images, Art Generation • Music Generation • Data Augmentation

FIGURE 5.2   Evolution of algorithms and use cases.

Source: Infosys.

4. Natural language processing
5. AI on the edge
6. AI life-cycle tools
7. AI governance

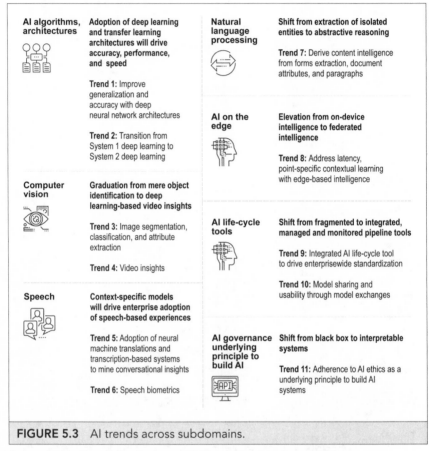

AI algorithms, architectures	Adoption of deep learning and transfer learning architectures will drive accuracy, performance, and speed	Natural language processing	Shift from extraction of isolated entities to abstractive reasoning
	Trend 1: Improve generalization and accuracy with deep neural network architectures		Trend 7: Derive content intelligence from forms extraction, document attributes, and paragraphs
	Trend 2: Transition from System 1 deep learning to System 2 deep learning	AI on the edge	Elevation from on-device intelligence to federated intelligence
Computer vision	Graduation from mere object identification to deep learning-based video insights		Trend 8: Address latency, point-specific contextual learning with edge-based intelligence
	Trend 3: Image segmentation, classification, and attribute extraction	AI life-cycle tools	Shift from fragmented to integrated, managed and monitored pipeline tools
	Trend 4: Video insights		Trend 9: Integrated AI life-cycle tool to drive enterprisewide standardization
Speech	Context-specific models will drive enterprise adoption of speech-based experiences		Trend 10: Model sharing and usability through model exchanges
	Trend 5: Adoption of neural machine translations and transcription-based systems to mine conversational insights	AI governance underlying principle to build AI	Shift from black box to interpretable systems
	Trend 6: Speech biometrics		Trend 11: Adherence to AI ethics as a underlying principle to build AI systems

FIGURE 5.3 AI trends across subdomains.

Source: Infosys Knowledge Institute, "AI-First to Be a Live Enterprise."

Enterprises can begin to experiment and scale AI with increased confidence, with advancements in AI capabilities provided by cloud providers as APIs, open-source frameworks and models, and niche AI platform services. This requires enterprises to build three kinds of capabilities: AI cloud, AI engineering, and model repository (with feature stores). AI cloud operates across private and public clouds and runs the AI workloads. AI engineering life-cycle tools automate the entire development and deployment of AI services and data catalog. Model repositories and feature stores curate data-sets, keep track of the latest models, and drive feature engineering to fulfill AI-driven business capabilities.

Latency on the Edge

As a species, we produce an estimated 2.5 quintillion bytes of data each day, enough to fill 10 million Blu-ray discs, which if stacked in a pile would be over twice the height of Manhattan's Freedom Tower (where Infosys has an office on an upper floor).[13] In our always-on, ever-connected society, enter-prises are bombarded with huge amounts of data from sensors, smartphones, social media, Internet of things (IoT) devices, and structured operational transactions. AI engines distill strategic value from this data to deliver zero latency insights, train algorithms, and update event-driven actions of mission-critical applications.

AI improves user experience through intelligence at the edge. Edge-based AI plays a critical role in remote locations where network connectivity is unre-liable, yet sub-second response times are required for hyper-contextualization through user-specific data.

Smart reply, smartphone autofill on smartphones, voice recognition, voice assistants, facial biometrics, and autonomous navigation—each uses local, natively deployed AI models to improve response to user actions. In the absence of a local AI model, the inference or prediction must be accessed remotely, risking outcome accuracy and user experience.

This differs from traditional analytic tools that operate on data at rest, inactive data stored in any digital form. Since not all data collected is rele-vant for future use, this need for real-time analytics has driven the shift from batch processing to real-time data streaming.

As enterprises experiment and scale AI, a significant constraint is data availability to train AI models. Enterprises have become data hungry and seek to use data strategically to link disparate systems and create a connected data ecosystem.

Connecting Data Through the Knowledge Graph

Billions

Earlier we looked at how 100 billion neurons generating more than 100 tril-lion connections give humans an edge, plus our ability to rewire neuronal pathways and information flows, create new connections, and adapt to expe-rience. Information runs between neurons for everything we see, think, or do. Similar to human beings, enterprises also connect business, operations, and knowledge using the knowledge graph. The knowledge graph is a collection of entities, things, and artifacts that are linked together based on their relationships with each other. The knowledge graph provides a programmatic way to link entities and their relationships using human experts and algorithms. The amazing capabilities of knowledge graphs are now possible through a new class of graph databases.

Just like in the human brain where neurons move information at different speeds, the data from diverse source systems within and outside the enterprise are brought into the knowledge graph at different speeds and freshness, based on what each source system supports. The goal is to link and connect the data in real time so enterprises can use the graph to make data-driven decisions and sense, process, and respond to changing business stimuli.

Data must be connected to create an AI-driven core, and the enterprise knowledge graph is the vehicle to do so. It links all information across sources spanning employees, customers, partners, networks, devices, and the interactions between them. The knowledge graph is used to connect these islands of information to improve visibility and then drive intelligence from this enriched view. Architecturally, the knowledge graph sits within the technology layer and maps relationships between data sources, including entities, interactions, events, and information content. Provided in Figure 5.4 is a representative knowledge graph model for employees.

The knowledge graph is used for a diverse set of use cases. These include customer 360-degree visibility, knowledge asset search, recommendations, and enabling Q&A-based conversations.

Infosys has over 240,000 employees, each with specific skills, and working on distinct projects, who develop specific software for a range of clients. All this data can be modeled as a network—a graph—so that each employee is linked to their specific skills, projects, and other artifacts. The knowledge graph drives contextualization and search, depending upon the situation, where relevant information is prioritized and shown to users.

Why is this the optimal approach? In a relational database, finding and managing multiple relationships becomes difficult, and suboptimal due to time and cost. A knowledge graph models relationships and simplifies the search process. If an HR employee searches for a candidate with journalism skills, they may not find someone in journalism, but they may find someone who is a blogger, since certain skills are common to both. This provides the organization a way of unearthing subtle relationships difficult to find through a relational model.

Knowledge graph technology is used extensively by the major technology firms to drive their core business. Google search and Microsoft Bing are both

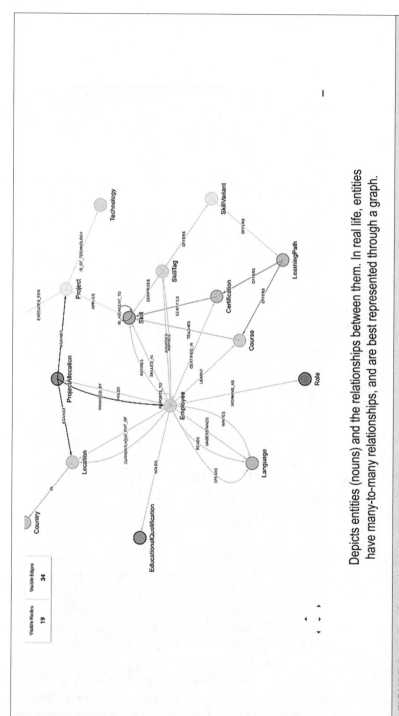

FIGURE 5.4 Employee knowledge graph.

Depicts entities (nouns) and the relationships between them. In real life, entities have many-to-many relationships, and are best represented through a graph.

Source: Infosys.

powered by a knowledge graph that is used to support search and answer questions at global scale. Facebook has the world's largest social graph that connects Facebook users with their friends, interest, music, movies, and so on. In a networked world of relationships, the knowledge graph is supreme, and it has become an important component of our digital journey at Infosys. For enterprises seeking to become more like the previously described hyper-scalers and adopt the Live Enterprise model, knowledge graph implementation is a significant step in the right direction.

Bringing a Knowledge Graph to Life

While designing and building the knowledge graph, keep the user in mind, as well as the purpose for which it will be used. This fit for purpose focus identifies the relevant entities, their relationships and source systems, and sources structured and unstructured data from core systems and brings them into the knowledge graph. The graph is loaded based on ability of source systems to supply data in real time or periodic intervals.

Both raw and computed data are maintained using a combination of analytical and graph databases. During loading, data de-identification is performed where required to meet privacy and security needs. Once the knowledge graph is active, it is continuously observed and tracked for coverage, correctness, usage, and consumption.

As the knowledge graph is populated and enriched with critical volumes of data, machine learning and deep learning capabilities systematically improve the graph's accuracy and outcome of the features and functions it supports. The knowledge graph becomes a primary source for the digital brain to sense what is happening in the enterprise ecosystem and quickly respond.

Digital Brain

Curated Knowledge and Intelligence

The digital brain is a set of deterministic and machine learning, deep-learning-driven code that continuously senses and looks for significant signals, trends, and patterns. The digital brain processes this input to determine if any action is required, and if so triggers actions and nudges. It then monitors the response to these actions and learns and evolves from them.

While the AI field itself is evolving and artificial general intelligence is not yet mature, the idea is to make decisions autonomously where AI augments and amplifies human intelligence. To enable these decisions, the digital brain continuously curates organizational knowledge. It captures and analyzes enterprise ecosystem data using machine learning, deep learning, and automated reasoning to orchestrate intelligent responses to emerging events.

Referencing our three-horizon framework, Horizon 3 (H3) systems evolve from semisupervised to unsupervised, transparent, multitask learning systems. Semisupervised machine-intelligence-based examples generate textual, audio, and video content, plus video-based insights generation, like activity recognition and video summarization.

Connected data systems perceive changing patterns and act where the rules are clearly understood, while deferring to its human partners when decisions are ambiguous or require higher-order thinking. This connected data becomes the feeder to the enterprise digital brain, increasing responsiveness by expediting decision making, while also recognizing new patterns that lead to innovation and evolve the business.

The Force Behind Sentient Routines

Every company needs a digital brain—a nexus for continuous, automated learning from data across business units and product lines, providing the enterprise higher cognition. The success of tech titans like Google and Amazon is driven by their ability to quickly connect the dots between microprocesses to exploit. A core component of the Live Enterprise model, the digital brain adds this intelligence, using automated reasoning to aid users through nudging and guided feedback. Refer to Figure 5.5 (see next page) for a conceptual design of the brain.

The digital brain comprises three key components—inceptor, inciter, and cognizer. The inceptor is constantly monitoring the knowledge graph, the event gateway, and any other source that publishes signals. The brain agents are developed to look to identify different kinds of signals, patterns, anomalies, and any event of interest. After identifying the signal, the agent invokes the resolver to process the signal. Depending upon the type of signal, the resolver invokes either deterministic or cognitive processors to process the signal. The processor determines if any action needs to be taken, then it invokes the action summarizer to determine the steps or processes to be executed and uses the inciter to execute them. The actions can either be executed through nudges or rich cards, or bubbled up as notifications like messages, alerts, or actions displayed in the experience layer for users to inform and act upon. The cognizer enables a conversational mechanism for the users. For example, users can ask a question that is processed and translated by the cognizer to understand the intent, process, and response to user queries. The cognitive processors use several classes of AI services—vision, text, speech,

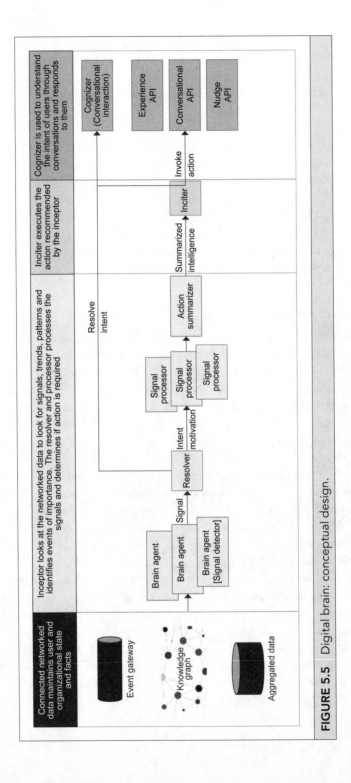

FIGURE 5.5 Digital brain: conceptual design.

language, recommendations, decisions, and operations. These services add cognitive capabilities to the digital brain, which is continuously learning and improving from the interactions.

The digital brain makes decisions that could be automated or made based on available data. When unacceptable risks occur, decisions are pushed out to human actors who use this knowledge to make decisions. It nudges the user to act, and it decides automatically where decisions have to be made to approve routine, not significant, actions. The experience configurator responds as well and actually pushes these experiences to individual users, whether internally to an employee or externally to a customer.

Using flight ticket booking as an example, the digital brain is the architectural intelligence layer that understands a user's search history and transaction-level activity, which it uses to guide the experience. The brain suggests hotels and taxis that the user might book by looking at historical market data—user preferences and where they stayed in the past. Then the digital brain identifies an insight—perhaps this person always stays at a Marriot hotel, and booked a particular location in Miami on a previous trip. This is the level of granularity the digital brain can recommend while booking travel.

Sometimes these insights from the brain are based on what a user is doing in a particular transaction, linking it to insights that the platform already has, based on current context. If a user searches a city and a particular location on a given day, the digital brain's recommendation service informs the person, "If you are booking in this location, here are potential options where our company has a corporate agreement."

These sentient routines use automation within the digital brain to nudge the user. Design principles like proximity to source, zero latency, and guided practice ensure the user can perform the task, the information is accurate, and support is available if they are unsure how to use the function. The architectural process layer can then execute promptly with minimal or no intervention. The digital brain construct is primarily a business, not technical entity, and everything is designed to increase decision-making capability and impact.

Goldfish and Hyper-Personalization

Herbert A. Simon was a Nobel Prize–winning economist and AI founding father who studied the decision-making processes in economic organizations.[14] He asserted that information consumes the attention of its recipients and famously predicted that the greatest challenge to marketing was going to be a "poverty of attention" driven by a wealth of information, "and a need to allocate that attention efficiently among the overabundance of information sources that might consume it."[15] That is now a reality, as the earlier mantra of "information is power" has become "drowning in data, starving for time."

According to a recent customer experience impact survey,[16] 86 percent of customers are willing to pay more for a better customer experience. This provides organizations an opportunity to differentiate through hyper-personalization—the next stage in the evolution of personalized marketing. Why is hyper-personalization important?

- ▶ According to LinkedIn Marketing Solutions, user engagement with content has decreased by 60 percent, with information overload causing consumers increasingly to tune out.[17]
- ▶ Research by Microsoft reveals companies now have only eight seconds to capture and hold the attention of a customer—*meaning we now have attention spans one second shorter than a goldfish.*[18] To be noticed and maximize customer attention without being distracted, communication must stand out and break through the noise.
- ▶ According to Google, "best" search phrases increased by 80 percent in two years on mobile devices.[19] Consumers are searching online to make informed purchasing decisions, where it appears no decision is too small.

Kittens and Kardashians

In the online battle against kittens and Kardashians for buyer attention, hyper-personalization leverages AI and real-time data to supply more relevant content, product, and service information to every user. The likes of Amazon, Starbucks, and Spotify owe much of their success to predictive personalization, where AI and machine learning drive recommendation engines analyzing multiple data sources focused on the individual consumer. Starbucks creates personalized customer interaction programs to foster an emotional connection with the brand. This is made possible by Starbucks cultivating a strong AI-led, customer-first philosophy across its customer engagement campaigns.

With customers using multiple devices that provide businesses with information about their life style and behavior, enterprises are investing heavily to connect enterprise-wide data to provide an omnichannel contextual experience. Connected enterprise data forms the digital brain and enables continuous, automated learning from data across business units, departments, product lines, and services.

To design EX at Infosys, we studied how people interact with data. For example, our executives look at KPIs on their smartphone, notice a change, ask the smartphone why, and the device responds. The learning system behind these interactions continues to evolve, because as new signals come in, the knowledge graph expands.

The knowledge graph and digital brain create perceptive experiences and make intuitive decisions. It's like a human being, where our brain impacts every aspect of what we do. It's essentially the way the brain itself works, with distinct short-term and long-term memory. Short-term memory is a collection of what the user is doing right now and provides the context that then gets applied to the long-term memory. Rajeev Nayar is an Infosys vice president and AI leader who led the development of digital brain architecture for the company. According to Nayar, "The knowledge graph is essentially that long-term memory. We developed a framework around the concept and how these brains are built."

AI Services

At Infosys, the knowledge graph and digital brain connect and link all information in the architectural intelligence layer. In this layer, we also established extreme automation through AI capabilities that bring together multiple technologies on a single platform: big data, analytics, machine learning, deep learning, and cognitive automation with robotic process automation and natural language processing.

A global consumer goods company enhanced their existing recipe site to sign up unregistered consumers through an exclusive experience, and used unique recipes and products to turn them into loyal customers. They created a taste graph that was constantly enriched through agents that identified local recipe origin, consumer affinity toward brands, and trending topics across products and recipes. Core digital brain services intelligently perceived relevant signals like party planner posts from consumer clicks and pushed contextualized exclusive proposals to their consumers. The taste graph, along with digital brain services, enabled the client to promote specific brands across locations and demographics. Consumers experienced the brand, contextualized to their taste through connected data across channels and touch points, and based on preferences derived from the taste graph.

It is an understatement to say airline operators seek to minimize the time that their planes spend on the ground. But this is challenging, due to complex maintenance, repair, and overhaul (MRO) activities, which differ significantly across aircraft types. A major aircraft manufacturer recognized this challenge as an opportunity as well. This client realized that if all MRO documents were stored securely in one place, they could solve this problem for themselves and for other airlines. Through cloud services, the company developed a system that enabled engineers to access the MRO information of every manufacturer's plane with ease, and made all data available securely in one place.

The solution not only solved the MRO challenge for our client, it also created a $25 million incremental revenue pipeline, plus an additional $1 million in annual cost savings.[20]

As the digital brain develops from an infant to a child and to digital adulthood, it evolves beyond what-if analysis to instant simulation to evaluate alternatives and options to complex problems.

Instant Simulation

The Strong Stone and 37th Move

South Korean Lee Se-dol was a 9 dan professional Go player—which means he was *very* good. As the second winningest Go player ever in international titles, Lee's nickname was *Ssen-dol* ("The Strong Stone").

Go is an abstract, two-player board game invented 2,500 years ago, where the objective is to surround more board territory than the opponent. Considered one of the four essential arts by aristocratic Chinese scholars, the number of board positions in Go is approximately 2×10^{170}, orders of magnitude greater than the number of atoms in the known universe (10^{80}). Put simply, Go is complex, *very* complex, a googol times more complex than chess—essentially, Go is to chess what chess is to checkers.

In March 2016, Lee competed against Google DeepMind's AlphaGo,[21] a computer program with deep neural networks taking the Go board as a real-time input, and processing it through many network layers with millions of neuron-like connections. In the 37th move of the second game, AlphaGo made a "very strange move" to the right of the board. It was so strange that Lee left the room for 15 minutes to compose himself and plan a response. The move proved pivotal in the relationship between humans and AI. Watching live, fellow Go expert, Fan Hui commented, "It's not a human move. I've never seen a human play this move. So beautiful."

In one of history's greatest duels between carbon and silicon, AlphaGo won the game, eventually winning the contest 4–1. Three years later, Lee retired, referring to AI as "an entity that cannot be defeated." AlphaGo relied on a mix of AI, machine learning, and deep learning. Although these technologies joined forces to defeat Lee Se-dol, they have subtle yet profound differences.

AI, Machine Learning, and Deep Learning

Imagine a set of three nested, Russian matryoshka dolls. The largest represents AI, the next is machine learning, and the smallest represents deep learning.

Put simply, AI is essentially machines doing tasks that typically require human intelligence. AI includes machine learning, where machines learn through experience to acquire skills independent of human involvement. Deep learning is a subset of machine learning, where artificial neural networks learn by analyzing large amounts of data.

Deep-learning algorithms are inspired by the human brain. Similar to how we learn from experience, deep-learning algorithms perform a task repeatedly, with each iteration tweaked a little to improve the outcome. It's called *deep learning* due to the neural networks having various deep layers that enable the learning.

Accuracy, Performance, and Speed

Instant simulation is where users conduct software simulations by running what-if scenarios in the flow and on the fly. These simulations are used to predict system performance in current production environments. The engine comprises system performance models and is built using real-world performance test results and forecasted workload. In cases where the system performance does not meet predefined service level agreements (SLAs), proactive corrective action can be taken before issue actually arise.

Monitoring a real-world production environment provides data on workload and performance, and a large set of this data can then be used to predict workload. This modeling and simulation-enabled performance testing is further used to strengthen test results and provide informed recommendations to improve performance. These models can be revised to overcome the differences between test and production environments using industry benchmarks.

Zero Latency

Platform adaptive features rely heavily on real-time data collection and processing to produce powerful insights that shape user experience. Using the principles of sentience (see Chapter 3), these signals deliver rich experience in real time. Adaptive learning uses the concepts of zero latency and instant simulation.

Zero latency is the state where a system responds instantly to information input. Zero latency avoids multiple layers of processing before anything meaningful is extracted. Instead, it uses the data available at the point of origin as efficiently as possible to minimize iterations. Instant simulation then flows from zero latency. The platform evaluates data and creates what-if scenarios in situ to guide users through alternate learning paths that may prove more appropriate.

This is driven by data platforms that evaluate distinctly different alternatives instantly while in the flow. Deep-learning and transfer-learning architectures enable instant simulation that drives adoption and improves accuracy, performance, and speed.

Adoption of deep-learning-based solutions to solve enterprise-class problems is driven by availability of graphics processing unit computing (GPU), availability of labeled data, and fast-paced innovations in algorithms. These solutions promise higher accuracy and better generalization characteristics compared to classical algorithms such as support vector machines, Naive Bayes, and Random Forest. However, the need for a large set of labeled data and the cost of GPU computing are still significant barriers to mainstream adoption of deep learning. Transfer-learning-based models have made significant headway to overcome the limitations of insufficient labeled data and GPU availability. Addressing complex problems in computer vision, natural language processing, and speech domains has become feasible with evolving architecture like Transformer,[22] a neural network architecture well-suited to understanding language.

In the insurance industry, simulation models evaluate risk while minimizing reliance on old claims records. This allows insurers to offer adequate coverage and better serve high-risk customer segments. Advanced modeling forecasts diverse risk scenarios, from damage due to faulty plumbing, to production shortfalls in a wind farm. Importantly, it prevents overselling, especially in health insurance, where brokers often pitch inappropriate plans or oversell coverage. Simulations enable insight-driven pricing models to use personal data and consolidated statistics, which optimizes the cost of personalized health plans.

Simulation has transformed industrial services to understand likely performance for individual assets. To achieve enterprise-scale simulation, digital twin models are required for every asset in their portfolio. GE has created digital twins that simulate full-scale, complex system interactions via simulation and determine optimum performance indicators for high-probability scenarios. By leveraging large data sources for weather, performance, and operations, these simulations play out possible scenarios and assess their potential impact.

Power generation companies run instant simulation to plan service-versus-efficiency trade-offs so that electrical power is delivered through minimal fuel consumption levels or to optimize price. Railway companies also run instant simulation to optimize fuel costs and emissions via variables like train weight, car configuration, route topography, and environmental conditions.

Consider the traditional recruitment process, where the hiring manager documents job profiles and requirements and then shares it with a hiring manager, who then posts it across multiple job sites and sources suitable profiles by applying human intelligence. After sourcing the profiles, the recruiter sends it back to the hiring manager who shortlists a few profiles and then schedules interviews with candidates to find the right fit. Typically, the entire process takes several weeks. AI services extract the knowledge from the candidate profiles automatically and load it into the knowledge graph. Then, real-time matching is done to find the best-fit candidates by leveraging organizational data in the graph. It is important to remove biases from the data to ensure fair outcomes. At Infosys we used implemented AI-first processes in our recruitment platform using knowledge graph and sentient process reimagining, and it delivered significant benefits. The talent matching to job profiles is done in real time and has decreased the overall cycle time.

AI Must Be Ethical

Explainable AI

As AI systems gain widespread adoption, the need increases for explainability and trust in the decisions made by these systems. Explainable AI (XAI) addresses the major issues that hinder our ability to fully trust AI decision making and ensures better outcomes for all involved.

The next decade will be marked by rapid advancements in AI and a corresponding compound effect on the global economy. By 2030, AI is estimated to raise global GDP by $16 trillion.[23] With AI systems increasingly central to critical decision-making systems, the decisions and outcomes generated by these systems become critical too. However, in the recent past there have been examples where the outcomes led to highly visible ethical missteps. These included an AI hiring algorithm biased against specific races and genders, prison sentences having twice the false-positive rate for black defendants as for white ones, and car insurance automatically classifying men under 25 years as reckless drivers.

As a result of these widely publicized examples, AI attracted significant negative press because of failed systems, resulting lawsuits, and other societal implications, to the point that regulators, official bodies, and general users seek ever greater transparency in decisions made by AI-based systems. In the United States, insurance companies must explain their rates and coverage decisions, while the European Union introduced the right to explanation in its General Data Protection Regulation.[24]

Doubts still remain, however, whether humans should be confident enough to trust AI yet. This skepticism has driven a need for transparency in machine learning, which has led to the growth of XAI to demonstrate how AI benefits society instead of harming it. Two of the biggest issues that XAI addresses are bias in AI systems and opaque AI decision making.

Deep Learning and Black Boxes

Deep learning originates from the connectionist approach to AI, where models comprise layers of nodes that use inner products and nonlinear functions to perform basic operations. Inside a neural network, there are no separate or discernible logical entities but rather an indistinguishable mass of numerical values. Users feed inputs into the neural network in the form of vectors, which are numbers derived from original data sources and listed in fixed sizes. As a result, there is no direct way to trace the reasoning implicitly used by the neural network to reach its conclusions.

Despite early attempts to extract rules from neural networks, with millions of nodes, these networks have become too large and diverse for users to attempt rule extraction. As a result, the term "black box" describes the opacity of the internal workings within these systems.

Confronting Bias in AI

Everyone suffers some level of cognitive bias, errors in thinking where the context and framing of information influence our judgment. Wikipedia lists 185 kinds of cognitive bias, ranging alphabetically from *agent detection* ("the inclination to presume the purposeful intervention of a sentient or intelligent agent") to the *Zeigarnik effect* ("that uncompleted or interrupted tasks are remembered better than completed ones").

Although unsurpassed in their modeling capacity and scope of applicability, deep-learning models are mysterious "black boxes" for the most part, which raises disturbing questions regarding their veracity, trustworthiness, and bias, particularly in the context of their widespread use.

XAI is critical to assist with the bias inherent to AI systems and algorithms—which are, after all, programmed by human beings whose backgrounds and experiences may unintentionally lead to AI systems exhibiting bias. Additionally, the teams delivering AI systems from inception to deployment generally don't represent society at large, and this creates an environment ripe for skewed datasets and algorithms that reflect inherent systemic bias.

One example comes from Amazon, which used AI in an experimental hiring tool that rated job applicants on a scale of one to five, with five being the best qualified.[25] It wasn't long before the company spotted bias—the

AI rated men more highly for software developer jobs than women. Why? Amazon's system had observed the résumés submitted to Amazon over the past decade—a dataset largely composed of male applicants—and used that filter to judge candidates. As a result, Amazon's system had developed a bias toward men, with two applicants from women's colleges downgraded simply because of where they went to school. Amazon changed its system to make it gender-neutral, but as this program evolves, there is no way to guarantee that future systemic bias won't once again rear its ugly head.

To mitigate the risk of bias, XAI should be applied throughout the AI life cycle, as shown in Figure 5.6.

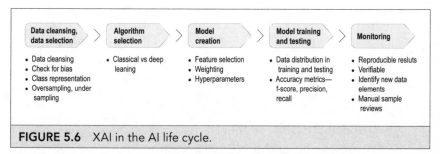

FIGURE 5.6 XAI in the AI life cycle.

Source: Infosys, "Infosys Live Enterprise—a Continuously Evolving and Learning Organization."

XAI Design Principles

For humans and AI systems to work collaboratively, a high degree of trust is needed in the decisions made by these machines. To develop this trust, enterprises must apply XAI to answer questions about how AI systems make decisions, and require AI models to adhere to six major design principles. (See Figure 5.7.)

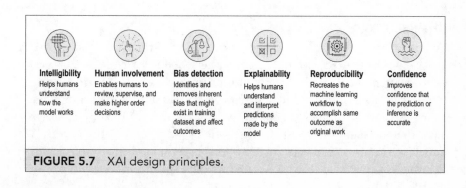

FIGURE 5.7 XAI design principles.

1. **Intelligibility.** An understanding of the working of the AI system, in terms that humans can interpret.
2. **Human involvement.** Though AI models are built to operate independently without human interference, human dependency is a necessity in some cases. For example, in fraud detection or cases where law enforcement is involved, we need some human supervision in the loop to check or review decisions made by AI models from time to time.
3. **Bias detection.** An unbiased dataset is an important prerequisite for an AI model to make reliable and nondiscriminatory predictions. AI models are being used for credit scoring by banks, résumé shortlisting, and in some judicial systems; however, it has been noticed that in some cases, the datasets had some inherent bias in them for race, age, and sex.
4. **Explainability.** XAI comes into the picture when we talk about justifiable predictions and feature importance. XAI helps in understanding how the model is thinking or which features of the given input it is emphasizing while making predictions.
5. **Reproducibility.** The machine learning model should be consistent every time when giving predictions, and it should not go haywire when testing with new data.
6. **Confidence.** The measure of certainty that the model associates with any given decision. Generally, uncertainty comes in two versions: epistemic, where the uncertainty stems from the inherent variability of data, and aleatory, where it originates from the system's inability to use prior learning for the input data.

Essentially, it's a question of trust, and the answers to questions of trust will influence the trajectory of AI in society and whether it is seen as virtuous or villainous in this exponential decade of change.

Trust and Ethics

Albert Einstein observed, "Whoever is careless with the truth in small matters cannot be trusted with important matters."

In matters small and important, it is essential that AI is fair, trustworthy, and impartial. As humans and machines work alongside each other more and more, we must be able to trust our AI systems. For that trust to be possible, we need to understand the decisions these systems make. Our ability to trust AI suffers in the absence of explainability. Our expectation is that the machines we work with perform as expected, and we can explain their reasoning.

Fairness is an aspect closely tied to trustworthiness and has more to do with whether the AI system has been designed with the user's interests in mind, than with the transparency of the technology itself. A strictly AI-based evaluation of personal loans, for instance, might prioritize lender profitability, rather than the applicant creditworthiness.

The requirement of fairness has become central to AI implementations. The objective study of fairness translates our subjective notions into statistical measures that can be applied to datasets on which AI models are trained. These measures are then used to evaluate datasets for fairness, with resampling and calibration methods employed where necessary, as corrective measures.

Fairness is also tied to the notion of impartiality, and for AI systems to be impartial, bias must be removed from the datasets used to train them. As a consequence, the focus turns to the data rather than the AI models themselves. Recent years have seen big strides in the formalization of bias identification and the removal of partiality from data. Multiple methods and tools systematically analyze datasets for bias—and employ corrective measures wherever required.

AI systems that are unexplainable are unacceptable. Ultimately, for systems we can trust, AI must be built on a solid ethical foundation.

As Einstein said, "Relativity applies to physics, not ethics."

RECAP: Intuitive Decisions

- Sentience is enabled by AI and automation and generates data-led insights, which are acted upon with maximum human intuition and minimum human intervention. This helps organizations develop intuition to drive decisions swiftly and accurately, and act with resilience in the face of disruption.
- The knowledge graph links all data spanning employees, customers, partners, networks, and devices, plus the interactions in between. An AI-driven core connects these islands of information in real time, allowing enterprises to make data-driven decisions, plus sense, process, and adapt to changing business stimuli.
- The digital brain uses machine learning and deep learning as a nexus for continuous, automated learning from data across business units and product lines. The digital brain processes this input to determine if any action is required and if so, aids users through nudging and guided feedback. It then monitors the response to and learn and evolve from them, providing the enterprise with higher cognition.
- The knowledge graph and digital brain continuously curate organizational knowledge to create perceptive experiences and make intuitive decisions. They capture and analyze enterprise data using automated reasoning to orchestrate intelligent responses to emerging events.
- AI must be ethical and explainable. For humans and AI systems to work collaboratively, a high degree of trust is needed in the decisions made by these machines. To develop this trust, the Live Enterprise applies XAI to answer how AI systems make decisions. XAI delivers this by adhering to six core design principles: intelligibility, human involvement, bias detection, explainability, reproducibility, and ultimately, confidence.

6

HYBRID TALENT

A World of Lifelong Learning

Hybrids Breed Resilience

Science has discovered that hybrids often play a vital role in fortifying species, sometimes doing so at astonishing speed in response to environmental threats. The classic example is the cichlid fish found in East Africa's great lakes, which hybridized at astonishing rates in response to climate change.[1] Hybrids can adapt quickly, with genetic micro-changes driving resilience in response to danger or profound change. As we have seen in previous chapters, resilient businesses imitate nature. Disruptive technology and the global pandemic have hastened the evolution of hybrids—including hybrid talent models.

Transforming the World: SDG 4

In 2015, the UN General Assembly adopted the 2030 Agenda for Sustainable Development. This new framework included 17 sustainable development goals[2] (SDGs) to attain by 2030, with the fourth focused on education: *Ensure inclusive and equitable quality education and promote lifelong learning opportunities for all*. While the idea has wide support, with 260 million children unable to access school in 2018, and 1.6 billion children out during the height of COVID-19,[3] new models are clearly needed to make this a reality. Mixed—or hybrid—models have proliferated, powered by tech.

Education does not end with childhood and is just as big a force into adulthood, in any society, from illiterate adults in sub-Saharan Africa to middle-class workers in Western societies who feel the digital age is leaving them behind. This is the challenge and opportunity for business and government leaders: to provide on-ramps to the digital superhighway for massive numbers of people, while meeting their talent needs to grow businesses to thrive in the next decade of the twenty-first century. The clock's ticking, education must not end at school, and business plays a key role to deliver lifelong learning and talent development.

Remaining Relevant in Today's World

Lifelong learning describes learning that can happen at any time in an individual's life. It could be at school, at university, in their first jobs after university, anytime during their professional career, and even after retirement. This happens because the individual is intent on learning something new to remain relevant—more so in the face of the unprecedented changes brought about by the Fourth Industrial Revolution. Impeding the learning process means obsolescence, lack of a job and financial security, and irrelevance in the future of work.

Lifelong learning empowers employees with the right set of tools to improve their own performance and grow within their company, or increase their external marketability. It also allows them to stay relevant in a dynamic and rapidly changing environment of increasing digitalization. Beyond technical skills, lifelong learning also enables people to develop leadership skills, as well as coaching and mentoring.

Every year, the growing workforce across the globe must move beyond knowing what they know to learning new horizon skills (niche skills, or skills of the future). They also need to learn and understand a company's evolving ethics, values, and work culture. Technology is all-pervasive, and the rate of change of technology is faster than what an average person can consume. This creates anxiety, stress, and a fear of missing out. According to one of our research contributors, Ferose V. R., senior vice president and head of SAP Academy for Engineering, "Becoming a lifelong learner becomes the most critical skill to remain relevant in today's world."

Since the Live Enterprise model is based on rapidly evolving self-directed work teams who continually learn, it is worthwhile to understand how they do so, using the six principles of adult learning developed by pioneer Malcolm Knowles:[4]

1. **Need to know:** Adults need to know the reason for learning.
2. **Experience:** Adults draw upon their experiences to aid their learning.

3. **Self-concept:** Adults need to feel responsible for their decisions on education, involvement in planning, and evaluation of their instruction.
4. **Readiness:** The learning readiness of adults is closely related to the assumption of new social roles.
5. **Orientation:** As a person learns new knowledge, he or she wants to apply it immediately in problem solving.
6. **Motivation:** As a person matures, he or she receives their motivation to learn from internal factors.

Notice the emphasis on motivation and ownership by the learner, not on policies and edicts from employers. Digital platforms should be designed to embed these principles into the adult learner's experience.

Emerging Talent Models

Blurred Lines

Like the emergence of hybrid species in nature, we are today witnessing a workforce shift where companies evolve to a mix of permanent staff and freelance talent working synchronously. This phenomenon will accelerate as better talent platforms are enabled that will allow more on-demand models to function, giving people better opportunities to learn, deploy their talent, and get paid.

Freelance workers already make up a third of the US workforce, and some estimates suggest the number was in excess of 43 percent at the end of 2020. This implies that employees around the world seek higher levels of flexibility in work hours as well as roles. Whether by choice or perceived necessity, they are more willing to take up new roles and learn on the job. The far-reaching implications of global change translate to increased demand for gig workers in the future. These roles can only be filled by individuals who learn quickly and continuously to keep up with the skills that the jobs of the future require.

At Infosys, we have been using freelance talent for quite some time. We use this talent pool either as a means to meet variations in demand or to fill in positions requiring specialized skills. The kind of roles we see increasing will be concentrated in areas of new technologies as companies and governments ramp up their digital spend. These will include jobs related to AI, data analytics, product engineering, cloud computing, and sustainability, as well as jobs focusing on the intersection of the human and technology, such as interface design and consumer behavior analysis. While not all of these jobs will focus on freelancers, the growth in these roles will increase opportunities for talent.

With companies now much more comfortable with a remote workforce, traditional boundaries between full-time talent and freelancers will blur. The future workplace will have hybrid teams that are multilocational, diverse in terms of education and backgrounds, as well as a combination of full-time and temporary workers.

This is also an opportunity for leaders to build a better future in terms of reskilling and upskilling, prioritizing work, improving the quality of jobs, as well as a new approach to education and its linkage to jobs. Crucially, it also gives business a stake in tackling SDG 4, quality education for all.

Establishing a Talent Model

Lifelong learning is the North Star for organizational talent development. These forces are disrupting and changing the talent needs of every industry, with the frequent introduction of emerging technologies, new delivery models, changing talent demographics, and geopolitical challenges. As a result, the core principles in establishing a talent model are presented in Figure 6.1.

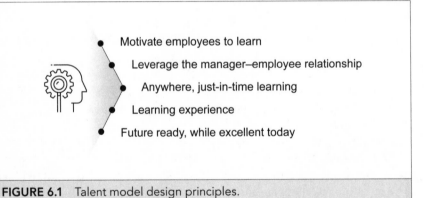

FIGURE 6.1   Talent model design principles.

Source: Infosys.

1. **Motivate employees to learn.** Success in establishing a talent model requires understanding what employees need, accessing their motivations, and removing all barriers and friction to learning. Ensure learners are able to access resources anytime, anywhere, and on any device—taking complete control of how they manage their individual learning journeys.

2. **Leverage the manager–employee relationship.** For learning efforts to be effective, an active role for managers should be created to help support and guide their teams in their learning journeys.
3. **Anywhere, just-in-time learning.** Trends indicate that employees prefer to learn on-the-go, at their convenience, and just-in-time. For this to happen, content needs to be organized in micro-learning modules and meet the needs of different personas within the organization.
4. **Learning experience.** Most employees are used to digital experiences on platforms like YouTube, Netflix, Amazon Prime shopping, and learning platforms like Udacity. Digital learning solutions must be designed to provide similar experiences and feel.
5. **Future ready, while excellent today.** Agile ways of working marked by shorter and continuous release cycles require balancing today's challenges with tomorrow's opportunities. Learning programs and courses must be forward-looking to excite digital native learners with fresh content and exciting formats, yet also designed to meet the needs of those who are less tech-savvy and need to learn mature, well-established capabilities.

Measuring Effectiveness: Sense, Feel, Respond

Talent model measurement systems should provide methods to allow predictions and alerts to make just-in-time, yet informed decisions. Like a live organism, the idea here is to constantly listen and sense the learning telemetry, evaluate metrics, analyze to make informed decisions, and respond through predictions or recommendations to stakeholders.

Learning effectiveness is measured using the three-pronged approach of sense, feel, and respond.

In the *sense* step, the learning unit constantly listens to its multiple diverse data sources to collect data and micro-feedback. In the *feel* step, the data collected in the previous step is analyzed and processed to decipher patterns, and then correlations are made to make informed decisions.

The *response* step delivers via predictions, recommendations, and by way of return on investment in learning. Depending on the stakeholder, responses vary, as expectations differ from stakeholder to stakeholder. Return on investment may be in the form of monetary value or fulfillment of expectations, based on the availability of accurate data through the relevant systems.

Measuring learning effectiveness allows organizations to accurately evaluate the efficiency of their learning interventions. Measurement also provides micro-feedback and recommendations to personalize learning experiences. A live learning function uses AI capabilities to gather data, prepare it for analysis, and process to yield useful insights.

Remote Work Opens New Avenues for Talent Availability

Talent acquisition (aka recruiting) is an existential challenge at most organizations, especially for high-demand technology skills. The old rules of office work and employee relocation have been questioned for some time. A silver lining of the pandemic has been the grand experiment—for the most part, successful—of remote work. Beyond the cost and productivity benefits, the most obvious of all is that employers can cast a much wider net when seeking new employees. Across the globe, the geographic variable is fading in the equation of many recruiting organizations. While there are a substantial number of professional roles that may need proximity for in-person work (like engineering labs), the model has changed and acceptance of remote work has skyrocketed.

As the initial euphoria of remote work announcements faded—no office for a year! Forever!—the realization set in that for most people in most roles, neither 100 percent in-person nor 100 percent remote work is the right answer. Behavioral psychologists will weigh in on the long-term effects of working remotely, and the right mix will emerge over time and evolve based on individual preferences.

The Talent Famine

Hybrid, modular, or quick-assembly talent is the future of the workforce. Beyond an individual "full-stack" worker with both STEM skills and empathetic creativity, hybrid talent is also defined as a seamless mix of humans, machines, and the gig economy to bring the right talent at the right time for the task at hand.

Hybrid talent is at the forefront of the so-called war for talent. However, for the digital jobs of today and tomorrow, our research has shown there is actually a talent famine, with millions of positions going unfilled, despite the job losses associated with the economic aftermath of global pandemic. With employment's impact on society at every socioeconomic level, this epic demand-supply mismatch has become the human capital challenge of the decade.

To fill this gap, a variety of new models have entered the market to provide alternatives to traditional pools like the major universities. Liberal arts colleges, community colleges, private certifications, and even online learning platforms have become providers of digital talent at all levels, and these pathways improve access to traditionally underserved populations. Ivy Tech Community College of Indiana is the nation's largest singly accredited state-wide community college district, with 100,000 students earning associate's degrees and related credentials. They provide a bridge from underserved communities to the digital on-ramp through practical skills-based curricula and close relationships with regional businesses. With 97 percent of the graduates remaining in-state and employed in well-paying jobs, Ivy Tech is simultaneously fulfilling their mission to the students, businesses, and communities in which they operate. Practical models like these are providing employers more sources of talent, especially for the so-called digital backbone jobs that pay less initially but provide valuable experience and a pathway to more lucrative roles. Some large enterprises and regional economic development groups also provide their own professional training programs to bridge students from educational institutions to true job-readiness.

This new approach to professional education focuses on practical learning, where foundational professional skills are complemented by specific technology skills—more just-in-time, less just-in-case skills. For experienced employees, lifelong learning and access to anytime, anywhere learning platforms enable reskilling and a workforce that can adapt to whatever business or technology requirements arise. The "anywhere" aspect is critical, given the pandemic drove home the point that a high percentage of work—and learning—can be done remotely from an employee's home.

Hybrid Talent

Characteristics of Hybrid Talent

As the volume and pace of information continue to grow, enterprises and their employees are caught in a dilemma of general versus specialized knowledge. The so-called T-model is often put forward as the ideal, where a broad understanding of the whole (the horizontal part of the T) is complemented by deep expertise in at least one area (the vertical part of the T).

However, as Infosys evolved our people supply chain and project delivery capabilities, we believe more will be required in the future of work, which will have both rapidly evolving projects and extreme automation. This pair of conclusions required us to look beyond full-time employees for other workers to create high-performing teams. First, this includes the gig economy and its vast supply of specialized skills. However, beneath the attractive veneer of skills on demand, it is difficult to integrate these external staff, especially for complex programs where governance and continuity are important. The other worker type is machines, such as robots.

As automation increases, robots become more team member than tool, and the research shows there are definite dynamics for human–robot interaction. In her behavioral research on human–robot teams, Dr. Nancy Cooke directs Arizona State University's Center for Human, Artificial Intelligence, and Robot Teaming. On the subject of carbon–silicon, human–machine collaboration, Dr. Cooke found compelling evidence that humans take on the "personality" of their robot coworkers, and this does little for the empathy level in the team.

Investment in employee development is certainly important, but not sufficient to address the flexibility and automation required. That is why hybrid talent is the future, and this combination of *employees* + *machines* + *gig economy* provides not only the scale but also the flexibility to fulfill staffing needs. Depending on the nature of the work and over time, the mix of hybrid talent—the ratio of employees, bots, and gig workers—will evolve.

Adaption, the Most Important Skill

The hybrid talent model is built on three pillars:

1. Promote micro-change routines, which over time build a culture of lifelong learning, and emphasize micro-feedback, helping people improve through small changes on continuous basis.
2. Adopt an open, collaborative, and multiexperience learning mindset across multigenerational learners, as they seek guided practice and experiences with tech trends such as edge computing, hyperautomation, and practical blockchain.
3. Elevate corporate trainers to learning champions, viewing their roles differently to simulate learner behaviors and learning patterns, enabling them to provide learning with minimal latency and instant simulation.

In the words of Infosys founder N. R. Narayana Murthy, "The most important skill required is the ability to adapt to new technology quickly, master it, and ride the wave of progress. Only those companies that do this can indeed succeed."

Addressing human factors will help companies succeed here. Anticipating human behavior and motivation, as well as AI capabilities and limitations, should be core talent levers that drive the creation of effective lifelong learning models.

Talent success depends on a confluence of work, workforce, and workspace built on a foundation of lifelong learning in direct response to business demand. Table 6.1 shows the major talent initiatives for each of the three areas.

TABLE 6.1 Hybrid talent levers.

Work	Workforce	Workspace
• Humans + machines collaboration • Agile delivery cycles, fail fast and learn faster • Convergence of technology, creative, and design skills • Open-source adoption, societal and client value • Anytime, anywhere working model • Distributed agile at scale • Outcomes driven through hyper-productivity	• Managing multigeneration workforce • Marketplace for the gig economy, which is a workforce, not vendor, seamless weaving into and out of projects • Blended workforce with a shift to Z-shaped skills • Rise of new-collar roles from alternate talent pools across community colleges, liberal arts, historically black colleges and universities • Problem-solving mindset	• Digital and collaborative workspaces • Smart campus infrastructure • Hierarchical to networked matrix models • Remote-first operating model • Employee experience across physical, digital, and emotional perspective

Intelligence, Sentience, and Micro-Change

Hybrid talent is built on the triangulation of intelligence, sentience, and micro-change.

First comes the intelligent use of data and technology. Many people processes are executed with dubious quality and can be optimized using the data and computation tools that are widely available. For example, promotion decisions are still made in many companies using gut feel, with a few indicators like time in role and employee review. However, using an algorithm to aid a promotion decision will ensure a better choice, or at least a more informed and defensible one for the manager.

Second comes sentience. Creating an organization that can analyze data from customers, internal operations, and other sources can generate enough insight to become self-aware. For example, how can corporate HQ know quickly that customer service in a distant outlet is performing poorly?

Third is the role for micro-changes in an organization's talent strategy. With micro being the new mega, micro-changes can bring about exponential macro transformation. For example, companies that did well in the pandemic allowed local managers to make quick, decentralized decisions on how they could repurpose their business to continue operations, even when it meant changing product offerings, pricing, and staffing policies.

Arbitraging Ambiguity

Humans should have different roles and responsibilities than robots and AI. ASU's Nancy Cooke also stresses that humans should do what humans do best, and the AI and the robots do what the AI robots do best, or things that humans don't want to do, like dull, dirty, dangerous things.

As software intelligence matures, machines take on the tasks that solve known problems, such as purchase order creation. As robo-execution becomes the commoditized norm, leaders create value by gravitating to areas of uncertainty and opportunity. This arbitrage of ambiguity provides the psychological space needed to nurture divergent thinking and generate novel ideas. Problem-finding complements problem-solving,[5] and a combined approach helps firms—and individuals—create and capture value.

AI augments human intelligence, it does not replace it, according to Vinay Menon, senior client partner and global lead for the AI practice at Korn Ferry, a leading organization consulting firm. AI treats decision making as a science, not an art, wherein lies both its strength and weakness. Data is no substitute for insight, and the latter needs moral and principled human intervention. In fact, the way companies manage their people strategy and human resources will determine the success of any AI program.

Z-Shaped Skills

Organizations develop problem-finders by offering learning and growth opportunities to a diverse candidate community—not just to those with advanced degrees or technical qualifications. These employees come from legacy workforces and include blue-collar workers and even displaced employees. Leaders help these "new-collar" workers nurture a mix of functional hard skills (like data science) and soft skills (like collaboration, critical thinking, change management, and communication). (See Figure 6.2.)

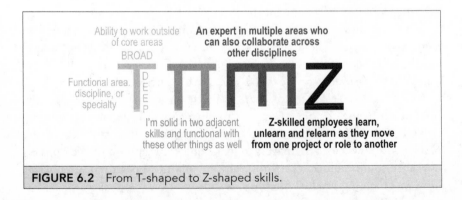

FIGURE 6.2 From T-shaped to Z-shaped skills.

This so-called Z-shaped skill set comes from business and digital literacy being a connector for enterprise creativity. The Z metaphor also extends to career development, as these Z-skilled workers straddle disciplines, zigzagging among individual skills as employees learn, unlearn, and relearn as they move from one project or role to another.

As machines take on more deterministic and analytical tasks, human creativity and multidimensional perspectives will differentiate performance. These skills are typically associated with liberal arts and design, yet they are needed for the digital jobs of the future. In our research, firms creating new business models ranked creativity, adaptability, and leadership as the most important soft skills. For those improving customer experience, empathy and communication ranked highest. Across the board, leaders valued collaboration skills over individual technical skills, with teamwork (74 percent), leadership (70 percent), and communication (68 percent) topping the list.

Nurturing and Thriving with Hybrid Talent

Three Horizons Making Learning More Meaningful

In Live Enterprises, digital technologies incorporate learning into the organization's ethos. Like everything else in this ecosystem, learning experiences are integrated across an organization, aligned across time, space, location, and culture. Employees are no longer sent to a central physical location for training, explains Srikantan Moorthy, executive vice president and head of US delivery operations and global head of education, training, and assessments, at Infosys: "The organization itself fosters an environment of continuous learning, inspiring employees to self-initiate their own learning paths to stay professionally relevant through lifelong education."

Thirumala Arohi, vice president and head of education, training, and assessment at Infosys, describes developing talent along three horizons—yesterday, today, and tomorrow—to continuously calibrate skills to meet changing demand. This segmented approach to talent development is strategic, rather than just theoretical or conceptual. It assesses how technology is changing and which skills are needed to evolve, and then it guides learner upskilling from the first horizon to the third, ready and future-proofed.

The Horizon 1-2-3 model is useful to organize and differentiate the many skills required across an organization. This breaks down the skill sets of the past, present, and future as follows:

1. **Horizon 1 skills (H1).** Core skills of the past that are increasingly making way for extreme automation. The H1 skills of yesterday are

not obsolete—yet. These are the core skills of the past that are still prevalent and used today, but they do not have a place in the future beyond the next two to three years. *Those with H1 skill sets will increasingly find themselves unemployed or unemployable.*

2. **Horizon 2 skills (H2).** New skills that are required to drive today's burgeoning need for new products, services, and processes. Today's skills often build on H2 skills and are new—or at least new at scale. They will typically be valuable for the next three or four years.
   H2 skills drive current needs for new products, services, offerings, and processes.

3. **Horizon 3 skills (H3).** Emerging skills or skills of the future that underpin the engines of growth in the digital transformation era. *As they develop employees, companies will need to align their skills with the expectations of tomorrow.*

Classifying skills into one of the horizons does not mean that they will remain there forever. They must be regularly calibrated and recalibrated across the different horizons based on market trends, customer inputs, employee needs, and internal strategies.

When analyzing the Horizon 1-2-3 model against lessons learned from the wide-scale adoption of cloud computing, we found the traditional recruitment strategy used by companies to evolve their workforce from H1 to H3 skills was deeply inadequate. This is particularly so in an era where the rate of technological change and adoption occurs at unprecedented pace and scale, and the core skills developed by university-educated employees become outdated in significantly shorter periods of time.

Companies struggle to not only identify and assess the skill sets of these three horizons, but also to maintain the correct balance between them. In effect, they need to balance legacy challenges, current requirements, and tomorrow's opportunities. To find this balance, companies must develop a skills acquisition strategy and adopt continuous learning.

In fact, continuous learning, upskilling, and reskilling are the only real options to balance the three horizons, plus move employees to fill the gaps and gray areas along this continuum. Organizations should take a critical look at their approach to learning and embrace a Live Enterprise approach to learning culture. This approach is not only necessary for firms looking to develop digital talent; practiced globally, it will also go a long way to fulfill the goal of UN SDG 4, lifelong quality and equitable education and learning for all.

To truly be ready for the future, companies must not only offer employee H1, H2, and H3 skill sets, they must deepen them too. Learning across all three horizons must be continuous, and a Live Enterprise at its core is a culture of continuous learning. Fostering this culture of continuous employee learning ensures that the enterprise itself continuously learns, evolves, and becomes more productive—enabling employees to adapt to an ever-evolving business and digital landscape. An effective learning journey begins with company culture, before the actual learning starts. It continues even after the employee completes specific training, applies it on projects, and contributes to organizational return on expectations (ROE).

Tracing the Learning Value Chain

Learning is an experience and a continuum, a journey without a final destination. *Learning needs analysis* involves connecting with a business unit or project team to understand factors like scope, coverage, mode, duration, and training competency level (i.e., beginner, intermediate, or advanced). *Learning experience and content design and development* is the next step in the learning value chain. Based on the needs analysis, this next step entails adapting existing content, developing entirely new or supplementary learning artifacts, and personalization to suit target learner profiles.

The third step is *knowledge dissemination*. This determines the pedagogy, mode of content dissemination, and conduct of assessments (such as formative or summative). It also considers the frequency, mode, and mechanisms for dissemination. The fourth and final step is *measurement of learning effectiveness*. This measures effectiveness of the previous three steps in the learning value chain.

The Three Rs of Measurement: Redefine, Redesign, and Refine

Measuring learning effectiveness in this manner enables more intuitive decision making, a responsive learning value chain, plus an enhanced perceptive learning experience. However, measurement of the learning value chain is only the beginning of the journey.

Leaders must redefine what it means to learn. Hybrid talent can no longer be isolated in specialist roles where they only practice a single skill set. By the same token, skills must be role-based, not seniority-based. The agile way of working must be adapted to ensure employees with diverse skill sets are learning from each other in diverse and multifunctional teams. Likewise, the level of support an organization gives its employees for learning must be redefined. Weekly learning targets (five hours a week in some companies) or performance-based evaluations that measure employee competence for a new skill set should be linked to bonuses, career impact, and other incentive structures.

Organizations must redesign the entire employee learning journey. From the time they join a firm, employees should embark on a learning journey that allows them to confidently build H2 and H3 skills. No learning platform should exist only for its own sake—organizations must redesign and evolve its content offering to ensure users will actually upskill themselves after completing the courses. This means testing learners in a practical way to ensure that a course achieves the level of upskill required for operational competence.

Employees and their organization jointly pursue a continuous journey to refine their skills. This requires formal and informal collection of feedback and data from all courses, learning products, and initiatives. Ongoing refinement of an organization's culture of learning will aid enterprises to deliver on UN SDG 4 and related goals by 2030.

Redefining Career Architecture

We have discussed how the business world is quickly changing, and the impact it is making on the fabric of work, workplace, and workforce. Multiple forces are reshaping how organizations function, including new technologies, changing business needs, an evolving talent market, and greater employee expectations.

Organizations need to find new ways of functioning to succeed in such an environment. In the past, organizations were designed for steadiness using levers such as defined job descriptions, hierarchies, and business functions. As new technologies emerge, skills and capabilities continue to become more transient. This requires us to rethink the fundamental organization mechanics—how we can build organizations that are agile, flexible, adaptable, and continuously evolving.

To provide corporate resilience and employee career development, organizations should deliver on four career architecture initiatives: remodel organizations for digital, jobs for digital, specialization as talent currency, and building a skill-based talent ecosystem. (See Figure 6.3.)

As organizations prepare to deliver on their digital ambitions, the infrastructure they require to do so is also continuously evolving. Organizations are forced to reassess their traditional approach of defining rigid career pathways, hierarchies defined by distinct job levels, and processes that often require high levels of governance, enablement, and execution.

In the reimagined organization of the future, many of these fundamental elements will take on a new shape—we will see capability tracks replace

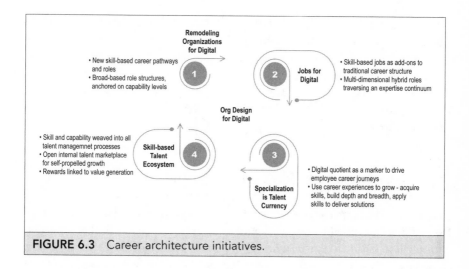

FIGURE 6.3 Career architecture initiatives.

functional tracks that exist today, and jobs will be redefined to be skill-led. Job level as an identifier of competence or hierarchal standing will be replaced by new-age identifiers such as skill and capability levels. These will become hallmarks of organization constructs that are skill-led.

The authors see capability tracks across cloud, data, design, and platforms emerging as integrated digital spaces. These capability spaces will house a range of skill-based jobs that traverse through a continuum of capability and expertise. The cloud capability track of the future, for example, will enable one to start as a cloud engineer, grow to become a cloud technology manager, and further advance to become a polycloud specialist or a healthcare cloud specialist, while having developed the ability to apply the cloud ecosystem across platforms and domains.

Jobs for Digital

With the increased focus on digital transformation, customers are more actively involved with businesses and are looking to join hands with partners who are agile and flexible. As customer challenges evolve, a new category of skill-based roles is required to build a specialized workforce. To this end, traditional roles are being replaced with supplemental skill identities in the form of skill tags or skill badges, to provide skill identity to individuals based on their knowledge and expertise in new and emerging skill areas.

First, skill tags address single-dimension spaces of technology, industry domains, or human-led design—like those of a Service-Now software developer, a domain consultant, or a digital interactions professional. At higher levels of complexity, skill tags start to reflect hybrid roles that require a combination of competencies across deep technology, multitechnology, industry, and process knowledge, creative thinking, and solutioning skills. As new technologies and spaces of work emerge, more such jobs will be defined as add-ons to a basic scaffold. These jobs infuse agility and flexibility into the organizational structure, since they remain agnostic with regard to job title or career grade.

Specializations as the New Currency for Talent

Navigating the organization construct of the future will be a function of the capability that a person demonstrates. New-age jobs will be defined based on skill and capability requirements—the readiness of incumbents to perform these jobs will also be assessed against the same yardsticks. As the very nature of jobs change, requirements for specialization will become the norm at every level—whether entry, middle, or senior. Employees will be continually encouraged to reach for career experiences that help them move from a T-shaped practitioner to a comb-shaped practitioner with specializations in multiple areas, with the objective of gaining more digital competence, becoming future-ready and adept at playing hybrid roles that emerge from changing client demands.

As the founder of Alibaba, the world's biggest online company, Jack Ma believes the 3Q philosophy of talent is the crucial human hedge against the rise of the machines. First comes the intelligence quotient (IQ), good, old-fashioned business smarts. Next comes the emotional quotient (EQ), the understanding of people. Then there's the love quotient (LQ), the ability to recognize and respect the talent in others. Combined, the 3Qs keep us relevant, providing the edge over tech and algorithms in terms of creativity, innovation, and constructive thinking. However, we believe there's something more, a missing factor. Capability to move ahead in a career is now also a function of a fourth element, the digital quotient (DQ).

In effect, talent is the sum of the 4Qs, intelligence, emotion, love, and digital: $T = IQ + EQ + LQ + DQ$.

Ferose V. R. is senior vice president and head of the SAP Engineering Academy, and uses multidimensional talent discovery to drive cultural change. For a company with 30,000 engineers serving 440,000 customers, the 4Qs are in the crosshairs of Ferose's talent strategy: "Our core insight was the best engineers are not just good technologists or good coders, but we call them multidimensional engineers, engineers who have compassion, who build communities, who have courage, are curious."

DQ is an indicator of digital competence demonstrated by acquiring knowledge, applying it to real scenarios, and further supporting organization transformation through high-quality solutions to generate value.

DQ at the individual level helps the individual guide their career path. DQ at a team or enterprise level gauges digital preparedness of the business. As the fourth element, DQ highlights an individual's position on the digital skills continuum on multiple levels. First comes *competence*, the breadth and depth of an individual's skills. Then comes *impact*, how these skills affect projects and clients. Ultimately, there's *value*, how DQ generates added value via the individual's ability to apply their expertise in high-impact areas.

But it doesn't stop there. From the individual to the enterprise, DQ is a metric applicable on micro- and mega-scales:

- ▶ **Individual DQ.** Assessment of digital readiness helps determine what's next in an employee's digital journey, with career progression potential and rewards linked to individual DQ.
- ▶ **Team DQ.** Collective DQ is a measure of a team's digital strength, with a structured managerial approach able to guide individuals and rapidly scale team DQ.
- ▶ **Business unit DQ.** DQ helps identify and retain existing digital talent. As the sum of individual DQ and factors such as leadership assessments and collective intellectual capital, it indicates a business unit's digital maturity by providing insight on digital talent gaps and helps nurture a talent pipeline.
- ▶ **Enterprise DQ.** Delivers insight on organizational talent gaps and how to cross the chasm to execute a robust digital strategy. Enterprise DQ identifies where to focus investment on digital skills initiatives to achieve maximum ROI. Enterprise DQ also indicates future talent readiness and enterprise adaptability.

Building a Skill-Based Talent Ecosystem

For a skill-led organization construct to thrive, a powerful talent ecosystem needs to be in place—one in which skill and capability is seamlessly weaved into all aspects of talent management processes. In this new construct, the meaning of career growth will shift from being a mere change in one's career level to instead reflecting the growth in their capability. Employee career growth will be multidirectional—dotted with their journey through a skill value continuum of gaining skill depth and breadth in current skills, enhancing capabilities in adjacent skills, and diving deep to build specialist expertise.

Open internal talent marketplaces will ensure that employees are not required to follow a single upward line of growth, but instead progress through a career grid that incorporates responsibilities, larger teams, newer experiences, and different types of problems to solve. With these new organization constructs, rewards and incentives will become more linked to the value that individuals generate—careers, learning, and rewards will reform accordingly and create a virtuous cycle of retention and growth where businesses value these investments in their people.

Removing the Friction from Learning

All-Inclusive, Accessible Anytime, Anywhere

Employee learning should be all-inclusive—any content, at anytime, anywhere, at any pace, on any device. Nandan Nilekani, cofounder and chairman of Infosys, believes that it is the responsibility of organizations to make learning frictionless. "The only friction between an employee and their learning should be their motivation," and the organization should take care of the rest.

When sentience and responsiveness are integrated across an enterprise, employees personalize learning opportunities and readily access organizational knowledge repositories. Platforms can proactively reach out to learners, making recommendations for how to build their skills. This facilitates the innate drive for learning and knowledge by promoting self-learning and self-assessments. It is also a flexible model, addressing the fact that what works for one learner at one time, might not work the next, even for the same individual.

Convenient, personalized learning content also ensures that learning is inclusive. This approach meets the learner where they are—regardless of ability, location, or mode. Digital accessibility ensures that websites, mobile apps, and electronic documents can be navigated and intuitively understood by all users, including those with visual, motor, or cognitive disabilities.

Byte-Sized, Just-in-Time Learning

Learner expectations are changing. Education has generally followed the traditional sage-on-stage model—a teacher or an expert taking center stage, conveying lessons to a classroom of students. The learning outcome is dependent on instructor ability to transfer learning content effectively to learners. But in the Fourth Industrial Revolution, post-COVID-19 world, learner experience is changing rapidly, and instruction models must also. Emerging technologies, new delivery models, and geopolitical challenges are disrupting and changing the talent requirements across industries.

From a corporate workforce standpoint, learners also need frequent upskilling in the face of continuous market changes and rapid technological advancement. The reality of the agile world with active projects and deliverable deadlines don't allow employees to take blocks of time away to focus on learning initiatives. This has forced the transition for learning to a series of byte-sized chunks, rendering the traditional continuous course model obsolete for many individuals and companies.

A large percentage of learners prefer the guide-on-the-side to the sage-on-stage. To accomplish this in large organizations, this new learning model must be delivered through powerful digital platforms. Learning digitization has rapidly progressed from legacy learning management systems (LMS) to massive open online course (MOOC) platforms, with large volumes of relevant content. Unfortunately, often these courses don't meet the needs of corporates who wish to make these learning programs an inherent, consistent part of their organizational strategy.

As training needs and expectations continue to evolve, LMSs and MOOCs have given way to advanced learning experience platforms. These platforms contextualize learning to employees, align the offerings to business strategies, and measure the learning impact across organizational metrics.

Fun, Relevant, and Experiential

Traditional learning models have tended to be so serious that sooner rather than later, learning fatigue sets in. But when fun forms the core of learning, learners often don't realize they are learning. Playful, personalized learning meets modern expectations for lessons that feel like experiences, not clock-watching sessions. Just as a consumer can select a movie on several devices at their convenience, learners can also select from multiple options to build knowledge that applies at work. Best practices from old-fashioned, offline learning can be brought online with games, contests, socializing, and other ways to provide deep engagement.

Structured learning follows these same principles: people pursue objectives, face constraints, understand them, and strive toward criteria that indicate that they are progressing (even winning) and receive rewards when they reach their goal. And just like keeping score during a physical game, leader boards and badges inspire learners to compete with peers, or even themselves, pushing themselves to do and learn more.

Social Learning

The social learning theory of Albert Bandura,[6] based on earlier work by B. F. Skinner,[7] describes a learning process where new behaviors are acquired by observing and imitating others. We learn best when our actions are reinforced, proposing that, in addition to the observation of behavior, learning also occurs through the observation of rewards and punishments (a process known as vicarious reinforcement). Some learners excel at learning alone, while social learning in cohorts is for learners who prefer to learn in groups. Cohorts help learners colearn with peers and collaborate with them, even across time zones and borders.

Principles underlying the enjoyment of social media can also be adopted for learning. Social networks share their learning experiences and encourage competition among members of a group or network. People of all ages are used to interacting on social media, giving opinions, and asking for feedback. Modern learning platforms emulate this model, enabling people to share expertise, teach each other, and provide each other feedback and encouragement. These platforms have messaging and calling capabilities to further encourage collaboration, both synchronously and asynchronously.

Organizations seeking high performance must adopt social learning platforms, not just to fit in with the values and digital consumption styles of its workforce, but also to keep up with the learning demands of business and culture. This enhances inter-team collaboration, while also opening up opportunities for learners to directly contact experts in a location-agnostic manner.

Content Curated for the Individual

The best learning experiences are tailored to an individual's needs, providing the exact information the learner seeks. Learners want real-life, curated content, and employees can learn from each other when organizations enable the best practitioners, regardless of age, experience, or background, on their teams to become training experts. Content can also be curated through external partners, such as MOOCs.

MOOCs are free, online courses aimed at unlimited participation and open web access. They deliver a flexible, affordable way to learn, evolve, and grow employability. Due to COVID-19 and the need for contact tracing, for example, in May 2020 Johns Hopkins University launched a six-hour online course for the traceability of people and goods. According to Professor Anant Agarwal, CEO of edX, an online learning destination founded by Harvard and MIT, "Internal learning platforms, hands-on learning on projects and MOOCs—all three will have a role to play in the future of work for learning."

MOOCs reduce training cost by an order of magnitude. External content can be curated for teams, or for individual types of learners, through a group of internal curators. These specialists customize content by taking into consideration several factors for learning personas, from generational needs to learning preferences to industry distinctions.

To deliver this curated content that respects employees as experts, organizations must think through design of how content is delivered. As internationally recognized training designer Cathy Moore describes, the best learning design focuses on design of the experience, not of the information. Content, delivery, assessment, rewards, and interfaces should be designed as experiences that test the right skills for the right employee at the right time. These experiences should have a clear purpose, with well-defined vocabulary, topics, relationships, connections, objectives, and flow.

RECAP: Hybrid Talent

- Work, the workforce, and the workplace are undergoing transformation, with companies evolving to a mix of permanent staff and freelance talent working synchronously. This phenomenon will accelerate with better talent platforms, allowing more on-demand models to function and give people better opportunities to learn and deploy their talent.
- Hybrid talent is the future of the workforce, a seamless mix of employees + machines + gig economy, providing the scale and flexibility to meet workforce needs. Depending on the nature of the work and over time, the mix of hybrid talent—the ratio of employees, bots, and gig workers—will evolve.
- Just-in-time learning will become the norm, with learning experiences delivered via an anytime, anywhere learning model. A new category of skill-based roles will build a specialized workforce, with traditional roles replaced by supplemental skill identities. Digital quotient is an emerging means to measure capability in these skill areas.
- The most important skill required is the ability to adapt to new technology quickly, master it, and ride the wave of progress. Such Z-skilled talent is the most effective for digital work, with Z-skilled employees able to learn, unlearn, and relearn as they move from one project or role to another. New HR policies, career structure, compensation structure, and hiring mechanisms are required to bring in Z-skilled talent and nurture them.

7

DESIGN TO EVOLVE

Making It Happen

The Woodwide Web

The largest organism on earth is the honey fungus—almost three miles across, with its home in Oregon's Blue Mountains.[1] It's a killer, a parasite colonizing and culling trees and woody plants. Above ground, all we see is dead trees and mushrooms. Down in the underworld, fungi connect as a vast, entwined network of mycelium, tiny fungal threads that wrap around tree roots to create a "mycorrhizal network" that connects plants in a vast ecosystem. In healthy forests, trees and fungi operate a mutually beneficial barter system, with fungi fueled by the sugar trees photosynthesize from sunlight. In exchange, fungi help trees suck up water and share nutrients such as nitrogen and phosphorus.

The mycelium is a connector, the system underground that connects trees to one another for the benefit of the whole forest, the whole ecosystem. Famed forester Peter Wohlleben describes this network as the "woodwide web." By plugging into this network, trees increase their resistance to disease.[2] Research indicates that when attacked by harmful fungi, plants release chemical signals into the mycelia to warn their neighbors. Through the mycorrhizal network, trees with deeper roots, so-called mother trees, detect distress signals from their neighbors and send them nutrients too.

Where human neurons pulse signals through our brains at 250 miles per hour, the electrical impulses of trees move at a much slower pace, a third of an inch per minute.[3] Regardless, in the woodwide web, the mycorrhizal network is the reference architecture for life, delivering micro-changes and resilience at forest scale. With 1.5 billion years of practice on the clock, it's well optimized to evolve too.

The Foundation Designed to Evolve

Aadhaar, the Indian unique identification system, now has over 1.2 billion enrolled members and has seeded over 250 additional schemes, delivering high-velocity access to government and private sector services.

In effect, Aadhaar has become the mycelium in Indian civil society, a digital mycorrhizal network shifting the equilibrium of state and citizen at scale. It took only 6 years to reach the billion, instead of the 46 years predicted by the experts. How was Aadhaar able to make this leap in under a decade?[4] It was designed to evolve from the start.

At Infosys, we were fortunate. Nandan Nilekani, Dr. Pramod Varma, and Sanjay Purohit, founders and mentors of the Live Enterprise genesis, had tested and scaled its key principles in the country of India and on societal scale platforms. These learnings and best practices were then applied to define the vision for the Live Enterprise model that was ultimately adopted at Infosys.

Adoption

The Next Big Leap

After Aadhaar and the India Stack, the challenge was to leverage the learnings elsewhere. When Nandan Nilekani came back to Infosys, he said, "Why can't we apply the India Stack learnings in enterprises that are large, complex, and have a history that constrains their ability to make nonlinear improvements?" That's how the principles mutated from a societal platform, where they were considered for the public good and societal public purposes, and then were reapplied in the corporate world. While not all the principles were applicable in a commercial enterprise, many of them were, and the primary goal was to shift the landscape equilibrium.

We brainstormed as to what could be the next potential leap—where are enterprises headed? That spawned more research, specifically on the future of AI and potential conceptual constructs through which one could prepare a journey. Through that process the idea emerged that while the industrial economy was shaped by Adam Smith's invisible hand, we hypothesized that the digital age could be constructed by the invisible brain. However, even the most intelligent brain is not enough, because results require action and periodic course correction. We thought through the digital equivalent of an organic being, where intelligence is complemented by decisions and activity. We developed principles to direct these decisions and activities. Then we imagined how to unleash the potential of our 240,000 employees—all connected, complemented and augmented by technology. This enterprise would be sentient, but an organism requires more than awareness. It also needs energy and motion, and to embody evolution, which is why we chose "Live" as the theme. It is a journey, not a destination.

Conceptualizing Live Enterprise

All of this thinking, principles, and ideas went into conceptualizing the Live Enterprise model at Infosys. We reimagined Infosys to be an ecosystem of humans and things that are connected with each other through a network that is continuously emitting signals, and is observed, processed, and acted upon by a digital brain. This brain manages the collective knowledge and state of the enterprise ecosystem, learns from each interaction, and drives value exchange in each of these interactions. All of this was designed with a platform mindset to build a digital runway for the company to eventually help Infosys have the agility of a start-up and be responsive and networked. It was also designed to increase velocity of ideas and innovation, and bring in extreme automation. Importantly, we applied this model and thinking to productize and mature our platforms, before sharing externally or taking the message to clients to assist on their own digital journeys.

Figure 7.1 (see next page) was used to define the Live Enterprise vision to Infosys employees during the initial kickoff meeting for the Live Enterprise. As is evident from the diagram, we envisioned Live Enterprise to be a connected, networked ecosystem of employees, partners, clients, and things that are all connected to each other, and value change occurs in every interaction. All these interactions are captured in our knowledge graph and digital brain, which observe, learn, curate, and respond to the stimuli in the ecosystem to make every interaction valuable.

Live Enterprise Architecture

The Resilience to Thrive and Survive

In early 2020, the Infosys Knowledge Institute published research assessing the digital maturity of large companies. Surveying the views of 1,000 executives, the Digital Radar report categorized companies into watchers, explorers, and visionaries.[5] The research found that 68 percent of enterprises

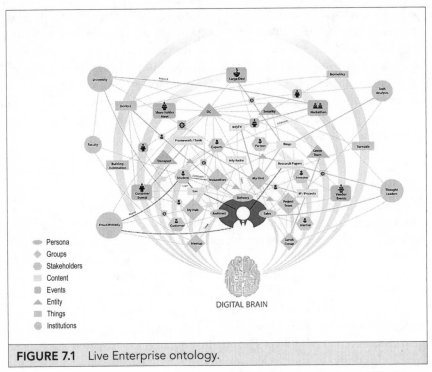

FIGURE 7.1   Live Enterprise ontology.

Source: Infosys Knowledge Institute, "Infosys Live Enterprise—a Continuously Evolving and Learning Organization."

were still in early stages of their digital journey, yet every leader sought ways to accelerate and scale.

While enterprises continue to leverage technology to improve productivity, the most successful businesses also transform to improve customer experience and employee engagement. These findings are consistent with what we hear from our clients, who deal with the duality of accelerating digital initiatives while maintaining operations stability in their new normal. The enterprises that survive will be those that navigate this duality and become resilient. In human terms, when an arm gets injured, the rest of the body makes up for that injured arm and copes until it gets healed. Business resilience means ability to respond to market changes and uncertainty, without stepping off the treadmill of continually rising expectations.

This duality required defining and developing an evolutionary architectural approach using Live Enterprise principles with the goal to make the existing IT landscape robust and resilient, abstract complexity, and establish a foundation to build new capabilities. The architectural layers and services were developed incrementally over a period of time and it continues even now.

Inspiration in the Natural World

This transformation of an incumbent enterprise to the Live Enterprise model that thinks and operates like digital natives requires major change. We used the tongue in cheek analogy that "it's like performing heart surgery while the patient is running on a treadmill." To perform this transformation in a nondisruptive manner, we looked to natural life for inspiration—to make our enterprise a lifelike, responsive, resilient being, and at scale.

Just like the mother trees in the forest network, enterprises have enterprise resource planning (ERP) systems that are core to the business. If they are fit for purpose and business, then instead of replacing them and starting from scratch, we recommend an approach to strengthen them and build new Live Enterprise capabilities around them. This will further strengthen their resilience and connections within the enterprise ecosystem.

The enterprise-like mycelium creates shared digital infrastructure that operates the entire enterprise technology ecosystem across hybrid cloud and edge. This will provide a set of platform services that can be used by the enterprise to deliver perceptive experiences, responsive value chains, and intuitive decision-making capabilities.

Figure 7.2 (see next page) depicts the reference architecture for a Live Enterprise. The architecture augments an existing IT landscape and creates new services around it, and in the process transforms it into a Live Enterprise model.

Enterprise IT Systems

These are the systems that run older mission-critical applications and tend to be part of systems of record. At Infosys we work with 1,400-plus clients, and as in a recent study we conducted to study and analyze enterprise IT landscapes, we found four patterns around the core systems that support business operations today.

1. **Mainframe centric core systems.** Typically seen in financial services, insurance, and healthcare industries.
2. **ERP-centric core systems.** Typically seen in manufacturing, life sciences, and consumer goods industries.
3. **Best-of-breed and customer core systems.** Typically seen in telco, logistics, resources, and utility industries.

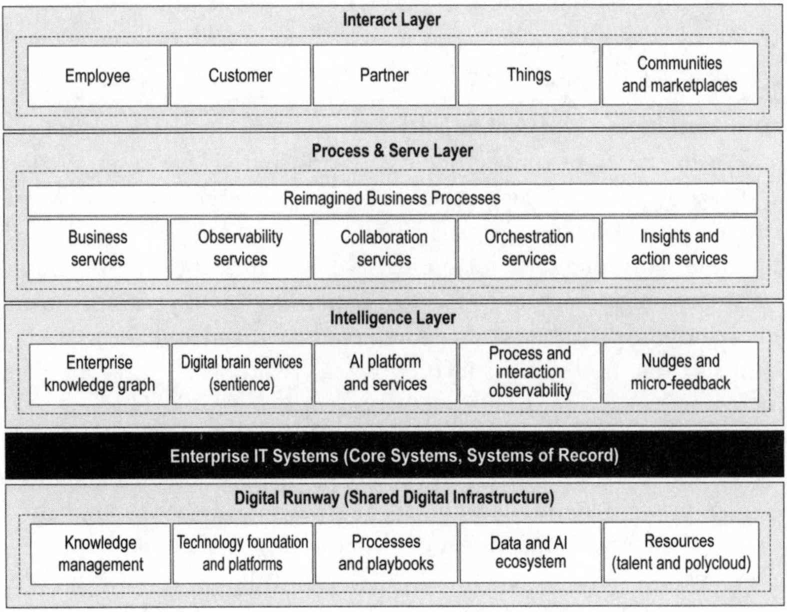

FIGURE 7.2   Live Enterprise reference architecture.

Source: Infosys.

4. **Combination** of all four core systems.

A big bang modernization approach is not recommended, given the risk and complexity involved. We suggest an evolutionary approach to modernize core systems to simplify and reduce technical debt, improve efficiency through automation, optimize run cost, and make them resilient.

In our experience, a one-size-fits-all modernization approach for the four patterns does not work. A differentiated approach may be required, depending upon the core systems technology.

Mainframe-centric core systems can be modernized through an accelerate, renew, and transform (ART) approach:

▶ **Accelerate.** Accelerate modernization for enterprises having a small mainframe or AS/400 footprint, where the applications and data can be migrated and rehosted on the cloud using so-called lift and shift techniques. However, if the mainframe footprint and consumption is significant, then the mainframe portfolio should be optimized and simplified through decommissioning.

▶ **Renew.** Revitalize existing mainframe applications by provisioning existing functionality as APIs, bringing in mainstream engineering practices like DevSecOps to the mainframe world and reducing technical debt for core business services.

▶ **Transform.** Transform and reengineer the existing mainframe application using an incremental approach and migrate to industry platforms or develop using open-source and micro-services-based architecture on the cloud.

ERP-centric core systems are undergoing modernization at three levels—migrating the ERP systems to strategically run on a hybrid cloud ecosystem from the on-premise infrastructure, developing perceptive experiences and responsive value chains. This enables orchestration of ERP services through the intelligence, process, and serve layers and by integrating with new technology and industry platforms.

The best-of-breed and custom core systems are undergoing consolidation, rationalization, APIfication, and modernization to move to the cloud using lift and shift, modernization, and reengineering techniques.

One common theme across all these patterns is that core systems are simplified and modernized to provide data and APIs to reimagine the experience and business processes. These capabilities are provided in the Live Enterprise model through the interact, process and serve, and intelligence layers. This minimizes the impact to the core systems, yet still brings in the ability to sense, process and respond using open-source and cloud-based architecture.

Interact Layer—Driving Connections and Collaboration

Emperor penguins live collectively in vast breeding colonies of up to 100,000 breeding pairs.[6] In the Antarctic, they huddle together to escape the icy winter air temperatures that plummet to –30 degrees Celsius, with huddling patterns differing according to the breeding cycle, the biggest occurring during egg incubation. Each huddle is constantly changing, in response to both the outside air temperature and penguins overheating. Every minute or so, a penguin shifts position, triggering a wave of *Tetris*-like movement across the huddle. Those in the middle get too hot, move to the outside, cool, and find their way back into the crowd.

Huddling improves group and individual survivability, increases huddle density, and maintains the orderly arrangement of the group. However, huddling only works if all penguins work in unison and react instantly to messages, both verbal and nonverbal. This type of sentient empathetic intelligence is intrinsic to the Live Enterprise, with all users cooperating rapidly to visual and system cues across a range of channels.

Like penguin huddles or the woodwide web, a Live Enterprise is connected, and this connectedness drives interactions and collaboration between humans, things, and data. We discuss the first two of these here and address data later in the chapter.

Human connectedness relies on organizations putting digital tools in the hands of every human user so they can access information and services anytime, anywhere, using any mechanism desired—and ultimately perform these actions by themselves. These tools should enable a collaborative process and also promote collaboration across key business processes.

Collaborative culture doesn't happen by chance. With Gartner research indicating 82 percent of companies intend to allow remote work, they need to innovate and personalize team building to maintain an engaged, shared culture.[7] The initial conditions necessary for user engagement are access, interaction, and empowerment. Engagement is where routines and habit shifts happen. Once engaged, users feel the power and want to pursue it, and simply don't feel like going back.

To feel this engagement users require an experience that is both innovative and personalized. They want a better experience at all touchpoints, like one-call resolution and streamlined processes. A sentient platform with embedded automation and intelligence is the way to leverage the need for user sentiment.

As hierarchies have become self-directed work teams, organizations also start asking new questions, demonstrating a genuine curiosity to understand their employees. Codifying sentient principles allows assessing behavior and outcomes even at large volumes. These questions address what employees and partners say, do, think, and feel. Armed with that information, even if only directional indicators, leaders can maximize opportunities, or make early course corrections and get ahead of impending problems.

These answers improve capability for employees to interact with and continuously learn from their ecosystem. Each interaction and its associated intelligence are recorded and linked through the knowledge graph to drive a better experience, pan-enterprise visibility, and operational efficiency (acknowledging the privacy considerations involved). This harnessed knowledge is a complex but valuable asset.

Like most large organizations, at Infosys over the years we had developed dozens of applications to serve our employees. While each was clearly identified on the corporate intranet, the list was confusing to even company veterans—and required a laptop network or VPN connection. Taking a consumer mobile-first mindset, we converted dozens of separate applications into three employee mobile-first experiences: personal productivity (InfyMe), learning (Lex), and new hire onboarding (LaunchPad). This simplification effort had a profound effect on how employees saw the company—not only did efficiency improve, colleagues saw how one area related to others and made better decisions. Users also benefitted from sentience, where the goal is for an enterprise to act much like starling murmurations over Gretna Green that move together in beautiful synchronicity, each individual matching the speed and direction of its nearest neighbors.

In addition to humans, in a Live Enterprise *things* are also connected, driven by APIs. In a nutshell, APIs reflect a group of operations that developers can use, along with a description of what they do. API-driven means easier integration, and they can be instantiated at the click of a button, enabling any physical device to connect.

When an employee enters the turnstile at the Infosys campus (or any of the many other campuses globally), the combination of their badge and biometric data (pre-COVID, anyway) grants them access. This is a simple yet pervasive example of the Internet of things at work, and these sensors are things that enable more than access. Capacity, attendance, security, safety, space management, hoteling of workspaces, and traffic flow are all enriched through the steady stream of data provided by these and countless other sensors that quietly capture presence, movement, environment, equipment performance, and other relevant characteristics. While we all see the explosion of low-cost, high-quality sensors—another dividend of the smartphone wars—it is less widely known how IoT has become driven by APIs. The benefit of ubiquitous API-driven IoT is the ease of integration and ability to instantiate them at the click of a button. This means an employee can click, view, and operate a building's air-conditioning, and an enterprise can enable any physical device through APIs.

To drive reuse and speed to build and deliver newer experiences, the page or screen should not be designed as a monolith, as it becomes complex to maintain and manage over a period of time. Instead we recommend adopting the micro-front-end architecture pattern that enables a page or screen to be unbundled into different pieces of front-end feature and functionality, which can be developed independently by different teams and packaged in a standardized manner and then composed together. This promotes reuse and collaboration between the user experience teams. The micro-front-ends in turn interact with the micro-services provisioned by the process and serve layer to fulfill the functionality required by the interact layer.

Process and Serve Layer—Orchestrating and Powering Interactions

The process and serve layer acts as the glue that connects and powers the user experience by enabling and orchestrating the APIs provided by the intelligence layer, core systems of record and the digital runway. As organizations start reimagining the experience, it also requires the underlying processes to be reimagined, reconfigured, and orchestrated to enable anytime, anywhere perceptive experiences. To provide this flexibility, it is important to unbundle the entire business process, features, and functionality into a set of services that can be developed by independent teams to provide discrete functionality and can be stitched together in different combinations over time to enable the continuous evolution of experience and features.

Unbundling of functionality should be done into these two types of services:

- ▶ **Atomic services.** Deliver one and only one purpose, where the purpose is less, yet the offered value is high. It limits access via a well-defined (and limited) set of APIs, is removable and replaceable independent of other elements, and is reusable across applications, contexts, domains, and even platforms.
- ▶ **Composite services.** Deliver a cohesive set of purposes using an assembly of services and service components deployed together in a single service, accessed through APIs, and removable and replaceable independent of other elements.

While traditionally the focus has been to design and implement micro-services and specifically, pattern-based business and orchestration services, we recommend three new categories of services to incorporate Live Enterprise capabilities:

- ▶ **Observability services** that emit and provide usage and consumption information across all layers to understand how the features and functionality are used, what is working and what is not, and the adoption trends. The process owners and product managers use this information to determine which features to enhance or rework, which ones to stop investing in, and which ones drive the most value.

▶ **Collaboration services** that provide the ability to meet, share, discuss, listen, ask, learn, introspect, and brainstorm. These services should be weaved into the user experience. This is to ensure that collaboration happens at the point where work is done and users don't have to move to different tools to perform these activities.

▶ **Insights and action services** that provide the ability to sense, process, and respond to the events and signals coming from the connected humans, things, and their interactions. One of the important capabilities within the Live Enterprise model is to change user routines one at a time. Nudges triggered by the digital brain are used by these services to take users through guided practice and start driving the change.

This critical role to hide the complexity of the core systems of record makes it easier for the reimagined experience to consume the features and functionality in an integrated manner, irrespective of the system where the information or functionality resides. At Infosys we have a number of core systems that support our key business operations—ERP, customer relationship management (CRM), and custom applications. We made a decision early on that we would not replace the core systems, but use the process and serve layer to hide the complexity and use the intelligence layer to make information, insights, and actions available in an integrated manner through graph, digital brain, and nudges. We also use the observability services to continuously observe, learn, and evolve, and the collaboration services to bring users together to collaborate and be hyper-productive.

Intelligence Layer—Driving Sentience

We earlier mentioned the connectedness of humans and things. Data is the next degree of connectedness. Data remains a significant challenge to organizations, especially the need to develop data into insights and then convert insights into actions. Today most of the transactional data is distributed across multiple core systems, and it is difficult to get a real-time and connected view of data across the systems. Traditionally, enterprises have used data warehouses and data platforms to develop integrated view of the data required by the business, but that approach takes too long and maintains only the historical data that is best suited for reporting or analytics.

For a Live Enterprise, connected real-time data is required to be able to sense, process, and respond to evolving events, situations, and user needs. Taking inspiration from the Google search engine that uses the knowledge graph to link all the things, people, and places at scale, we thought why not use the same approach and technology to link all the data across core systems through an enterprise knowledge graph. A knowledge graph comprises the entities (nouns) and the edges (relationships) between them and can be stored in a new class of databases known as graph databases.

Beyond Google, today this technology is extensively used by LinkedIn, Facebook, Microsoft Bing, and other technology majors. At Infosys, the Infosys knowledge graph connects all the significant enterprise entities and has around 20 million nodes and 90 million edges and is continuously growing. This drives all the sentient features experienced by our employees.

Mahatma Gandhi once said, "Truth is by nature self-evident. As soon as you remove the cobwebs of ignorance that surround it, it shines clear." By clearing the cobwebs around people, data, and things, an enterprise arrives at its own truth through the principle of *observability*.

Once an organization connects humans, data, and things, it can then observe the data streaming from each of these inputs. This is similar to the human central nervous system, where five senses capture external signals as input. Humans, data, and things capture these signals for an enterprise, and observability enables its analysis. There are three elements to this observability. The first is to simply analyze the data itself, to understand what's going on. The second is how well the most important features delivered to users are used and serve the required purpose. The third element addresses quality and service availability.

Once organizations start observing, then they can also sense, process, and respond—gaining sentience. If sufficient signals are in place, they can be acted upon. The digital brain constantly observes the knowledge graph and data streams to scan for signals of interest. When a signal is identified, the brain analyzes and then acts upon it in a deterministic or exploratory manner and then recommends an action. Deterministic decisions are based on predefined rules. However, with advancements in AI especially in the areas of vision, text, speech, language, operations, decisions, and recommendations, a higher percentage of decisions can be made using these technologies. Advancements in predictive modelling, machine learning, deep learning, differential programming, and other probabilistic methods enable more and more processes to be reimagined in AI-first way.

Early in the Infosys journey, we found that EX needed to change, and we knew this was a massive change. That required changes in the habits, conversation, and the routines of the organization. In essence, the question became, "How do you change behavior of 240,000 people?" That simple yet profound question required us to create a choice architecture and nudge architecture. These items were similar to what was created for India Stack changes at societal scale. The nudges are used now to drive desired change one nudge at a time.

It is difficult to discover patterns within the flood of data and knowledge rushing at and across an organization. But as more intelligent systems are established and automated processes implemented, the impact of each employee is amplified for the enterprise overall.

Live data from the knowledge graph creates potential user journeys for each employee, based on their previous queries and activity. User communities are spun up to allow employees with common interests to ask for advice and learn from each another. Collaboration APIs enable employees to create and publish new collaboration groups and channels, along with APIs to set up meetings in calendar applications.

These interactions put all employees on the same level, no matter their area of expertise. Employees learn from one another, dig deeper into complex business challenges, and refine previous solutions. Codifying the emotional state of mind for employees is an exciting prospect, leaving repetitive work to the past, freeing the workforce to do purposeful work that has real meaning. Like any AI-driven proposition, a reference to analyzing employee emotional state carries with it heavy ethical baggage. However, this model assumes proper governance, and all the information already exists—the knowledge graph simply makes sense of it all.

At Infosys, employees engage with the platform through the interact layer that provides in-the-moment insights and collaboration and contextual search that shows relevant information to users. The digital brain makes each interaction a value-adding exercise so that employees focus on creativity and innovation.

While the interact, process and serve, and intelligence layers bring in the new capabilities required to be sentient and live, the digital runway provides the foundational services required to design and implement these layers at an accelerated pace.

Digital Runway—Shared Digital Infrastructure for the Company

The traditional approach followed in most organizations is to focus on features and functionality. While initially seeming more efficient, this approach makes it difficult to evolve and change as the features and functionality change over time, or newer functionalities are required that were never considered at program start.

In the Live Enterprise model, getting the architecture right is critical, and we start by developing a shared digital infrastructure for the company determining which platforms, features, and functions can be developed in the future. We call the shared digital infrastructure for the company a "digital runway" that helps increase velocity of developing new ideas and innovations and taking them to the market in a shorter span of time.

The digital runway comprises five components—knowledge, technology services and platforms, processes and playbooks, data and AI, and resources. We cover this topic in detail in the chapter on the digital runway.

All five layers of Enterprise IT systems, intelligence, process and serve, interact, and digital runway layers consume the services provided by the digital runway. As an example, one of the key technology services is the Polycloud platform. The Polycloud platform provides a thin layer of abstraction over the public and private clouds and provides an API-based mechanism to deploy, manage, and govern applications and data in a secure and compliant manner.

Key Architecture Characteristics

To ensure that the architecture is realized correctly and is communicated to stakeholders, we have defined a set of characteristics that help ensure that the capabilities required for a Live Enterprise are embedded into its design and implementation, as shown in Figure 7.3.

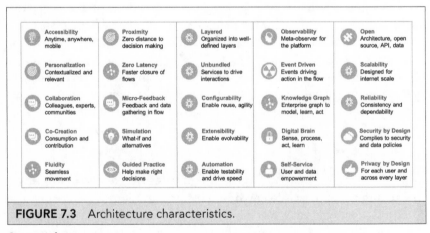

FIGURE 7.3 Architecture characteristics.

Source: Infosys.

Evolving Architecture and Capabilities

At Infosys we have realized the Live Enterprise architecture model over a period of time. The traditional approach is to spend significant effort and time to build the foundation layers first and then go vertically above to other layers. This approach takes longer, and it will take a significantly longer time for value to be realized. In our experience we have found that if we design and build enough capability in each layer that is required to deliver an end-to-end minimum viable product that can be rolled out to the users, then we can incrementally roll out new features on an ongoing basis every few weeks. As we learn from these rollouts and understand what is or is not working, the capabilities in each layer can be further enhanced or refactored to meet the evolving business needs. This approach helps us perform rapid experimentation, deploy features to end users quickly, learn from these experiences, and continuously evolve.

Infosys has navigated its journey to adopt the Live Enterprise model by executing three key tracks, each running in agile sprints of six weeks:

▶ Reimagine experience (interact layer)
▶ Reimagine processes (process, serve, and intelligence layers)
▶ Digital runway (shared digital infrastructure of the company)

Each track has micro-changes within each release. With micro-change interventions performed to accompany agile sprints, change occurs one step at a time aligned with the agile build, which brings about the larger changes. After experimenting with different durations, we found six weeks as the optimal cadence to provide a new release that allowed users to gain confidence in the efficacy of incremental innovation. Over time, additional capabilities are introduced across the organization, covering both current operations and new capabilities.

These sprints are crucial to transformation. The whole sprinting nature to make a change at scale every six weeks is an amazing discipline. The fundamental point is that micro-change at scale, every six weeks, is truly transformative. If the equilibrium of the company moves by an inch or even a millimeter every six weeks, the collective effect of that movement over a year is a transformative result for the organization—micro and mega—because it results in a compounding, not simply linear effect.

Across the tracks, three underlying themes stand out. First, architecture is unified, but not uniform. Second, the model shares the ability to solve, so the entire organization learns and is able to solve its own problems. Third, micro-change occurs at scale, which was covered previously. These three important elements of the overall journey can be easily overlooked because people tend to see only things on the surface and can forget that the underlying building blocks are architecture, learning, and micro-change at scale.

As Infosys applied the Live Enterprise model internally, we experienced that the most challenging aspect is to change mindset and community norms. As a result, we plan enablement and full adoption to be achieved over a number of sprints so that people can learn to think and act differently. This allows individuals time to tackle a small problem first, before being asked to be part of adoption at scale.

Driving Change One Step at a Time

Using the previously mentioned approach at Infosys, we reimagined the employee experience and are moving away from 100-plus different applications to fewer mobile-first experiences that enable our employees to operate anytime, anywhere. LaunchPad is a mobile app that has been used to onboard 50,000 new employees globally, and this has also helped our sustainability goals by avoiding the printing of 2.2 million sheets of papers per year. Once an employee joins, InfyMe is used for personal productivity, Lex is used for learning, and Meridian is used for workplace activities. Today InfyMe is used by 180,000-plus employees globally, Lex is used by 200,000-plus employees and Meridian is used to perform workplace collaboration and events across the company. Reimagining business processes has made many of our processes zero latency and helped us move to a self-service model, bring sentience into sales and delivery, and to make data-driven decisions.

The shared digital infrastructure enables us to run the entire company on our Polycloud, supporting multiple public and private clouds, using the Live Enterprise store to curate 15,000-plus assets to accelerate ideation, cocreation, and client work and to democratize access to data and services. The Live Enterprise Application Management Platform (LEAP) is used to manage the existing IT landscape and is secured by cybersecurity platforms. Infosys has now been able to take these platforms create market offerings, and use them to accelerate digital transformation work for clients.

Designing for evolvability is required to accomplish the vision of a live enterprise that is continuously evolving and learning, with a robust foundation. The next chapter goes into detail on that foundation, the digital runway.

RECAP: Design to Evolve

- An architecture-first approach establishes the right foundation through the unbundle–rebundle approach. Business and technology capabilities are unbundled into modular, layered services and then rebundled to create value-additive services, features, functions, and experiences. These foundational services become part of the digital runway.
- The Live Enterprise reference architecture has five layers: Interact, Process and Serve, Intelligence, Enterprise IT Systems, and Digital Runway. These layers are designed to provide flexible, scalable capabilities.
- The Live Enterprise model builds on existing enterprise IT capabilities by augmenting and bringing in newer capabilities. Layered architecture enables features and functions to be built as the company scales, with telemetry to continuously learn, understand what is working (or not), and evolve.
- Architecture is unified, but not uniform, sharing the ability to solve so the entire organization learns and can solve its own problems. Micro-change management directs investment, reimagines lagging areas, and celebrates blockbuster innovations.

8

DIGITAL RUNWAY

Ultraviolet Sunflowers

Legendary painter Vincent van Gogh arrived in the south of France in 1888, in search of warm weather and artistic inspiration. Over six months, he painted seven still lifes of sunflowers, his favorite plant, infused with yellows of ecstatic beauty that captured the sun and warmed his troubled heart. While he saw the sunflowers in a special way, in one respect he did not see them at all. This is because humans see in the visible light element of the electromagnetic spectrum, the cones in our eyes perceiving radiation in wavelengths from 380 to 700 nanometers. Sunflowers, however, are meant to be seen in ultraviolet light of 10 to 400 nanometers—invisible to our eyes.

Bees see in color, and like humans, bees are *trichromatic*—meaning they have three photoreceptors in their eyes, enabling them to see three primary colors. Unlike humans, the bee's primary colors are blue, yellow, and *ultraviolet*. Butterflies go even further than bees, being blessed with the widest visual range in nature due to eyes with five photoreceptors perceiving ultraviolet, violet, blue, green, and red.[1]

With flower evolution shaped by the need to attract pollinating bees and butterflies, pigments in flower petals absorb ultraviolet light to create patterns. Known as "honey guides" or "nectar guides," bees associate these ultraviolet "runways" with sugar and are guided at speed with pinpoint accuracy to the center of the flower (bees see five times faster than us, thanks to color vision that's the fastest in the natural world[2]).

Mutualistic Relationships

In effect, van Gogh's sunflowers provide bees and butterflies with ultraviolet on-ramps and bull's-eyes. It's a perfect trade—bees get all the nectar they need, and the flowers reproduce—a "mutualistic relationship" shaping the 75 percent of our food crops reliant on pollination by bees and butterflies. In effect, these ultraviolet runways help create a hyper-productive economic ecosystem worth over $200 billion a year.[3]

Applied in the enterprise context, bees and butterflies are the teams working to solve customer problems or building new products, and the flower bed is like a digital runway that helps the teams find the right shared digital infrastructure ingredients. Knowledge, tools and technologies, playbooks, data, and AI services can be used and combined in interesting ways to accomplish their goals. These teams then contribute back by sharing the learnings, best practices, and any new digital services that they develop or enhance that could be of use to the entire enterprise ecosystem. This confluence enriches the digital runway on an ongoing basis and helps accelerate the velocity of ideas and innovations across the enterprise.

The Digital Runway

Shared Digital Infrastructure

In large global organizations, we tend to see very good ideas and innovation happen on a regular basis, but in isolated pockets. It is straightforward to rapidly experiment, innovate, and develop point solutions. However, it becomes a significant challenge when one has to unbundle them into shared digital infrastructure services and then scale, productize, and roll it out across the global organizational footprint. Few companies are able to do this successfully so that global users can use these unbundled services to rebundle and solve problems specific to their customers, lines of business, and geographies. The ones that have succeeded have built an enterprise digital launch capability for their company, which they use to increase the velocity of new ideas and innovations across their customer base in a short span of time.

Amazon has developed digital platforms for their company using their famous two pizza team size rule and innovates at a rapid pace to develop newer platforms, features, and functionality. The digital platform provides the tools that can be used by hundreds of independent and globally distributed teams to rapidly experiment and roll out successful ideas to their entire customer base.

We call these corporate digital platforms the *digital runway*, which provides the tools to scale ideas and innovations, and also provides the ability for teams to independently use these tools to solve their customer problems in their context and part of the business.

Digital runways provide a shared digital infrastructure for the company by curating and organizing knowledge, platforms and services, processes and playbooks, data and AI services, and other resources. All these elements come together in a cohesive manner and in a scalable model that drives the velocity of new ideas and innovations, aggressively using the shared digital infrastructure. This also enables ideas that have worked well in one area of business or platform to be quickly scaled to the rest of the organization, as they are based on the same digital infrastructure.

Digital runways curate the strategic and shared software- and hardware-driven resources available as APIs that can be consumed by different teams within an organization to innovate with new experiences, value streams, and products. Where ultraviolet runways provide platforms to pollinate flowers, a digital runway provides the platform as a service to the company upon which new projects to be launched and delivered at accelerated pace and at scale. The shared digital infrastructure (digital runway) has five categories: knowledge, platform services, process, data and AI, and resources (see Figure 8.1). Note that that technology is only a portion of the shared digital infrastructure.

Knowledge	Platform Services	Process	Data and AI	Resources
Business	Digital workplace	Process reimagining using sentience principles	Transactional, operational, and analytical data	**People and communities**
Product engineering	Experience and interactions			Employees
Code	Insights and actions	Anytime, anywhere operating model	Knowledge graph	Consumers
Learning	Manage and modernize	Distributed agile	Strategic research and insights	Customers
Ideas and innovations	Secure and protect	Micro-change management	AI cloud	Partners
Research	Experiment and innovate	Rapid experimentation and innovation	Social and digital engagement	Alumni
Market insights	Learn and change	Talent transformation	Data catalog	Gig workers
Case studies	Distributed engineering		Feature store	Academia and students
Competitor insights	Live Enterprise store		Model repository	Special interest groups
				Infrastructure (Polycloud)
				Innovation
				R&D
				Development and test
				Production
				Disaster recovery

FIGURE 8.1 Shared digital infrastructure.

Source: Infosys Live Enterprise Shared Digital Infrastructure.

Knowledge

All the organizational knowledge and context that exists within employees, undocumented knowledge in manual processes, and the documented and digitized knowledge across formats should be curated, linked, and classified as per a standard taxonomy for the organization. It is practically impossible to standardize all knowledge assets in shared digital infrastructure. However, from our experience, we have found the following techniques useful:

▶ **Common asset markup language.** Define a common language for all enterprise assets so that consumption can be driven based on the metadata of visibility, accessibility, and search. Derived fields in the asset markup are continuously updated based on the runtime usage and annotations enriching it on a frequent, even continuous basis.

Assets can be classified as knowledge and product artifacts; reusable pieces of code and IP; physical devices like a phone, laptop, or smart card; or even legal and regulatory agreements. The class of assets may vary depending on the industry and market in which the organization operates. Asset markup language defines a common standard so these assets are identified, curated, and made discoverable, but remain accessible based on visibility permissions. The asset markup makes it easy to search, find, link, and connect organizational assets and enriches the enterprise knowledge graph.

▶ **Text analytics services.** Users mine the vast repository of knowledge artifacts and emails, with shareable ones used for knowledge exchange. These services are used to mine and curate nuggets of information and insights. Also, this enables the build of the asset markup for existing artifacts and to allow enterprise-wide search.

▶ **Enterprise knowledge graph.** Curates and links all knowledge artifacts using the asset markup and the metadata curated from text analytics services. The knowledge graph is updated continuously as new knowledge artifacts are produced, and existing ones get updated on an ongoing basis. Text analytics services have crawlers that continuously mine and update the knowledge graph periodically.

Do these ideas work? At Infosys, using the InfyMe app for personal productivity and the Lex app for continuous learning, our employees search through all organizational knowledge assets to find the best-fit case studies, projects, proposals, learning paths, and ideas. These are powered by the Infosys knowledge graph and HINT text analytics services. The result has been significant improvement in search speed and accuracy, enabling our employees to find better information, faster, to execute their work.

Platform Services
Platform services provide centralized software and hardware infrastructure abstracted as APIs that enable value additive features, functionality, and

interactions in a plug-and-play-based model. To realize the vision of a Live Enterprise, platforms need to get the architecture right and design for evolvability rather than features and functions. In our experience, features and functions evolve over a period of time, and platform architecture has to be robust enough to allow rapid evolution and with lower change costs.

Platforms may may become monoliths, so they should be unbundled into a set of services, as a platform is only as effective as its individual services. Based on our experience building the Infosys shared digital infrastructure services and experience building similar platforms for our clients, the platform services in Table 8.1 are required or helpful for an organization to create their own shared digital infrastructure. Based on the nature of a specific business and the industry, the list will need to be customized, with additional services identified as required. These platform services can be rebundled to develop higher-order industry-specific services, solutions, and platforms to accomplish business objectives.

TABLE 8.1 Platform services to create shared digital infrastructure.

Category	Brief Description
Digital workplace	Platforms and services required to manage employee life cycle and the workplace operations. Onboarding and offboarding, personal productivity, space management, Live Enterprise workplace.
Experience and interactions	Platforms and services required to enable anytime, anywhere user experience that is sentient and provides the foundational services required to build any transactional application.
Insights and actions	Platforms and services required to manage data, be sentient, and perform actions. Knowledge graph, digital brain, and AI services.
Manage and modernize	Platforms and services required to modernize the existing IT landscape and also to manage the operations to be resilient. Live enterprise application management, data modernization, legacy migration.
Secure and protect	Cybersecurity platform and services required to secure the live enterprise. Security metrics and KPIs, incident management, threat scanning and hunting, security controls and policies, threat intelligence.
Experiment and innovate	Platform and services required to enable rapid development, cocreation, and innovation pilots. Living labs and playground.
Learn and change	Platform and services for learning, career planning, and assessment. Learning, assessment and certification, change management, personal development, and knowledge management.
Distributed engineering	Platform and services required to automate the entire engineering process and manage the hybrid cloud. DevSecOps, Polycloud, and distributed agile.
Live Enterprise store	A store to manage all the shared digital infrastructure assets to enable easier discovery and reuse.

Source: Infosys.

Process

Process defines the ways of working and operating model required to combine the knowledge, platforms, data, AI, and resources to produce meaningful outcomes. The processes are codified into playbooks that are repeatable and powered by platforms through guided practices. The playbooks and guided practices are continuously refined based on the usage and learnings, with the objective to drive more collaboration between stakeholders and to bring collaboration into business processes.

The playbooks essential to guide Live Enterprise transformation are listed in Table 8.2.

TABLE 8.2   Live Enterprise process playbooks.

Area	Description
Process reimagining using sentient principles	Framework and playbook to reimagine business processes using the five sentient principles.
Anytime, anywhere operating model	Operating model and readiness assessment to enable employees to work anytime, anywhere and the technology and enabling capabilities required.
Distributed agile	Distributed agile software engineering model to allow small hyper-productive teams to deliver work packets using "micro is the mega" approach.
Micro-change management	Approach and playbook to contextualize the micro-change management approach for an organization and to drive it at scale using the change platform and services.
Rapid experimentation and innovation	Playbook to observe technology trends, identify disruptors, do rapid experimentation, and build innovative pilots along with users and clients.
Talent transformation	Playbook to enable existing employees with legacy skills to learn and apply new-age skills and uplevel them into hybrid talent.

Source: Infosys.

Data and AI

Data is a strategic asset in the Live Enterprise model, and all organizational data should be managed and governed in a strategic way. While a data-based product organization is the ideal approach to organize and manage the data, where that's not feasible all data should be brought together from source systems and linked through a knowledge graph. Data is the foundation based on which AI services are trained and deployed. The technology platforms required to manage, govern, and secure the data per organizational and regulatory needs should also be built as part of the technology platforms.

The services described in Table 8.3 are required to manage and provision data strategically.

TABLE 8.3 Services to strategically manage and provision data.

Area	Description
Transactional, operational, and analytical data	SQL, NO SQL, and real-time transactional analytics databases.
Knowledge graph	Graph databases to manage the knowledge graph.
Telemetry	Telemetry service to instrument and capture telemetry events.
Strategic research and insights	Curated data sources that provide financial intelligence of companies, strategic insights, social intelligence.
Data catalog	Raw training data sets required for AI services.
Feature store	Data store required for feature engineering of AI services.
Model repository	Model repository to continuously track and curate the best models for usage across AI services.

Source: Infosys.

To enable AI-first business processes and capabilities powered by data, an AI Cloud is recommended. The AI Cloud strategically brings together the AI hardware and software stack (across private and public cloud) as platform services that can be used to accomplish three major objectives:

- ▶ Enable AI to scale from point solutions to enterprise level AI
- ▶ Innovate AI by democratizing and making the AI cloud and services accessible to rapidly experiment and innovate at affordable price points
- ▶ Accelerate AI by providing AI engineering, technology, and industry-specific services available out of the box

Continuously curate data and the latest models to improve AI service outcomes. It's also important to de-risk business operations by investing and building capabilities to enable responsible AI.

Resources

Expertise and talent are vital to bring organizational initiatives to life. For a Live Enterprise a new kind of talent—"hybrid talent"—is required, bringing together a combination of skills and expertise to make it happen. The platform enables more interactions between community members and drives value exchange as this new talent collaborates, learns, contributes, and grows. Software and hardware infrastructure are the other critical resources required for shared digital infrastructure. A cloud abstraction layer is required to position an enterprise to operate across the hybrid cloud and edge. This layer is also known as Polycloud and enables enterprises to operate across public and private clouds in a consistent, compliant, and secure manner. The intent is to minimize vendor lock-in and use the cloud strategically for services where it provides competitive advantage. As more workloads are deployed and distributed across the hybrid cloud and edge ecosystem, the need increases to move and migrate the entire stack in a compliant manner across cloud providers. Polycloud platform investments should increase capabilities, provide more choices and build a strong cloud community that ultimately drives internal and external innovation.

To drive collaboration within enterprises, the platforms should connect users to other users with similar interests, nudge them to join communities focused on mutual interest areas, and streamline collaboration.

Shared digital infrastructure components can be rebundled in interesting ways to experiment, pilot, and scale initiatives at an accelerated pace. As an example, after adopting the shared digital infrastructure at Infosys, new business initiatives are launched in weeks instead of months and have accelerated the pace of service offering launch and innovation.

Well architected and implemented Live Enterprise capabilities provide velocity and evolvability, yet an architecture-first mindset is required to get this right.

Architecture-First Approach

Embrace an architecture-first approach, where architecture and technology stack decisions like build versus buy versus rent are made based on what's right to meet business and architectural requirements, rather than buying ERP software or a platform and thinking that it will take care of all the quality of service and evolvability requirements.

From our own Live Enterprise transformation journey and large transformation work done for our clients, we have curated a set of architecture strategies that can be useful to get the architecture right the first time.

Unbundle

Most enterprises we have studied or worked with have linear business processes supported by monolithic IT systems that operate in silos, and while this may have worked well historically, it is not best suited for the future. To transform and unlock value, unbundle architectural and business capabilities into atomic services, or micro-services.

Atomic services serve only one functionality of higher value, are accessible through well-defined interfaces (APIs), and are removable, replaceable, and reusable across different applications, processes, and platforms. An example is a service that executes user authentication and authorization.

One of the big barriers to unbundling is large monolithic applications (like mainframe applications) that have minimal documentation and are difficult and expensive to change. It is difficult to tackle large monoliths in one project, and we recommend unbundling the monoliths into a set of services by curating knowledge and using modernization patterns like firelaning and strangling. These services also help to move away from technology lock-ins to an open and standards-based architecture.

A global retailer unbundled their core business processes and business functions into more than 20 service areas. They also implemented a delivery model where each of the service teams was responsible to define, develop, and run their technology operations.

Isolate Services

Once the unbundling is done into a set of atomic and composite services, each of these services should expose a well-defined interface that is externalizable, interoperable, and independent of other services in the enterprise. This provides the flexibility required to replace or refactor, with minimal impact on the ecosystem and remove interface lock-ins that exist.

With the pace of technology change and evolution picking up significantly in the last few years, new innovations in software and hardware stack are happening continuously. This results in more major upgrades, more alternatives, and at times changes in licensing models and policies with newer releases. Some of these changes result in technology lock-ins or impact dependent modules or services requiring changes. We recommend to abstract and develop an isolation layer from the lower-level software infrastructure components like operating system and platform services, as well as software tooling like databases, middleware, and third-party utilities. With more and more organizations moving to the cloud and leveraging their platform capabilities, it's important to isolate the usage of platform features to ensure portability across cloud providers.

Standards Based

Once the isolation is done, it's important to bring standardization across all the architectural layers:

▶ **User experience.** Fragmentation of user experience across newer channels like chatbots and voice-driven apps should be minimized. Consistent and seamless user experience across channels and devices should be defined and evolve the experience layer based on user environment and needs, but ensure that they leverage the same APIs.

▶ **Interfaces.** One of the challenges in most enterprises is the widespread presence of point to point and nonstandard interfaces. If the case, the first step is to simplify the integration points and standardize to externalized APIs, and then the renewal or modernization of the underlying implementation can be done over a period of time. Use standard protocols (like HTTP/REST) and industry standards (like PSD2) to standardize integration and enable interoperability.

▶ **Data.** The data structure and schema should be standardized through industry standard data structures, format specification, and vocabularies (like OData), to enable interoperability and openness in data exchange.

▶ **Security.** Standardize security services for data security in flight and at rest (encryption and decryption), certificates, virtual identities that are revocable, identity and access management, biometric and face detection, antivirus checks, document protection, and device management.

▶ **Hardware.** We see a significant shift of enterprise workloads from proprietary hardware and appliances to commodity hardware, and this movement has been significantly accelerated by the cloud providers. With increasing support for infrastructure as code across compute, storage, memory, and network on commodity hardware and container technologies, it has become easier to architect and deploy Internet-scale platforms and services on this hardware.

▶ **Cloud neutral versus native.** With the major cloud providers now aspiring to become the platform of choice for developers, careful consideration should be given to determine when to be cloud neutral versus using cloud native services. It is recommended to take a cloud-neutral approach to embrace cloud to ensure portability across cloud providers. However, when time to market is important or the infrastructure and platform services are more mature or only available on the cloud platform, then cloud native services could be a viable option. Even so, design them in a way that they can be replaced when better alternatives become available.

Open Source as Strategy

To realize the unbundled, isolated, and standard-based services, enterprises typically conduct a "build versus buy versus retain versus rent" analysis. In our view this requires careful evaluation to ensure that the products and platforms don't have a monolithic architecture. We strongly recommend considering open source as a strategy to design and implement differentiated and noncommoditized business and technology services.

Open-source software currently provides a credible alternative to move away from the proprietary software and lock-in. The rate of innovation in the open-source space is much higher than what we see from product and platform vendors. It has become the de facto standard in the areas of operating systems, UX technologies, API and microservices, big data, analytics, DevOps, automation, and AI. With the availability of hardened and supported versions of open-source software, the risks associated with open-source software have also been mitigated to large extent.

Everything as Code

Mark Andreesen in 2011 shared his now famous viewpoint that "software is eating the world," and this has indeed come to pass. With the dominant design of the software-defined data center, software-defined network, and containerization, today most of these resources are available as APIs, and almost all could be codified and driven by software.

Some of the emerging patterns in everything as code are as follows:

▶ **Infrastructure as code.** Codify the infrastructure in declarative specifications that can be used to create, manage, and burn in environments and underlying infrastructure. It is managed in the code repository, versioned, and used to drive extreme automation.

▶ **Configuration as code.** Define configurations like Jenkins and environment configuration in a simple readable format that is versioned and can be executed to automate the process.

▶ **Security as code.** Codify all security controls and policies so that they can be applied and monitored automatically.

▶ **Policy as code.** Codify all the privacy, regulatory, and organizational policies.

▶ **Monitoring as code.** Codify the monitoring aspects like what to monitor, when to alert using a high-level configuration syntax, and automation of the monitoring of each container or instance.

Rebundle

Once the digital runway starts providing unbundled services that are isolated, standardized, and implemented using extreme automation, the project teams working to solve employee, client, or partner problems can rebundle the services they need from the shared digital infrastructure to solve their specific problems.

Due to the COVID-19 outbreak almost all universities, schools, and colleges sought an education platform that enabled them to enroll students, run assessments to shortlist, and then operate classes in a digital-first anytime, anywhere model with students attending classes from all over the world or in their local community. At Infosys, we developed a new education platform quickly in weeks, by rebundling learning, collaborations, commerce, and onboarding/offboarding services. This was first for ourselves, and then we shared our learnings with our clients. This would simply not have been possible with the traditional IT approach.

Ecosystems

Traditional processes are linear in nature. However, in a Live Enterprise business processes are ecosystem-driven to integrate processes, together with the evolving business models of marketplaces and circular economies. The architecture must be open and standards-based to enable ecosystem integration and make it easy to plug and play with ecosystem participants.

Architectural Language

The right words change mindsets. When it comes to applying the architecture-first mindset across a large enterprise, it's important to choose the right language and words. Use terms like *configuration*, *extensibility*, *observability*, and *sentience* rather than customization, dashboards, and reporting. Repeating and reinforcing these words will ensure teams internalize these concepts and embed them into the design and implementation of platform services.

Architecture by Design

Chunking in Nine

George Miller is regarded as the "Father of the Cognitive Revolution," heralding a new era of psychology theory and research. His famous paper on memory capacity demonstrated that human minds can parallel process between five and nine pieces of information at any one time.[4]

Miller's paper also introduced the concept of "chunking," the breaking up of information into smaller chunks to help commit information to memory. In effect, chunking optimizes memory by breaking down information into chunks of five to nine items. To get the architecture right for a live enterprise, we have identified nine architecture-by-design principles. Architects, designers and developers should think about these aspects from the outset and ensure that these principles and practices are purposefully weaved into the architecture, design, and code. These principles have been developed based on inputs and references from Infosys experience and from external sources like Societal Platform, AWS Well-Architected Framework, Google Cloud best practices, Twelve Factor principles, and US Air Force Data Reference Architecture.

Evolvability by Design
Evolvability by design is accomplished by applying the following concepts.

Atomic. Single-purpose atomic services that have high value and well-defined interfaces are replaceable and can be reused across platforms and solutions. An example is an encryption service that is responsible to encrypt and decrypt data across the enterprise.

Configurable. Personalize, modify, and configure the service to run differently across different environments and context. For example, configure a different payment gateway to be used for making payments online without impact to the features or functionality.

Extensible. Evolve by extending existing services and functionality with minimal downtime of the platform. For example, additional user details have to be stored and processed for compliance reasons, and this can be implemented as a plugin that will be registered with the platform.

Refactorable. Enables the code to be refactored by new and existing developers with minimal impact to external services using the API interface. For example, the algorithm used to search information across documents can be replaced without impact to the interface and users.

Generizable. Services should be abstractable from their current context and environment so that they can be generalized and reused across different contexts and platform. For example, an accounting service developed for one system should be reusable in another context with appropriate configuration.

Automation. Any software engineering process that is repeatable should also be fully automated to deliver everything as code, applied during the DevSecOps life cycle to enable platform speed and scale. This becomes critical to drive hyper-productivity as engineering teams expand.

Versioning. All externalizable APIs should be versioned and natively support backward compatibility. It is important to implement the versioning strategy early, as multiple versions of an API may co-exist in production environments to support multiple API clients.

Upgradable. Upgrade and rollback of services at scale, across all environments, should be fully automated and nondisruptive. As new services are released periodically, production environments need the ability to upgrade without breaking existing interfaces and ensure options to revert to prior versions.

Debuggable. Generates debug information at runtime, based on configurations to enable remote diagnostics and troubleshooting. It should be possible to configure this at runtime so that for a slice of users or interactions, diagnostic information can be captured. This is extremely useful to operations teams, when the software is deployed in remote locations or edge cloud and provides useful information to debug without requiring any changes to the code.

Testable. Fully automated functional, performance, stress, endurance, and regression testing to enable speed and scale for new features and refactoring. Testability is critical to ensure resilience, especially as organizations evolve to an operating model where software releases occur more frequently, even daily.

Scalability by Design

Scalability by design is accomplished by applying the following concepts.

Responsive to scale. Designed to manage increase in interactions over time and sudden surge in volumes and scale with increase in storage, memory, and compute. Software should be horizontally scalable to handle load increases without requiring code changes.

Reliable. Consistent behavior and performance over a period of time across different contexts and releases. All software releases should be tested for reliability on an ongoing basis to ensure user experience does not degrade with ongoing releases.

Resilient. Self-healing and ability to recover from certain types of failure, like a node going down on surge in load, with minimal or no impact to end-user experience. Production software and hardware failures happen over time, and design for broad fault tolerance ensures that platform services can abundantly handle and recover from failures when they occur.

Performant. Consistently delivers high throughput and response times as expected of the service. Users expect subsecond response times from digital services, and deep architectural analysis should be done early to consider end-to-end response time including latency, processing time across layers, and external dependencies.

Fault tolerant. Designed to ensure no single points of failure, and when faults, errors, or exceptions occur, the service handles it with minimal or no degradation in user experience. Both software and hardware components need consideration across layers, plus redundancy for each critical service, based on business and operational requirements.

Observability by Design

Observability by design is accomplished by applying the following concepts.

Telemetry. Instrument code across architectural layers to emit information that can later be analyzed to get system insights and improve the platform features. Systematically plan feature prioritization, change management and continuous user experience improvements based on telemetry information.

Monitoring. Monitor as code across all services to capture the health and diagnostic information that can be used to troubleshoot and heal in case of any faults or errors. Monitoring information should be processed in real time and routine actions should be taken automatically wherever feasible, minimizing the need for human intervention.

Traceability. Globally unique identifiers to trace user interactions across layers, events, and asynchronous processes and the ability to track them at runtime based on context. As systems become more event-driven and distributed, traceability is required to quickly troubleshoot and resolve issues.

Insights. Real-time data analytics of the information gathered to understand the usage and runtime behavior to improve the services and platform. Business, engineering and technology metrics should be monitored on an ongoing basis to identify areas for improvement, measure outcomes delivered, and communicate to stakeholders.

Trust by Design

Trust by design is accomplished by applying the following concepts.

Open. Open and externalizable APIs, open standards and frameworks, open-source usage and contribution, open data standards and empowerment, and codified, community-led governance.

Consistent. Consistency of system behavior through externalized APIs and standards to build trust amongst the platform users and community.

Cocreative. Promote cocreation amongst the platform teams across the enterprise through collaboration, communication, learning, sharing, and reuse of services. Platform architects should use services developed by other platform teams to accelerate the velocity of platform features delivered.

Consumable. Easy to consume services by other platform users through simplified setup, self-service, proper documentation, and implementation support. As more and more platform services take an API-first approach, a consumable approach is essential to drive usage and better developer experience.

Digitally trusted. Trust between platform ecosystem players established through identity (for individuals and organizations) and immutability (for transactions or assets) and can be machine verifiable.

Sentience by Design

Sentience by design is accomplished by applying the following concepts.

Proximity to source. All the information and insights required to make good decisions should be made available to users in the flow during the interactions itself. For example, if the manager is approving a travel request, then the manager should have a view to the budget available and all the requests pending approval and likely impact so that they can make an informed decision.

Zero latency. Straight through processing with zero or minimal layers and approvals required to complete the interaction or service request.

Instant simulation. Ability to do what-if analysis or evaluate alternatives when exploring different options to make right decisions. For example, the manager while approving travel requests should be able to do what-if analysis to ensure the right decisions are made based on business relevance.

Guided practice. Drive change in culture and behavior by removing nonproductive routines and taking users along guided paths to develop new routines. For example, LinkedIn asking its users to provide information to complete the profile every time a user logs in, to enrich the profile.

Micro-feedback. Gather feedback at the end of each interaction to learn and improve the interaction and underlying services. For example, Uber or Lyft asking for feedback about the ride at the end.

Usage for All by Design

Usage for all by design is accomplished by applying the following concepts.

Multitenant. Provides deployment choices at the time of setup and implementation based on customer, regulatory, and business needs. For global organizations operating across multiple markets, regions or for platforms, multitenancy considerations are required from the start.

Technology independent. Focus on the platform architecture to fulfill the business capability and requirements rather than rely upon tools, products, and vendors to fulfill these. Also, tool and product replaceability to evolve over time.

Commoditized technology. Use open-source technologies and solutions that can run and scale on commodity hardware. The cost per transaction to serve should work for customers whether small or large size.

Micro-footprint. Containerize and ensure each service requires minimal infrastructure footprint to drive adoption, across user classes and their deployment environments.

Metering. Enable throttling and runtime information gathering to enable switching features on and off, based on the subscription or licensing model enabled for the platform instance.

Internationalization. Natively provides internationalization supporting features support for multiple currencies, and localization of the user experience and layout.

Operational Excellence by Design

Operational excellence by design is accomplished by applying the following concepts.

Everything as code. As a practice, codify everything: DevSecOps, monitoring, configuration, security, policy, compliance, and testing as code to bring in extreme automation for speed and scale in releases.

Micro-release. Plan for frequent and continuous releases to consistently deliver new features to the users and enable micro-change management for released features to drive adoption at scale. A software release every four to six weeks ensures users continuously get new features and also enhances their overall experience.

Automated documentation. Annotate code to generate documentation automatically, so that the code is easy to read and is maintainable over time.

Anticipate failures. Design for planned failure and anticipate unplanned failures, and how to deal with them to minimize end user impact.

Security by Design

Security by design is the approach for platform services to embed security at the design stage. All security guidelines and practices are identified and codified, so that developers consider them and ensure compliance during the entire engineering process. This is accomplished by applying the following concepts:

Identity as foundation. Identity service to authenticate users through multimodal authentication and authorize actions across a centralized or federated model. Identity services should cover all key stakeholders— employees, customers, partners—and provide the flexibility to operate anytime, anywhere across the enterprise ecosystem.

Zero trust architecture. With enterprises now operating across hybrid cloud and edge and forming their own enterprise ecosystems, traditional perimeter-based security will not be enough. Ultimately, there is a need to trust no one and apply security controls and checks across all architectural layers and interactions that occur system to system, system to user, and user to user.

Multi Cloud and Data Security. Most enterprises operate across the hybrid cloud and edge, and manage this widespread data across public, private, and edge clouds. A critical success factor is to monitor and secure data, containers, AI services, and applications across multi-cloud environments. Autonomous techniques maximize the impact of emerging techniques like security as code, policy as code, and monitoring as code.

Privacy by Design

Privacy by design is the approach to embed privacy as core functionality into the design and architecture stage of business processes and new applications, products, and technologies. Privacy cannot be fully protected by existing policies and regulations alone, and it is necessary to introduce privacy as the default case into the design of processes and IT systems across the entire information life cycle.

Privacy by design (PbD) puts forth seven foundational concepts to mitigate privacy risks and achieve data privacy compliance.

- ▶ **Proactive not Reactive; Preventive not Remedial**: PbD supports proactive identification of privacy risk events in advance and taking necessary preventive steps, rather than being reactive and implementing remedial measures after an event occurs.
- ▶ **Privacy as the Default setting**: PbD requires privacy to be the default mode of operation, while building organization processes and

systems so that no specific action is required from a data subject to ensure privacy of their personal data.

▶ **Privacy embedded into design**: Privacy should be considered core functionality, starting from the design and architecture stage of any system or process, not to be added as an afterthought at a later stage.

▶ **Positive-sum, not zero-sum**: PbD believes that business functionality from stakeholders and data privacy are equally important. This means there is no need for trade-offs, and all interests and objectives are accommodated with a positive-sum mindset.

▶ **End-to-End Security**: PbD supports end-to-end security of personal data across the entire information life cycle.

▶ **Visibility and Transparency**: PbD supports complete transparency and visibility to all stakeholders.

▶ **Respect for user privacy**—PbD offers data subjects measures like privacy defaults and appropriate notifications to keep privacy user-centric.

Architecture Fitness Function

We have observed that often architecture and its related principles do not get translated properly into the code. A number of decisions made during the development life cycle can have a long-lasting impact on the architectural characteristics defined for the platform and services. A platform is only as good as the individual micro-services it supports.

To measure and ensure services are able to comply to this quality standard, the architecture fitness function should be defined and tested for each service. Test cases need to be developed to evaluate the ability of the platform services to fulfill these architectural requirements, and the fitness function can be calculated based on the test results. The architecture fitness function indicates compliance to architectural characteristics during the DevSecOps process and rates each service. This rating helps platform stakeholders understand how well the platform has been engineered and if it meets all the architectural goals.

Architecture fitness functions should be used continuously to ensure that the shared digital infrastructure services forming the digital runway are architected and implemented correctly. This is an integral component of the Live Enterprise model, and like all the model components, the value occurs when it is "live" and starts exhibiting the defined characteristics. The next chapter discusses implementation, collaboration, and adoption, where these principles come alive and become part of the enterprise operations, mindset, and culture.

RECAP: Digital Runway

- Corporate digital platforms act as a digital runway, providing the tools to scale ideas and innovation. Digital runways provide a shared company digital infrastructure by curating and organizing knowledge, platforms and services, processes and playbooks, data and AI services, and resources.
- These elements come together in a scalable model to increase velocity of new ideas and innovation, by aggressive shared use of the digital infrastructure. Platform services provide a centralized software and hardware infrastructure abstracted as APIs that enable value-add features, functionality, and interactions in a plug-and-play-based model.
- An architecture-first and platform mindset should be applied to ensure the platforms are designed for evolvability rather than features and functions. An architecture fitness function should be defined to continuously measure platform quality, plus include playbooks to define and codify guided practices.
- The digital runway requires a significant culture shift in corporate mindset. To deliver a change in culture and drive the business, there should be a persistent focus on the consumption, coverage, adoption, business impact, and usage of shared infrastructure.

9

MICRO IS THE
NEW MEGA

The Greatest Challenge

All Creatures Great and Small

In the natural world, evolution is the sum of changes on vastly different scales. Microevolution happens on a small scale within a single population, while macroevolution happens on a mega scale, transcending the boundaries of a single species. When it comes to cadence, microevolution is observed at short timescales, macroevolution over eons. Microevolution is driven by multiple mechanisms, including natural selection and mutation, all producing nature's countless variations. Macroevolution is defined as evolution above the species level, effectively microevolution *plus* 3.8 billion years.

In 2007, Lehigh University biochemist Michael Behe published *The Edge of Evolution*,[1] in which he reminded us that microevolution enables bacteria and viruses to evade our best-made plans to defeat them. Microevolution is agile, swift, and hyper-productive—with viruses, for example, being so diverse because they can mix genes and mutate at speed. This is the reason we need new flu shots every year, and more ominously, why COVID-19 was the novel coronavirus that shut down the world.

The macro and micro play out in business as well, and the evolution of the modern enterprise has followed similar patterns. From (relatively) slow changes constrained by paper-based communication and horse-powered logistics to instantaneous collaboration and Amazon Prime, the rate of market change has outstripped traditional macroevolutionary methods to manage it. A new approach is needed, and micro has become the new macro, or *micro has become the new mega*.

Resilience

COVID-19 not only redefined how we do business, communication, and culture but also shifted the tectonics of capitalism. From philosophical reframe to fundamental reset, the pandemic and its aftermath accelerated existing trends and exposed underlying weaknesses. Beyond the short-term challenges of health, cash flow, and consumer demand, the pandemic exposed the greatest strategic challenge of all: resilience.

As a result, traditional responses to change are no longer enough. Over the last 30 years, large incumbent companies have tried to be more like startups . . . and failed. All despite fully embracing trends like digital transformation, lean startup, and design thinking. While each approach has substantial merits, for most companies they have yet to deliver on their promise. As a result, traditional responses to change are no longer enough. Here's why:

Digital transformation falls short because companies reach a digital ceiling, with diminishing returns. They have a hard time taking improvements beyond so-called pilot purgatory, which can show progress but not result in widespread adoption and true change. Lean startup only goes so far, because while it explains principles to launch a new initiative or venture, it doesn't address how larger firms can change practices to become nimbler themselves to learn and evolve quickly. Design thinking provides initial energy and a framework, but typically doesn't help leaders scale the results beyond proofs of concept and localized projects. Individual creativity and qualitative intuition fall short when faced with the reality of systems integration and scale considerations.

We and our Infosys colleagues experienced these shortcomings firsthand during the transformation at Infosys and heard them voiced repeatedly in employee and client discussions. This experience led us to envision and develop a new, nontraditional change model for the modern era.

Mega-Visions and Micro-Thoughts

We looked to nature for inspiration, found microevolution, and called it "micro-change"—small, irreversible change from which you do not revert to the old habits.

Micro-change management is how the Live Enterprise model operates. The vision and aspirations are big, but the organization thinks "micro." Agile teams work on micro-problems, and they pivot to address user needs and develop a minimum viable product (MVP). These micro-problems are addressed by small, hyper-productive teams working on micro-releases to rapidly experiment and take concepts to market in weeks.

Crucially, this leverages a distributed agile model—a team distributed across two or more locations relying on digital technology to design, facilitate, and deliver. This model is ideal for smaller projects where team members work on a single functionality or solution at a time. Powered by the digital runway, the enterprise platform that provides a connected ecosystem, this activity is managed through micro-change management to optimize sprint planning meetings, daily scrums, sprint review meetings, and sprint retrospectives.

As seen in starling murmurations and Spotify, micro is the new mega, with agile predisposed to small teams working on rapid learning and decision cycles. Agile evolution is broken down into incremental micro-projects pulled together with a micro-front end and micro-service architecture, to create an environment of frequent micro-gains. This enablement is best delivered over a number of sprints so people can learn to think and act differently. In effect, micro-change management ultimately helps organizations evolve enterprise agile. Traditional change management does not work in this context, which is why micro-change management is so important—taking time to tackle a small problem first, and drive adoption at scale so the approach can be seen to deliver value.

The New Mega

Frameworking Change, Impact, and Scale

Peter Drucker famously said, "Culture eats strategy for breakfast." For the Live Enterprise model to be successful within an organization, the employees and teams working to define and execute the vision and strategy should believe in it and implement it effectively. One of the objectives is also to bring about cultural change, so that during transformation to be a Live Enterprise, this changes employee routines and eventually their behavior.

We use a simple framework to drive micro-change across the organization, depicted in Figure 9.1.

Each new micro-change initiative within the organization follows this four-step process. To ensure that the change programs deliver as intended, once change initiatives are rolled out to the users, the platform should use

1. Micro-changes	2. Routine +1	3. Behavioral approach to change management	4. Continuously measure, learn and evolve
Break down strategic initiatives into multiple **micro-change programs**, with each having a well-defined objective and outcome. Ask why a change is required, whether **incremental** or **exponential**, what value it will deliver, and what change in behavior is needed. These micro-change programs will lead to a **sigma of micro change programs** to accomplish the mega vision.	Each micro-change management program should drive a small change in a **routine**. Periodically augment with similar adjacent changes **(Routine +1)**. Eventually create a new routine and achieve **behavior shift** with minimal resistance.	**Behavioral approach** is a combination of **cues, hints, and suggestions**. **Positively nudge** the impacted stakeholders and supplement with **rewards and incentives** which create the excitement and improve outcomes.	As micro-change programs are rolled out, **continuously measure** to ensure they accomplish desired outcomes. If not, analyze data, rethink, and **improve through iteration**. Measure the change program through **platform services** for outcomes like convenience, adoption, behavior, and value.

FIGURE 9.1   Driving organizational change one micro-step at a time.

telemetry to automatically measure and determine how successful the change initiatives have been. If some of the change initiatives are not successful, then use micro-change management to drive adoption, and if that does not work, then based on micro-feedback seek to understand why it is not working and revise accordingly.

To measure the adoption of micro-changes, especially software-driven experience and features, we developed and used the evaluation tool shown in Figure 9.2. We found this two-dimensional framework extremely useful at Infosys. For example, it can be used to measure mobile app adoption against the app features and functions used.

In any large enterprise, for a pilot initiative or prototype consider limiting initial deployment to 2.5 percent of the overall pilot user base. For example, if the number of employees in an organization is 100,000 and a new health and wellness feature is planned for a pilot, then it should be rolled out to a test user base of 2,500. The learnings and experience from the pilot should be used to refine and scale the rollout across the entire user base.

When the micro-change adoption has reached between 20 and 40 percent, it becomes significant in the organization, and at 60 percent it becomes a standard. Once adoption reaches 80 percent it is considered assimilated into the organization and culture. To measure this in an autonomous manner, the software will have to be instrumented to produce telemetry information that can be used to measure and then act upon.

While user adoption at an overall initiative level is one facet, the extent to which the features and functions are used across the user base is also an

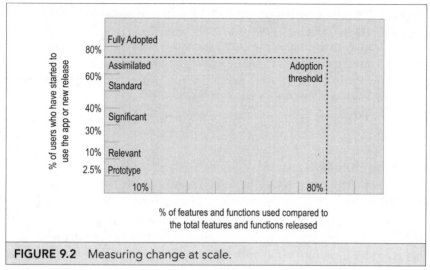

% of users who have started to use the app or new release

80% — Fully Adopted

60% — Assimilated / Standard — Adoption threshold

40% — Significant

30%

10% — Relevant

2.5% — Prototype

10%   80%

% of features and functions used compared to
the total features and functions released

FIGURE 9.2   Measuring change at scale.

Source: Infosys.

important aspect to continuously monitor. Thinking micro, it is worthwhile to look at each feature and function in isolation and determine why they are doing well or not, and for those not doing well, then either they should be reimagined or stop investing in those features and plan to sunset them.

A Precision Instrument

Traditional large firms require a cultural shift to become a learning organization. Learning in combination with a bias for action embeds and sustains relentless improvement. Cultural change is strategic and requires leadership commitment through a visible, active, and persistent role. Leaders shape the workplace environment so agile ways of working can take root. Micro-change management delivers incremental change from the bottom up, that is, the team level, with role model examples and guidance from leaders.

Conventional wisdom suggests a top-down approach as the strategy for organizational change management. Agile micro-change management, however, favors a bottom-up approach. At Infosys, we developed a successful bottom-up approach through many local and account-level events, viral videos on a dedicated WhatsApp channel, plus gamification via team webinars and quizzes. Individually, these can be dismissed as one-off, feel-good events. However, taken together, they influenced 240,000-plus employees through meaningful nudges that were relevant to them. The cumulative effect was lasting behavioral change and adoption of the broader goals for the agile transformation to the Live Enterprise model.

This approach considers the user experience rather than simply completion of transactions. Interactions are valued over transactions. Micro-change management moves beyond the pursuit of linear processes to an ecosystem approach, with open architecture that can sense, respond, and more easily adapt to change.

Nudging Human Nature

In the Live Enterprise model, as features and functions are released every six weeks, awareness level across the entire user base becomes a problem impacting adoption. Another challenge is that as we reimagine the processes and drive change programs, new routines will have to be developed and embraced by users to truly change the culture. Applying nudge theory and services, nudges can be instrumented into the reimagined experience and processes to drive desired changes in behavior.

Designed to make all major interactions available to employees on-the-go, the Infosys *InfyMe* productivity app was developed internally and is used globally by over 200,000 employees. With a large number of features released every six weeks, not all of the important features and functions were adopted by employees. For the features that were not working well, we used the micro-feedback and also held focused group discussions to understand how useful the features were and what can be done to improve further. For example, for a customer 360 feature, users indicated that they were not aware of all functionality, did not inherently trust the system data, and wanted a different hierarchy view of information. Based on this feedback, the team made user interface modifications, conducted awareness campaigns, and used nudges across interactions to drive usage, and today this functionality has been assimilated across the user base.

Compounding Microevolution

In the wake of the greatest business disruption in living memory, agile organizations have proven best equipped to survive. However, even before the COVID-19 pandemic, we studied the problem of large-scale change and found traditional methods fell short. Market forces were already moving too quickly and unpredictably for rigid forms-driven change management to succeed. Yet all the data pointed to change management issues as the leading cause of large program failure.

Despite being built for the incredible scale of 1.2 billion Indian citizens, the India Stack[2] programs showed that frequent small changes, each nudging the user to incremental behavior, not only succeeded but amplified success with a compounding effect. We call this approach micro-change management. Micro-change measures success via a framework composed of convenience, adoption, behavior, and value—each release delivering small yet compelling benefits to the target user community.

Micro-change measures progress in transformation programs via a framework of convenience, adoption, behavior, and value delivery, and these frequent releases have the cumulative effect to improve agility as well. Much like the exponential power of compound interest, people tend to underestimate the power of frequent micro-shifts at scale. Something small and done right consistently has a large impact, and a major insight at Infosys emerged that "micro is the new mega." As with any strategic initiative, leadership commitment is required, with a visible and active role to facilitate cultural change.

Micro-Change Management

Cycles Within Cycles

With every photon that hits the eye, our mind looks for meaning, for frameworks that help us navigate nature. This is why we created calendars, to study the heavenly cycles and bring order to our lives.

Over 35,000 years ago in modern Swaziland, someone carved 29 notches into a baboon bone to record the number of days between full moons.[3] About 4,500 years ago, Stonehenge in England recorded the Metonic cycle of 19 solar years,[4] with 29.5 stones in its outer circle giving even greater accuracy to the time between full moons. At the other end of the scale, 3,500 years ago, the Vedas in India recorded cycles lasting trillions of years, each divisible by 2,160, the number of years the equinoctial sun takes to process through one sign of the zodiac (or 30 degrees of the sky above us).

At Infosys, we also looked for the cycles within cycles that drive micro-changes. We navigated our journey to adopt the Live Enterprise model by executing three major tracks, each running in agile sprints of six weeks: reimagine experience, reimagine processes, shared digital infrastructure. (See Figure 9.3).

Each track has multiple micro-changes, in each release. With micro-change interventions conducted to accompany agile sprints, change occurs in micro-bursts, one step at a time in alignment with the agile build, which cumulatively evolve larger organizational changes.

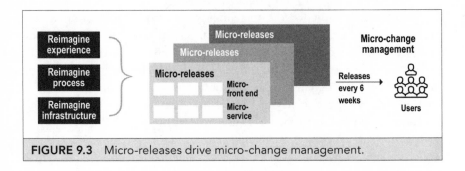

FIGURE 9.3   Micro-releases drive micro-change management.

After experimenting with different durations, we found six weeks as the optimal cadence to provide a new release. This allowed users to gain confidence in the efficacy of incremental innovation, and over time, introduce additional capabilities addressing current operations and new capabilities. This frequent cadence and regular tempo required a new architecture to modernize and manage technology, plus shift organizational posture and momentum.

Business Tracks in Rapid Sprints

While agile is more effective than waterfall and sprints are crucial to transformation, six-week sprints making change at scale requires amazing organizational discipline. If the momentum of the company moves by a small amount every six weeks, the cumulative effect over even a year is transformational, because the compounding effect is exponential, rather than linear.

Our experience has demonstrated three underlying themes of the Live Enterprise model. First, *architecture is unified*, but not uniform. This flexibility provides for small changes in the enterprise technology scaffolding, so the tech moves with business needs but retains structural integrity. Second, the model *shares the ability to solve*, so the entire organization learns and is able to solve its own problems. This distributed approach allows flexibility for resultant change to occur at the point needed, when needed, and then the learning is shared in the organizational body of knowledge. Third, *micro-change at scale is truly transformative* (see Figure 9.4). Many small, targeted changes with impact accomplish the need of the hour, and that provides credibility for the users who ultimately are the ones responsible to adopt the new way of working. These three elements of the Live Enterprise model are foundational, yet can be easily overlooked because people tend to focus on larger, more visible items.

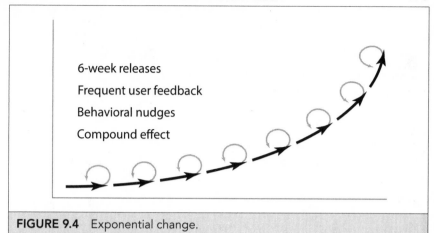

6-week releases

Frequent user feedback

Behavioral nudges

Compound effect

FIGURE 9.4 Exponential change.

Change Management Challenges

Communication insights and learnings on the digital journey are often lost in translation as they are shared with others affected by change. This is due to unclear language, technical complexity, or lack of preparation and implementation analysis. Micro-change addresses misalignment by measuring via telemetry, careful design, and rigorous testing as outlined in the change measurement diagram earlier.

If talent is the lifeblood of an organization, then it is also important to get it right for change initiatives. Talent is fundamental to any successful enterprise, yet supply gaps exist in high-demand areas such as data analytics. Skills shortages delay adoption of Live Enterprise principles, but organizations can fill at least part of their demand through reskilling. Reskilling requires decisive action to set up the right training program, then follow-up to ensure the newly skilled employees are allowed to work where needed, even if that means transferring to other units in the company. This sounds obvious, but incentives (or at least executive mandates) are needed to overcome talent hoarding by myopic managers.

Siloed teams and thinking lead to reluctance to share data and organizational inertia, exacerbated by skepticism and funding constraints. Deconstructing transformation programs into a micro-change management framework overcomes these problems by providing metrics that ensure accountability for change at both the individual and organizational levels. This micro-approach also allows managers to more readily track progress on learning, readiness, and adoption.

Organizational change management (OCM) strategy is typically a top-down approach, manifesting in an overarching company-wide communication campaign, company-wide events, and a digital OCM hub. This approach may have served its purpose when large programs were rigidly structured and tightly planned, but the frequent nature of change and evolution of agile concepts drove the development of micro-change management's bottom-up strategy. Tactically, a bottom-up approach includes local and unit-level events, viral videos on dedicated collaboration channels, and gamification via team webinars and quizzes.

Even with its merits, there are barriers to micro-change management that should be addressed through a flexible operating model, collaborative working, and updated policies:

- ▶ Broad organizational policies like performance plans and incentives, and budgeting and planning practices typically don't align to agile ways of working.
- ▶ Control or governance mechanisms may not shift to allow for self-organizing, autonomous, collaborative teams. They may fail to integrate the constant "adjust and adapt" cycle of agile, practiced in sprint retrospectives, beyond formal team organizational boundaries.
- ▶ Broader cultural and governance issues may discourage open sharing of information, or people may not collaborate across functional boundaries.

The Delta of Persuasion

In 2016, Cornell University released a paper on the thorny subject of changing minds.[5] Using an online forum over two years for their research sample, the findings suggested that numbers are important—you effectively have four chances to change an individual's mind before it seemingly snaps shut. Getting your argument in first also seems to have greater impact than those arriving late to the party.

If Cornell's research subjects were persuaded to change their minds, they confirmed this by typing "Δ," or delta, the fourth letter of the Greek alphabet that mathematicians use as the symbol for change.

The research considered the role language plays in persuasion—it has to be nuanced, considered, and calm. *The* works better than *a*, for example, meaning it helps to use the definite article. Contextual phrases like "for instance" add credibility, as do ones like "it might be," with cautionary phrases seeming to soften the sharper edges of an argument. Listening obviously helps with "opinion malleability" too. People using a first-person *I* are more entrenched in their views than those using an inclusive *we*.

When it comes to making this mental change, the research concludes it is vital to understand how community norms encourage a well-behaved platform so that useful rules, moderation practices, or even automated tools can be deployed in the future.

As Infosys initially applied the Live Enterprise model internally, we found the most challenging aspect was changing mindset and community norms. As a result, we now plan and deliver adoption over a number of sprints so people can learn to think and act differently. This allows individuals time to tackle a small problem first, before being asked to be part of adoption at scale—a nuanced, considered approach that softens the sharp edges of persuasion.

Culture and Servant Leadership

This change in thinking and community norms is the catalyst to a changed work culture, beginning with the organization's leadership. Senior leaders must be vocal champions of change and demonstrate agility in their own actions. They should create and communicate shared purpose, hold themselves accountable to deliver value, and establish a culture of transparency.

Cross-functional leadership is essential to micro-change management's ability to connect people who need to work together across boundaries or with those outside the enterprise. Successful transformations need strong and aligned leadership who share a compelling, commonly understood, and jointly owned business vision. Mentoring new managers in their roles over an extended period sustains transformation. Cross-functional leadership is optimized by creating a cohort of managers that meet through stand-ups (as frequently as required to make decisions faster), receive group facilitation on real-life cases from their own work, and reinforce learnings through weekly coaching sessions.

Plus-One Nudges

In 2008, University of Chicago economist Richard H. Thaler and Harvard Law School Professor Cass R. Sunstein published *Nudge: Improving Decisions about Health, Wealth, and Happiness.*[6] Triangulating half a century's research in policy, psychology, and behavioral economics, the book highlighted how indirect suggestion and positive reinforcement influence the behavior and decisions of groups and individuals. Thaler and Sunstein defined a "nudge" as any aspect of the choice architecture that alters people's behavior in a predictable way without forbidding any options or significantly changing their economic incentives. To count as a mere nudge, the intervention must be easy and cheap to avoid. Nudges are not mandates. In their words, "Putting fruit at eye level counts as a nudge. Banning junk food does not."

Put simply, a nudge is a stratagem to make judgments and choices easier, but not in a coercive way—a soft psychological push, rather than a shove. Nudges are behavioral micro-changes that are relatively easy and inexpensive to implement.

Micro-change management allows businesses to prepare, equip, and support individuals to successfully adopt changes that drive organizational success and outcomes via a digital platform. Again, this requires leadership commitment to a visible and active role to facilitate the cultural change.

With micro-change interventions carried out to accompany agile sprints, change occurs one micro-step at a time. Change interventions are instituted from the bottom up in micro-change, aided by change routines in the current process (Routine +1 or Plus-one). To motivate people to adopt the new routine, nudges are introduced as cues, hints, or suggestions. Nudges achieve incremental behavior shifts with minimal resistance, which leads to the ultimate behavioral shift and desired outcomes. People are reminded about goal importance through replicating successful nudges, by promoting these successes throughout the organization—and also by recording and sharing stories of "failed" nudges too.

Plus-one thinking aligns well with actual micro-change implementation. It considers where people are currently and their motivations. Plus-one is a change from which they don't feel like going back to the previous way of working.

The cues and rewards that support bottom-up change also lead to the ultimate behavioral shift and desired outcomes, as the very nature of micro-change and plus-one thinking is intended to be nonthreatening. This goes back to the concept of routines and that people do not make leaps, they take one step at a time. And for them, the micro-perspective makes change nonthreatening, just simple steps that they can do for a while until becoming part of their new meaningful, adaptive routine.

Cues, Hints, and Suggestions

Micro-change interventions are carried out to accompany agile sprints, so change occurs one step at a time along with the agile build. These micro-steps lead to a sum of micro-changes, which bring about larger change during the transformation—again taking us back to the concept of compound organizational evolution over time.

To keep pace with compound evolution, companies need a faster, more cost-effective and less risky way to cope with change. With micro-change management, change adoption occurs by changing a routine one step at a time, augmented by adjacent changes to the routine for every sprint. The

Aadhaar initiative reminds and reinforces the twin effects of compounding change—amount and speed.

In the new world where humans and machines (e.g., bots) coexist, while the micro-change management approach covers humans, technology practices are also needed so that frequent software changes do not impact the end-user experience. Some of the techniques mentioned in the digital runway chapter (configurable, testable, and so on) can ensure continuous micro-releases to users with confidence and minimal or no disruption.

"Micro is the new mega" deconstructs complex and large initiatives into micro-initiatives with clear goals and objectives, executing them with a rhythm of micro-releases every few weeks and supported by the micro-change management framework. Over a period of time, this results in changed routines, behavior, and culture—taken together, realizing the vision of the Live Enterprise.

RECAP: Micro Is the New Mega

- Micro is the new mega is the strategy of deconstructing complex and large initiatives into micro-initiatives with clear goals and objectives. These are delivered via a cadence of regular micro-releases, supported through the framework of micro-change management. Over time, this results in changed routines, behavior, and culture.
- Micro-change management delivers small, irreversible change by addressing micro-problems with small, hyper-productive, agile teams working on micro-releases to evolve and take concepts to market. With features and functions released every six weeks, new routines are applied via plus-one nudges, to reimagine the experience and process that drives changes in corporate behavior.
- When micro-change adoption has reached between 20 and 40 percent, it becomes significant in the organization and becomes standard at 60 percent. Once adoption reaches 80 percent it is considered assimilated into the organization and culture. To measure this in an autonomous manner, the software has to be instrumented to produce telemetry information that can be used to measure and act.
- The micro-change model shares the ability to solve, with the entire organization learning and capable to solve its own problems. Micro-change at scale is truly transformative, effecting small changes in the enterprise technology platform so the tech evolves with business needs but retains structural integrity.

10

THE TRIPLE HELIX

Extinction-Level Events

Creative Destruction

We started as a single-cell bacterium almost four billion years ago. Of an estimated 4 billion species since then, 99 percent no longer exist. We humans are the 1 percent.

In the last 500 million years, there have been five mass extinctions, each destroying at least 75 percent of life on earth.[1] The one we all know happened 65 million years ago—the Cretaceous event caused by a space rock hitting the Gulf of Mexico, signaling "game over" for 75 percent of species and sending dinosaurs the way of the dinosaurs.

An ominous lesson for us today, climate change played a role in every mass extinction, wiping the slate clean and allowing nature to downsize and evolve. Mass extinction essentially creates the space for survivors to spread into the environmental niches and thrive through less competition for food and resources, allowing rapid reproduction.

The Permian mass extinction cleared the path for the first mammals and dinosaurs, while the Triassic helped turn dinosaurs into chickens and a small, toothy rodent into you and me.[2] As Charles Darwin wrote in *The Origin of Species*, the "extinction of old forms is the almost inevitable consequence of the production of new forms."[3]

Why does this matter in a business book describing the Live Enterprise? In evolutionary terms, nature is the ultimate act of *creative destruction*. The famed economist Joseph Schumpeter in 1942 wrote that creative destruction describes the process of "industrial mutation that continuously revolution-izes the economic structure from within, incessantly destroying the old one, incessantly creating a new one."[4]

In economic and business terms, nature is the ultimate teacher, with 3.8 billion years' experience and a near-limitless research and development (R&D) budget.

Financial Fossils and Corporate Mass Extinction

Taking from the Greek for "life" (*bios*) and "imitation" (*mimesis*), Janine Benyus popularized the concept of biomimicry in her 1997 book *Biomimicry: Innovation Inspired by Nature.*[5] The book contends that nature is a model, measure, and mentor—the ultimate example of what works, what's appro-priate, and what lasts.

Animals, plants, and microbes are the consummate engineers. After billions of years of research and development, failures are fossils, and what surrounds us is the secret to survival.

What of the corporate fossil failures? Since 2000, over 50 percent of Fortune 500 companies have either merged or gone out of business, according to *Harvard Business Review.*[6] That same article reports that in 1958, corpora-tions listed in the S&P 500 had an average stay of 61 years. By 2011, however, the average was 18 years, and 75 percent of 2020's S&P 500 expected to be corporate fossils by 2027. During the writing of this book, Exxon Mobil was replaced on the Dow Jones Industrial Average by Salesforce. In a sign of the times, Exxon had been on the Dow Jones for 92 years, whereas Salesforce only went public in 2004—in this instance, data really is the new oil.[7]

No wonder Tom Siebel, founder of Siebel Systems and CEO of C3.ai, observed, "The fact is that we are experiencing, in the first part of the 21st century, a mass extinction event in the corporate world."[8] In Greek myth, Hesiod called the Titans "the former gods" (*theoi proteroi*). Looking at the fate of a long list of once-corporate titans—the likes of Polaroid, Compaq, Tower Records, Lehman Brothers, Blockbuster, Kodak, Nokia, and Toys "R" Us—Hesiod and Mr. Siebel might well be correct.

What's the secret to survival?

The New Triple Bottom Line

The Triple Bottom Line 1.0

People, planet, prosperity. The new triple bottom line.

John Elkington conceived this concept back in the 1990s—plus others such as the *green consumer, green growth,* and *environmental excellence.*[9] Essentially, the triple bottom line (often shortened to TBL or 3BL) is a sustainability framework to examine a company's social, environmental, and economic impact. Described by *BusinessWeek* as "a dean of the corporate responsibility movement for three decades," John is a global authority on corporate responsibility and sustainable development, and might be considered godfather to the environmental, social, and governance (ESG) focus of many companies today.

ESG criteria are also fast becoming a set of standards used by responsible investors to screen companies. Environmental criteria address carbon footprint, access to resources, pollution, and waste. Social criteria address how a company manages product liability, supply chain, employees, human rights, and the communities in which it operates. Governance deals with a company's leadership, executive pay, and shareholder rights.

Infosys has always recognized the interplay between business and society. As a Live Enterprise, we are aware of the role we perform in sounding the clarion call for effective corporate and societal action. We share our ESG vision and approach to stakeholder capitalism as an example of the link between Live Enterprise principles and ESG aspirations. (See Figure 10.1, next page.)

In effect, ESG metrics are a filter for investors to derisk investment portfolios, drive sustainable growth, and focus on the triple bottom line. Research seems to demonstrate a valid link between ESG and stronger company performance. In 2015, Oxford University concluded that "80 percent of the reviewed studies demonstrate that prudent sustainability practices have a positive influence on investment performance."[10]

The Thinking Ahead Institute concluded that as the talk on sustainability turns into action, leading firms will not only manage to close the "saying–doing" gap, but also the "doing–impact" gap, which is the shortfall between the initial action toward a more sustainable economy and the ability to create it. In effect, ESG and the triple bottom line have passed the relevance stress test, and the conversation has transitioned to impact.

Quality Control: The Triple Bottom Line 2.0

In June 2018, 25 years after coining the phrase "triple bottom line," John Elkington revisited the concept in the *Harvard Business Review.*[11] In a bold move, he proposed a "strategic recall to do some fine tuning" to his own idea. This was due to the belief that the original triple bottom line concept had been warped out of shape, effectively "captured and diluted by accountants and reporting consultants."

FIGURE 10.1   Infosys ESG vision and ambitions 2030.

Source: Infosys.

In researching this book, we sat down with John to elaborate and update his groundbreaking concept for the post-pandemic world. He explained, "Financial markets have embraced the concept of improving environmental, social, and governance performance, and that's progress. And ESG funds have done strikingly well during the pandemic. But every time you get businesspeople embracing a new agenda, they tend to dilute the ambition of new concepts."

As financial leaders pump out new funds, and companies embrace related goals and standards, they're also making new promises and commitments, and not always understanding what those commitments actually mean. While John Elkington and other sustainability pioneers are pleased this moment has been reached, they suspect there may be a major quality control issue.

Our experience working at the intersection of industry, tech, and sustainability leads us to agree with the honorable Mr. Elkington. That is why tools like a materiality matrix (see Figure 10.2) are useful to develop an accurate ESG lens and rank priorities in order of importance to business and stakeholders.

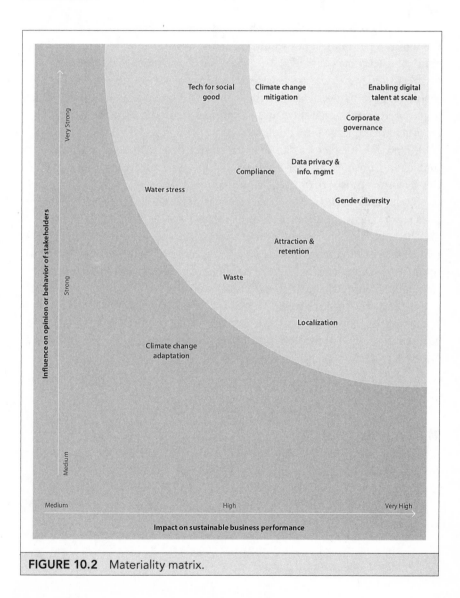

FIGURE 10.2 Materiality matrix.

A Genetic Code for Tomorrow's Capitalism

In effect, despite paying lip service to the triple bottom line, companies have often used it to reinforce the original paradigm of the single bottom line. Writing in *Institutional Investor*, Michael Porter, George Serafeim, and Mark Kramer of Harvard Business School identified examples of such "corporate window dressing."[12]

The carbon footprint of a bank, for example, is not material to a bank's economic performance, nor would reducing its footprint affect global carbon emissions. In contrast, banks' issuance of subprime loans that customers were unable to repay had devastating social and financial consequences. Yet ESG reporting gave banks credit for the former and missed the latter altogether, in part because the voluntary and reputation-focused nature of sustainability reports tends to leave out bad news.

Material ESG factors can also be misleading to investors who fail to understand business model differences. One ESG scorecard that asked for the "volume of fossil fuels used" captured all of Walmart logistics fuel usage, but none of Amazon's outsourced delivery system (even though Amazon does report the carbon footprint of its third-party deliveries)."

The triple bottom line was never supposed to be just an accounting system. It was originally intended as a genetic code, a triple helix of change for tomorrow's capitalism, with a focus was on breakthrough change, disruption, and asymmetric growth, with unsustainable sectors actively sidelined.

In effect, the triple bottom line was conceived to *evolve* the current system of capitalism, not reinforce it. In January 2020, just as COVID-19 forced Wuhan into lockdown, the World Economic Forum (WEF) met in Davos–Klosters to discuss a new form of capitalism.

Capitalism 3.0

The Preferred Path

On its 50th anniversary, the WEF theme for January 2020 was "Stakeholders for a Cohesive and Sustainable World." To support this objective, the organization developed its "Davos Manifesto 2020: The Universal Purpose of a Company in the Fourth Industrial Revolution," and redefined a company's role in society:[13]

> The purpose of a company is to engage all its stakeholders in shared and sustained value creation. In creating such value, a company serves not only its shareholders, but all its stakeholders—employees, customers, suppliers, local communities and society at large.

Going further, Klaus Schwab—founder and executive chairman of the WEF—pitched the Davos Manifesto as central to a better kind of capitalism, identifying two models of dominant capitalism and then adding a third as the preferred path and "better kind."[14] (See Figure 10.3.)

Capitalism 1.0 **Shareholder capitalism**	**Capitalism 2.0** **State capitalism**	**Capitalism 3.0** **Stakeholder capitalism**
• The Western Model, advocated by Milton Friedman, 1970 • Engine for economic growth • Misaligned incentives between owners and broader society	• The Chinese Model, directed by Deng Xiaoping, 1992 • Leverages the benefits of scale and policy influence • Ineffcient resource allocation, does not incent individual innovation	• The WEF Model, advocated by Klaus Schwab, 2020 • Integrated view of financial, social, and environmental interests • Unproven at scale; constraints due to increased responsibilities

FIGURE 10.3   The three models of capitalism.

▶ **Capitalism 1.0—shareholder capitalism.** Where a company's primary goal is to maximize profits—today's dominant model in much of the West.

▶ **Capitalism 2.0—state capitalism.** Where government centrally directs the economy—the model in China and some emerging economies.

▶ **Capitalism 3.0—stakeholder capitalism.** Schwab's "better kind of capitalism"—where companies act as trustees, focusing on customers, employees, partners, and society as a whole.

In effect, in early 2020 Schwab indicated the world was at an inflection point, where corporations must evolve from creating value for shareholders to benefiting wider society. So why the proposed shift to stakeholder capitalism, and how might capitalism 3.0 help society? Schwab explained that business leaders had an incredible opportunity to give stakeholder capitalism concrete meaning, moving beyond their legal obligations and upholding their duty to society.

Then global pandemic took much of the world offline.

A Tipping Point and Change in Cadence

In April 2020, the Infosys Knowledge Institute conducted primary research in seven countries, asking whether COVID-19 marked a tipping point toward stakeholder capitalism.[15]

Overall, almost 54 percent of respondents supported this view, with only 16 percent against, and the rest undecided. The C-Suite had the most positive sentiment toward stakeholder capitalism, with over 80 percent of senior executives in agreement, as opposed to less than half of vice presidents and managers. The push for stakeholder capitalism is clearly coming from the top. For some time, there has been a profound psychological evolution in executive thinking, where the people who increasingly occupy C-suites and boardrooms know ESG is an imperative and someone must act.

The pandemic, however, was the seismic shift that caused the WEF to accelerate the pace on stakeholder capitalism.

The Great Reset

In 2002, James Stock and Mark Watson wrote a paper asking, "Has the Business Cycle Changed and Why?"[16] They observed a reduction in business cycle volatility since the 1980s, likely caused by institutional and structural changes in the economy, most notably in central bank policy. Stock and Watson called the period the Great Moderation.

The Great Moderation came to a screeching halt with Lehman Brothers on Tuesday September 15th, 2008. The following day, global money markets froze, just as the UN General Assembly met for its 63rd meeting a stone's throw away from Wall Street in midtown Manhattan. Speaking as president of the European Council and president of France, Nicolas Sarkozy explained: "There is no longer a unipolar world with East and West. It's a multipolar world now," with "The twenty-first century world" no longer being "governed with the institutions of the twentieth century."

In some respects, the twenty-first century effectively began on January 23, 2020, with Wuhan going into lockdown, and the great and the good meeting in Davos to discuss capitalism 3.0. COVID-19, however, caused the WEF message to switch from stakeholder capitalism to the Great Reset, "an urgent need for global stakeholders to cooperate in simultaneously managing the direct consequences of the COVID-19 crisis."[17]

In effect, we transitioned from the Great Moderation to the Great Reset in a just over a decade.

System Reboot

The Great Reveal

Warren Buffett famously said, "You only find out who is swimming naked when the tide goes out."[18] How did the global economy look with the tide out?

1. **The World Bank indicated over 90 percent of the world's countries were in recession in 2020**—a new record exceeding the previous high of 84 percent set in the Great Depression.
2. **There is no precedent to the extent of synchronized global contraction.** This caused a major slump in world trade volumes, with the OECD estimating global trade volume contracted by 15 percent in 2020—a level previously unknown in the postwar era.
3. **Debt-to-GDP ratios reached uncharted territory.** IMF estimates revealed gross government to debt GDP ratios spiked to new records in the United States, Japan, Italy, France, and United Kingdom. According to the US Federal Reserve Board's Bureau of Economic Analysis, each US dollar of debt generated only 38.5 cents of GDP in the first three months of 2020.
4. **United States GDP fell at record levels.** The US economy shrank by a stunning 9.5 percent from April through June 2020, a historic contraction and a stinging reminder of how much was lost in such a short period.

The Greek term for "uncovering" is *apokálupsis* (or apocalypse), and in the most literal sense, 2020 was an era of economic apocalypse. COVID-19 was the Great Reveal on resiliency in a time of crisis. The pandemic, however, did not create but only revealed the underlying trends already in place, perhaps accelerating the trend mentioned previously that, in Tom Siebel's view, "we are experiencing, in the first part of the 21st century, a mass extinction event in the corporate world."

What Role Resilience?

Did focusing on the triple bottom line insulate companies during the economic apocalypse?

In April 2020, Fidelity International looked at more than 2,700 companies and found a positive correlation between COVID-19 financial performance and ESG rating.[19] Rating these companies across five ratings scales (A to E), A-rated companies outperformed the S&P 500 by an average 3.8 percent, with each ESG rating level worth 2.8 percent of stock performance versus the index.

In May 2020, BlackRock analyzed the performance of ESG indices and their non-ESG equivalents, with 51 out of 57 sustainable indices outperforming their non-ESG peers.[20] The analysis found a correlation among sustainability, quality, and low volatility, with factors such as employee satisfaction, strong customer relations, and board effectiveness playing a role in this outperformance—"which themselves indicate resilience." The report concluded, "We believe companies managed with a focus on sustainability should be better positioned versus their less sustainable peers to weather adverse conditions while still benefiting from positive market environments"—with sustainable companies expected to be more resilient in downturns.

In June 2020, Harvard Business School published an analysis looking at over 3,000 companies around the world, with an average market cap of $19 billion.[21] The report concluded that companies seen as protecting their employees and supply chain benefited from higher institutional money flows and less negative returns—with companies focusing more on customer satisfaction experiencing up to 3.9 percent higher stock returns.

Taken together, these are three strong endorsements for the new triple bottom line.

A Unique Window of Opportunity

Concepts like ESG, the triple bottom line, and materiality (relevance of sustainability to financial performance) aren't new, but have recently gained momentum. In August 2019, 181 North American CEOs signed the Business Roundtable Statement on the Purpose of a Corporation,[22] pledging to promote long-term value of their corporations for the benefit of all its stakeholders and not solely to maximize shareholder wealth. In the same month as the Wuhan lockdown, BlackRock—the world's largest asset manager—announced "Sustainability as BlackRock's New Standard for Investing."[23]

What changed with a global shutdown was the Great Reset as a unique window of opportunity to not only shape the recovery, but indeed the economic structure of the world itself.

Based on multiple evidence, it is clear that COVID accelerated several trends that were already in motion: technology trends like digitalization, as well as supply chain simplification. Companies that did well were the ones able to sense the market, adapt, respond, and stay resilient. US-based T3 Expo, for example, converted their entire convention facilities into a hospital for COVID-19 patients. When sports ground to an abrupt halt overnight, sailmakers such as Sander's Sails in England adjusted their skills and deliveries to create personal protective equipment (PPE) for healthcare workers when supplies were critically low. LVMH switched their operations to make hand sanitizer for French hospitals; Dyson and Babcock both switched from vacuum cleaners to ventilators, and the list goes on. Then there were those that didn't switch core operations, but continued to deliver business-as-usual services with zero outages and zero drop in service level agreements—such as Infosys, which switched 96 percent of our 240,000 global employees to fully operating remotely within four days of worldwide lockdown.

These were crucial times for the world and also informative moments for the Live Enterprise model, when the resilience of the organization to quickly adapt to these massive shifts was tested at scale. The COVID-19 crisis suddenly required most businesses to operate remote first, where all day-to-day work had to be done anytime, anywhere—while still performing business-critical operations at critical physical locations (like warehouse, delivery center, and pharmacy stores) in a secure and compliant manner.

Shared digital infrastructure helped companies quickly support and then evolve to build the new features and functions required to meet the new business needs. However, many cautionary tales emerged for organizations that lacked this infrastructure, as they struggled with significant manual effort to conduct business. For example, companies slow to adopt to the cloud were at a significant disadvantage, while those that did were able to move operations much faster and with lower risk.

Beyond simply sustaining operations, the crisis also required launching new services to market. The organizations with robust shared digital infrastructure significantly accelerated the velocity for new ideas and innovations, and at lower cost.

Schrödinger's Capitalism

We experienced a world where furloughed airline pilots delivered groceries, while hospitals laid off staff—in the midst of a pandemic. Workforces became more distributed yet more connected than ever before, and economies a curious chimera of capitalism 1.0 and 2.0, needing state capitalism to survive and shareholder capitalism to thrive.

During our research for this book, it was clear that current forms of economics and the shared understanding of capitalism proved to be unequal, even dysfunctional. Like Schrödinger's famous cat, capitalism 1.0 and 2.0 appeared both dead and alive at the same time.

COVID-19 demonstrated that companies can be lifelike, responsive, evolving beings at enterprise scale—and any company, however large and complex, can transform to be adaptive and resilient. By expanding focus from profits to customers, employees, and society, companies bring human concerns into harmony with business objectives. From firsthand experience at Infosys and client examples, we have seen early indicators that this holistic view will enable successful transition to capitalism 3.0, stakeholder capitalism.

This transition requires a different mindset on a global scale, different from earlier attempts, where leaders have moved beyond awareness to necessity and urgency.

The Genetic Code of Corporate Evolution

DNA—There and Back

With 3.8 billion years of experience, nature provides a vivid guide to evolution. Nature via DNA is the ultimate model for survival, a master class in resilience, innovation, and transformation.

Rewind to that first single-cell bacterium almost four billion years ago. Every one of the four billion species since then has shared a single trait—DNA. Deoxyribonucleic acid is the ultimate in resilience and creativity to celebrate diversity and reward relevance. Able to work in micro-changes, agile sprints, and across the eons, DNA is the clean code linking every living thing from dogs to daisies, narwhals to Nehru, and Buddha to Beyoncé.

Living organisms can be expressed as information, vast amounts of it. As human genome editing expert Jamie Metzl puts it, "We may never know everything about humans, but we are increasingly knowable." Every adult human has enough DNA to stretch to Pluto and back—17 times over—in ribbons only 10 atoms wide. DNA is compelling on its own merits as the code of life. For business research, DNA also holds a particular fascination because its four primary roles are highly relevant for business:

- ▶ **Replication.** When a cell divides, the chromosomes containing the DNA strands must replicate, or make copies, of themselves so that both daughter cells receive the full set of genetic material and maintain integrity. *Businesses need processes that ensure the same culture and results occur as they reach scale.*
- ▶ **Encoding information.** The base sequences of A, T, C, and G along a DNA strand are organized into units called genes. Only four base types, yet with established sequences, it can create billions of combinations. *Enterprises must evolve such flexibility at scale.*
- ▶ **Mutation and recombination.** DNA plays a role in the evolution of a species, and through the process of genetic recombination, segments of different chromosomes swap places with each other, creating new sequences of genetic material are essentially experiments in evolution. *Organizations also need a means to experiment and incorporate the successes into their own larger enterprise genetic code.*
- ▶ **Genetic expression.** DNA plays a role as a traffic cop for the types of proteins a cell will make, through interactions with proteins that cause only certain genes to express themselves. *Enterprises also have to determine which capabilities and skills to express, based on the needs of a customer, offering, or geography.*

Black Swans and Green Swans

Ever since Nassim Taleb's 2007 book *The Black Swan: The Impact of the Highly Improbable*,[24] the business world has been fascinated with the topic and looking (retroactively, it seems) for the next rare and unpredictable outlier event, to prevent it, profit from it, or at least survive. It was no surprise when black swan seers labeled COVID-19 such an event. In reality, it really wasn't, as it violated the first principle of black swans, that we don't see them coming—there were warning signs from previous, regional pandemics. As history shows, there will always be another earthquake, virus, or volcano, another shift in the financial markets causing the system to flash on red.

As a result, sustainability pioneer John Elkington inverted the black swan concept into a more positive vision. Instead of society breaking down, in *Green Swans: The Coming Boom in Regenerative Capitalism*[25] he articulates a future where "green swans" signal a profound market shift and catalyze exponential progress across the three dimensions of economic, social, and environmental wealth creation. At the same time, today's unknown "ugly ducklings" will leverage exponential technologies to accelerate breakthroughs and become tomorrow's celebrated success stories.

While Elkington's optimistic scenario is attractive, its realization will rely upon the Live Enterprise concepts discussed in this book. There's also a wider, demographic dynamic at play—given that business generations tend to be rather shorter than human ones—C-suites and boardrooms know change is coming, and at some point, they will have to act. This points to a psychological shift John Elkington describes as "seismic."

How seismic? John described a reframed triple bottom line of people, planet, and *prosperity* as "a genetic code, a triple helix of change for tomorrow's capitalism."

Plan B (Corp)

While companies are at different stages in their triple helix evolution, tomorrow's capitalism is coming—and for some, it's already here.

In 2006, three friends founded B Lab in Berwyn, Pennsylvania.[26] A nonprofit themselves, B Lab certifies companies "who meet the highest standards of verified, overall social and environmental performance, public transparency, and legal accountability." As the certifying entity, B Lab looks at companies and how they treat their workers, consumers, communities, environment, and governance. Across all these factors, companies answer and are assessed on a variety of different questions. They become B Corps only if they score above the B Lab threshold.

A B Corp is a company whose social and environmental performance has been certified by B Lab. Consumers may be familiar with certifications such as Fairtrade, LEED, or Organic, but these are concerned only with individual *products*. B Corp certification is about the company as a whole, an in-depth assessment of the extent to which the company is socially and environmentally responsible.

It's little wonder B Lab was added to Fast Company's prestigious annual list of the World's Most Innovative Companies in 2020.[27] The B Corp movement laser-focuses on creating a new kind of company with the triple helix baked into its DNA, via impact assessment and analytics tools that help companies measure their impact and develop plans to improve. The movement has grown exponentially, with a community of over 3,500 B Corps in 70 countries and 150 industries, with over 100,000 companies managing their impact via the B Impact framework. It's no coincidence that John Elkington's SustainAbility was the first B Corp in the United Kingdom.

Christopher Marquis, professor in Sustainable Global Enterprise at Cornell University's SC Johnson College of Business, produced a masterful exposition of the B Corp phenomenon in *Better Business: How the B Corp Movement Is Remaking Capitalism*,[28] calling it the "most impressive example of business innovation" he'd seen. Opening with the dry observation that "the B Corp movement is the most important social movement you've never heard of," Chris told us that B Corps mark a more systematic transition to stakeholder capitalism and independent validation that companies really are committed to the concept. Also, that these firms possess the right toolkit, standards, and metrics for companies to proactively meet the needs of tomorrow's consumers. Evolving the traditional company–stakeholder relationship, the B Corp movement also allows stakeholders to hold companies to account.

Who are these future consumers and stakeholders, and where's the momentum coming from? The ranks of B Corps are growing and attracting larger companies like Danone, Unilever, Procter & Gamble, Nestlé, and Gap. At the same time, Chris explained around 70 percent of millennials want to work in companies that have a social impact. In terms of demographics alone, millennials already make up almost half the US workforce, and will inherit $30 trillion in the coming decades—perhaps the biggest intergenerational wealth transfer in history. That's momentum, and look for B Corps to play a larger role to shape the stakeholder capitalism movement and the global economy overall.

Nature as Sustainable Economic Engine

There are other vectors of momentum too. Chris Marquis told us inflection points typically occur once a change has been percolating under the surface and not been fully recognized—akin to John Elkington's ugly ducklings and green swans. At some point though, an event connects the dots and leads to greater awareness and steeper growth trajectory.

Dr. Enric Sala is a former university professor who saw himself as simply writing the obituary of ocean life, so he quit academia to become a full-time conservationist and make an impact. As a National Geographic explorer-in-residence, he founded and leads Pristine Seas,[29] a project combining exploration, research, and media to inspire country leaders into protecting the last wild places in the ocean. To date, Pristine Seas has helped create 22 of the largest marine reserves on the planet—"national parks in the sea." After already protecting vast swathes of our oceans almost half the size of the United States, Enric wants to change the world again. In his book *The Nature of Nature: Why We Need the Wild*,[30] he explains how protecting wildlife and the environment is both ethically and economically crucial, that when we appreciate how nature works, we will understand why conservation is economically wise and essential to our survival. The Living Planet Index, for example, estimates the Great Barrier Reef supports 69,000 jobs and contributes $5.7 billion a year to the Australian economy.[31]

Enric described the COVID pandemic to us as

> the best wake-up call we've ever had, because it has shown us that the emperor has no clothes, that our socioeconomic system and most of our business approach was based on very shaky foundations, because we've been building for growth, not for resilience.

When it comes to resilience, nature is our best teacher. But what about the numbers?

Enric explains that the natural world provides free services to the global economy on the order of $125 trillion per year, and for every dollar we invest in protecting nature, nature will give us at least five dollars in return. This is why he's now looking to protect 30 percent of the planet in national parks, natural reserves, and marine reserves—a strategy that would help us prevent the looming extinction of one million species of plants and animals, plus the potential collapse of our life support system.

What about the cost? Protecting 30 percent of the planet would cost an estimated $140 billion a year—about the same as our annual spend on video games. Not only is nature a model, measure, and mentor, it may provide a fivefold return on investment as well.

WEF Redux: Metrics for Stakeholder Capitalism

What about governance and global leaders, the people tasked with bridging the disconnect between global problems and national politics? Enric explained that we humans are very good at ignoring information and making irrational decisions—so he flipped the mode of operations by first aiming for the heart, then the brain. He wants these leaders to fall in love with these wild places, so Enric takes them to the field with his crew. If they cannot come in person, then Enric takes these places to leaders through his films. Once they fall in love with these beautiful places, then Sala's team provides the scientific and economic information to show the benefits to the people and politicians.

Essentially, it's about hearts and minds, rational thinking justifying the emotional decision you already made—a play on confirmation bias. While emotion is one thing, this approach also requires robust, measurable metrics for companies to improve their ESG initiative results and reporting. In September 2020, the World Economic Forum aligned with the United Nations to provide such a framework. Called "Stakeholder Capitalism Metrics,"[32] this framework rests on four pillars.

1. **People.** Company equity and its treatment of employees and value chain—with metrics including diversity reporting, wage gaps, and health and safety.
2. **Planet.** Dependencies and environmental impact—with metrics including greenhouse gas emissions, land protection, and water use.
3. **Prosperity.** How a company impacts the financial well-being of its community—with metrics including employment and wealth generation, tax payments, plus research and development expenses.
4. **Principles of governance.** Purpose, strategy, and accountability—with metrics measuring factors such as risk and ethical behavior.

These four pillars are supported by 21 core and 35 expanded metrics drawn where possible from existing standards. As a result, not only has the inclusion of governance extended the *planet–people–prosperity* triple helix, but by tying the framework to the 17 UN sustainable development goals (SDGs), WEF has effectively also endorsed John Elkington's concept of regenerative capitalism. (See Figure 10.4.)

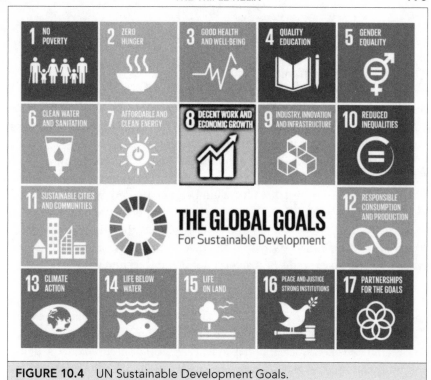

FIGURE 10.4 UN Sustainable Development Goals.

By drawing from existing standards, WEF aims to accelerate convergence in near-term objectives with the likes of the International Business Council—a community of over 120 global CEOs—in an attempt to speed and scale the ways companies measure and demonstrate their contributions toward shared economic, environmental, and social objectives. This has immediately galvanized a wider regulatory ecosystem. The European Union, for example, is revising its nonfinancial reporting directive,[33] with more mandatory reporting on sustainability. IOSCO—the global standard setter for securities markets regulation—is looking at how to harmonize financial and sustainability reporting, while the IFRS Foundation is aiming to broaden its globally accepted accounting standards to embrace sustainability issues.

While reporting is only one element of system change, it is a crucial one that is pivotal to the reinvention of the current system. The system, however, is doing what nature does best after an extinction-level event—adapting. Once again, we're reminded of Darwin's observation that the "extinction of old forms is the almost inevitable consequence of the production of new forms."

The Live Enterprise Is a Triple Helix

The End of the Beginning

In 1942, the Battle of Egypt signaled the first Allied victory against Nazi evil. Speaking to the British parliament after the victory at El Alamein, Winston Churchill cautioned, "This is not the end, it is not even the beginning of the end—but it is, perhaps, the end of the beginning."

January 23, 2020, perhaps signaled the end of the beginning—with Wuhan and WEF symbolizing a deeper current of change. The economists Nikolay Kondratyev and Joseph Schumpeter both said broadly the same thing—that economies never go in straight lines, but rather in cycles that move in "long waves." Wuhan and WEF signaled the end of a wave that began with the Bretton Woods Conference[34] in terms of geopolitics and Milton Friedman in terms of macroeconomics and technology.[35]

After working in leadership roles at the White House, State Department, United Nations, and World Health Organization, Jamie Metzl knows more than most about global affairs and societal impact. Like a real-life Jerry Maguire, Jamie stayed up all night in March 2020 to write and post a Declaration of Global Interdependence,[36] evolving a blog to a global movement in only 44 days. Launched in May 2020, OneShared.World is a long-term strategy for global systemic change,[37] and 1.2 million people participated in their September 2020 Global Interdependence Virtual Summit. Jamie told us that, looking in history's rearview mirror, 2020 will mark the end of the postwar world that began with Bretton Woods—"with the game now on to figure out what's next."

A Meaningful Difference and Lasting Change

Where most black swans take you exponentially where you don't want to go, green swans are the positive exponentials that take you very fast after a period of relatively slow development to places that you do want to go. While comprehensive sustainability requirements seem daunting, they are not only possible but realistic, with a clear mindset on capabilities and roadmap. The potential for companies to transform into a sustainable Live Enterprise model, with the ability to respond intuitively to disruption, started to become reality even as the pandemic loomed large. Beyond the profit motive, the sustainability perspective alerted leaders to the pressing need for a holistic approach that builds long-term resilience, generates economic opportunities, and provides environmental and societal benefits.

Success in the Live Enterprise model is measured through products created, services rendered, and impact on individuals, organizations, and the society at large. In that, a Live Enterprise has an important role to play in shaping and sharing solutions to address the world's most crucial challenges. The goal is straightforward, to make a meaningful difference and enable lasting change.

The double helix expresses itself in some complex mechanisms over time, but it is also an integrated set of solutions. This concept can be extended to the triple helix model, which is not just about financial performance, but also includes social performance and environmental performance. Leaders must address all three of those dimensions simultaneously to deliver the systemic change companies, capitalism, and wider society need.

To break through the digital ceiling, companies must bring a different mindset to their improvement initiatives. By expanding focus from profits to customers, employees, and society, companies bring human concerns into harmony with business objectives. This holistic, triple helix view (see Figure 10.5) enables enterprises to go beyond traditional success metrics and position themselves to achieve the emerging goals of stakeholder capitalism.

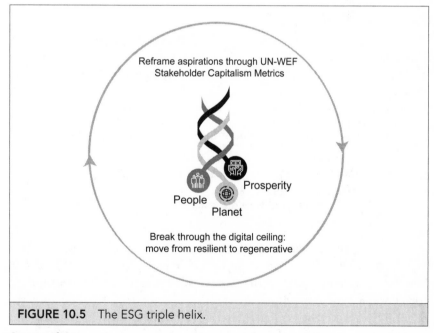

FIGURE 10.5 The ESG triple helix.

Source: Infosys.

When companies shift focus to stakeholders and not just shareholders and customers, decisions have greater impact. In fact, this emphasis on the triple bottom line of people, planet, and prosperity actually compels companies to increase digital maturity.

Our interviews with executives across enterprises, governments, and NGOs have reinforced the view that both sustainability and employee welfare have become essential considerations in customer preferences and regulatory requirements. Our research shows that this broader view, in combination with the digital initiatives outlined earlier, helps companies achieve better results—making ESG and the triple bottom line an imperative, not merely a nice side goal.

The nature and scale of the challenges we face are not going to be solved if we simply trade off the belief that the triple bottom line is about economics with an environmental and social add-on. Until we integrate all of this into real-world solutions, the model will progress incrementally as well-intentioned but not essential. It will succeed at scale only if these principles become integrated into the platforms of government, the mission statements of civil society organizations, and businesses around the world.

The Exponential Decade

In September 1962, President John F. Kennedy made a speech at Rice University in Houston. Russian cosmonaut Yuri Gagarin had become the first human in space exactly 17 months before, and in the new space race, America was losing.

Kennedy made a promise and bet the farm on the seemingly impossible:

> We choose to go to the moon in this decade and do the other things, not because they are easy, but because they are hard, because that goal will serve to organize and measure the best of our energies and skills, because that challenge is one that we are willing to accept, one we are unwilling to postpone, and one which we intend to win.[38]

It seemed impossible in 1962—expensive too, estimated to cost $28 billion in 1960s dollars, over $288 billion in today's.[39] On July 20, 1969, however, Neil Armstrong left the *Eagle*, made his small step, and with Buzz Aldrin walked the tranquil sea. After initial disaster, Kennedy's promise was fulfilled by investment, resilience, and a decade of exponential progress.

The triple helix may today seem equally impossible, but the business case is beyond doubt. However, there simply isn't time for organizations to evolve at a leisurely pace. The United Nations states it seeks *all 17* of its SDGs delivered by 2030—which calls for a very different mindset, a very different level of ambition and performance targets to the ones we've been accustomed to.

The challenges are also growing at a nonlinear rate, with companies needing to evolve exponentially to compete in their markets and to achieve the UN SDGs by the target date of 2030.

The 2020s must be another exponential decade. This is our moonshot. We can fulfill the UN SDGs before this decade is out, not because they are easy, but because they are hard, with the triple helix serving to measure the best of our energies and skills.

RECAP: The Triple Helix

- The original triple bottom line has evolved to a broader perspective of people, planet, and prosperity. This has moved ESG from side initiative to integrated board priority.
- The World Economic Forum (WEF) proposed stakeholder capitalism as a new system, where companies act as trustees to a broad set of constituents. Along with the United Nations, they published "Stakeholder Capitalism Metrics" with definitions and metrics across people, planet, prosperity, and governance.
- Research suggests ESG-astute companies are more resilient and deliver stronger financial performance: Fidelity (3.8 percent higher stock returns), Harvard Business School (3.9 percent), and BlackRock (significant).
- The Live Enterprise model offers a feasible path for companies to meet the daunting challenge of market success and UN SDG fulfillment by 2030.

EPILOGUE

From Responsibility to Regeneration

We live in a world that is evolving almost faster than we can comprehend: a time of vast opportunities and risks. Think of it as a twist on Moore's Law, with great danger baked into the formula rather than endless upside. This is an era of exponential technological change accompanied by equally exponential consequences—both financial and social—if we do nothing, or even too little.

This test of resilience challenges everyone, from families to businesses to governments. We all must collaborate to advance both global values and economic prosperity. Even as the world struggled with a devastating pandemic, many leaders worked energetically to meet the United Nation's 17 Sustainability Development Goals for 2030. To reach those targets, it requires more than government intervention. Beyond the responsibility of SDGs, regeneration as a goal is even more exponential and aspirational. Organizations worldwide must move purposefully onto the playing field and take leadership roles so that all can survive, then thrive. The triple bottom line requires a reboot to a "triple helix for value creation," as business sustainability pioneer John Elkington has eloquently argued.

Change on that scale may seem impossible, but "daunting yet achievable" is a better descriptor. Technological progress, evolving attitudes, and bold advances have already transformed companies and even countries. Think of India's Aadhaar national identity program, which facilitated greater access to loans, healthcare, and government services. Think of the India Stack set of open APIs that makes the Aadhaar system work for businesses, government, and more than 1 billion people. Forty-seven years of per capita GDP increases were accelerated into less than a single decade, thanks to these technological accelerators, the Bank for International Settlements determined.

Moonshots like this don't happen with the same traditional approaches and business models that have worked in the past. New thinking, not beholden to the past, leads to decisive change on an enterprise, national, and even global scale. It all starts with a purposeful vision, supported by a human-centered, technology-enabled model.

At Infosys, our goal was to leverage the skills, ideas, and innovation of our more than 200,000 employees to create a shared digital infrastructure powered by a digital brain and a form of sentience. While we continue our journey to evolve, the results of that Live Enterprise transformation and its new, faster metabolism is undeniable. Infosys market capitalization grew from $33 billion to $69 billion (over 100 percent) in three years. While financial valuations may vary, markets have also valued the increase in resiliency and the environmental and social strides the company has made to achieve the promise of stakeholder capitalism.

Although large-scale changes capture our attention, micro-evolutionary advances are the ones that sustain an organization and continue to push it forward. These small steps create large-scale transformation, particularly when they happen consistently and pervasively throughout a company. The "micro is the new mega" approach helps design and roll out an increment of change every six weeks toward a far larger, higher impact goal. This continuous change and ongoing learning process foster rapid experiments, scale successful ones, and prevent an organization from standing still or falling back into old habits. Linear progress gives way to compounding benefits. A good week leads to a great month and a record year.

And like all living creatures, organizations thrive in their optimal ecosystem. No one organism can survive on its own, no matter how agile or resilient. Partnerships enhance strengths and offset weaknesses. They build structures that elevate all involved; this is not a zero-sum game. Typically, creatures have little control over their ecosystems, but a Live Enterprise can create one of its choosing.

Taken together, the Live Enterprise can do what old-fashioned approaches cannot. This new operating model will:

- ▶ Create quantum organizations
- ▶ Deliver perceptive experiences
- ▶ Build responsive value chains
- ▶ Drive intuitive decisions
- ▶ Nurture hybrid talent
- ▶ Design to evolve architecture
- ▶ Build digital runways
- ▶ Drive change through micro is the new mega

We realize that some of the phrases sound like trite sayings, even marketing copy. However, each one has been tested in the real world, at our own firm as well as at leading organizations.

Organizations are eager to advance to the next stage of their evolution. What is missing is the underlying structure and new thinking to support these digital transformations. Too often, companies bump into the digital ceiling and discover that some of the lessons learned from agile startups are harder to implement than envisioned. Innovation and scale collide, creating neither.

Talent famines make it more difficult to find the right people for the right jobs. Looking in the same conventional places with the same basic assumptions is no longer enough to fill jobs at scale and meet the changing demands for skills. Unlocking existing organizational talent through continuous upskilling, providing an environment to experiment, and helping employees turn their ideas into reality is infectious and spreads like wildfire, rejuvenating the organization. The workforce should fuel growth and innovation, rather than be perceived as a burdensome cost center. The human side is also reflected in the move toward stakeholder capitalism, where profit is not the final answer.

There are no guarantees in life or business. Even past successes can fade faster than anyone could have imagined, and yesterday's leading companies can discover they are now playing from behind. The most interesting business cases are not just the astonishing successes but also the cautionary failures. Often, those that faded were unable to adapt quickly enough to a changing environment or simply didn't see a need for change. However, their extinction wasn't inevitable.

Even the most insightful futurist can't predict all the twists and turns ahead. Still, the most successful companies won't need to have all the answers. They just need to prepare for the possibilities, even those not yet known. By designing to evolve and having a right mix of people, processes, technology, and partners, a new generation of companies can thrive despite the unknown, rather than fail because of it. They can create a company that is sustainable financially, environmentally, and socially.

The consistent thread running throughout this book is one of resilience and regeneration, of companies needing to evolve like natural organisms at speed and scale. When Darwin published *The Origin of Species* in 1859, he emphasized cause and effect in natural selection—and as leading contemporary zoologist Thomas Henry Huxley argued, this was the "quintessence of Darwinism." His grandson Aldous Huxley wrote his own influential book, *Brave New World*, released in 1932—a time, not unlike 2020, of social and economic unrest. *Brave New World* portrayed a nightmarish vision of cloning, grinding conformism, and mindless consumption. His famous book is more a warning than blueprint.

Contrast that somber vision with Carl Sagan, who as a student read *Brave New World* and decided the future would be positive, even uplifting. Where Darwin envisioned the selective past and Huxley a dark future, the renowned astronomer and humanist Sagan gazed out there and related it to us down here. A NASA consultant since the 1950s, he was the visionary responsible for the famous photo of the earth taken by *Voyager 1* in 1990 from 3.7 billion miles away, at the edge of our solar system. Earth, small and blue, a tiny 0.12 pixels out of 640,000. Sagan named the image Pale Blue Dot and described its significance:

> Look again at that dot. That's here. That's home. That's us. On it, everyone you love, everyone you know, everyone you ever heard of, every human being who ever was, lived out their lives. . . . To me, it underscores our responsibility to deal more kindly with one another, and to preserve and cherish the pale blue dot, the only home we've ever known.[1]

Pale Blue Dot or Brave New World? While technology and market forces are disruptive, leaders have a choice in how they approach the future. Like Carl Sagan, the Live Enterprise model offers a science-based yet uplifting mindset, in this case to create an enduring, prosperous company. Further, it also provides a blueprint for individuals, governments, and society to evolve purposefully while addressing the structural problems and opportunities that will define the future of business, and ultimately life itself.

NOTES

Chapter 1

1. "Welcome to UIDAI," Unique Identification Authority of India, Government of India, last modified January 24, 2019, https://uidai.gov.in/.
2. "'Aadhar' Most Sophisticated ID Programme in the World: World Bank," daijiworld.com, last modified March 16, 2017, http://www.daijiworld.com /news/newsDisplay.aspx?newsID=442948.
3. "What Is India Stack," About Indiastack.org, accessed September 27, 2020, https://www.indiastack.org/about/.
4. Julia Clark, "The State of Identification Systems in Africa: A Synthesis of Country Assessments," World Bank Group, April 1, 2017, http://documents1 .worldbank.org/curated/en/156111493234231522/pdf/114628-WP-68p-TheState ofIdentificationSystemsinAfricaASynthesisofIDDAssessments-PUBLIC.pdf.
5. "Aadhaar-Enabled DBT Savings Estimated over Rs 90,000 Crore," *Economic Times of India*, last modified July 11, 2018, https://economictimes.indiatimes .com/news/economy/finance/aadhaar-enabled-dbt-savings-estimated-over-rs -90000-crore/articleshow/64949101.cms.

Chapter 2

1. P. Ward and A. Zahavi, "The Importance of Certain Assemblages of Birds as 'Information-Centres' for Food-Finding," *International Journal of Avian Science* 115, no. 4 (October 1973): 517–534, https://doi.org/10.1111/j.1474 -919X.1973.tb01990.x.
2. George F. Young, Luca Scardovi, Andrea Cavagna, Irene Giardina, and Naomi E. Leonard, "Starling Flock Networks Manage Uncertainty in Consensus at Low Cost," *PLoS Computational Biology* 9, no. 1 (January 31, 2013): e1002894. https://doi.org/10.1371/journal.pcbi.1002894.
3. https://www.ben-evans.com/benedictevans/2017/12/12/the-amazon-machine
4. "History: The Agile Manifesto," Manifesto for Agile Software Development, accessed September 30, 2020, https://agilemanifesto.org/history.html.

5. "Advancing the Practice of Agile," Agile Alliance, accessed September 30, 2020, https://www.agilealliance.org/.

6. Klaus Schwab, "Davos Manifesto 2020: The Universal Purpose of a Company in the Fourth Industrial Revolution," World Economic Forum, December 2, 2019, https://www.weforum.org/agenda/2019/12/davos-manifesto-2020-the-universal-purpose-of-a-company-in-the-fourth-industrial-revolution/.

7. "The Great Reset," World Economic Forum, accessed September 30, 2020, https://www.weforum.org/great-reset/.

8. George Gaylord Simpson, *The Meaning of Evolution: A Study of the History of Life and of Its Significance for Man* (New Haven, Connecticut: Yale University Press).

9. "Coronavirus in Mind: Make Remote Work Successful!" Gartner Research, March 5, 2020, https://www.gartner.com/en/documents/3981830/coronavirus-in-mind-make-remote-work-successful-.

10. "Coronavirus in Mind," Gartner Research.

11. "The Lean Startup," accessed September 30, 2020, http://theleanstartup.com/.

12. "What Is DevOps?" The Agile Admin, accessed September 30, 2020, https://theagileadmin.com/what-is-devops/.

Chapter 3

1. Gallup, "State of the Global Workplace," May 14, 2019, https://www.gallup.com/workplace/257552/state-global-workplace-2017.aspx.

2. As cited by Kerry Taylor, "Supply Chain Resilience: Pandemic Preparation and Recover," podcast interview with Jeff Kavanaugh, March 20, 2020, https://www.infosys.com/about/knowledge-institute/podcast/supply-chain-resilience.html.

3. Randall J. Beck and Jim Harter, "Why Great Managers Are So Rare," accessed September 29, 2020, https://www.gallup.com/workplace/231593/why-great-managers-rare.aspx#:~:text=Managers%20account%20for%20at%20least,severely%20low%20worldwide%20employee%20engagement.

4. A. H. Maslow, "A Theory of Human Motivation," *Psychological Review* 50, no. 2. (July 1943), 370–396, https://doi.org/10.1037/h0054346.

Chapter 4

1. Tori Peglar, "1995 Reintroduction of Wolves in Yellowstone," Yellowstone National Park Trips, June 30, 2020, https://www.yellowstonepark.com/park/yellowstone-wolves-reintroduction.

2. "The Value of Pollinators to the Ecosystem and Our Economy," *Forbes*, October 14, 2019, https://www.forbes.com/sites/bayer/2019/10/14/the-value-of-pollinators-to-the-ecosystem-and-our-economy/#22e0f7fc7a1d.

3. Nick Holland, "The Economic Value of Honeybees," BBC News, April 23, 2009, http://news.bbc.co.uk/2/hi/business/8015136.stm.

4. Owen Gaffney, "11 Reasons Bees Matter," World Economic Forum, February 29, 2016, https://www.weforum.org/agenda/2016/02/to-bee-or-not-to-bee-11 -reasons-pollinators-matter/.

5. "P&G Recognizes Top Performing Global Partners," press release, Procter & Gamble, January 9, 2015, https://news.pg.com/news-releases/news-details /2015/PG-Recognizes-Top-Performing-Global-Partners/default.aspx.

6. "Walmart Announces Sustainable Product Index," press release, Walmart, July 16, 2009, https://corporate.walmart.com/newsroom/2009/07/16/walmart -announces-sustainable-product-index.

7. "Trust-Based Relationships with Our Suppliers," Total, accessed September 29, 2020, https://www.total.com/commitment/shared-development/supplier -relationships-underpinned-by-ethics-and-sustainability.

8. Michael Porter, "Competitive Advantage" (New York: The Free Press, 2015).

9. "The Cambridge Declaration of Consciousness," July 7, 2012, http:// fcmconference.org/img/CambridgeDeclarationOnConsciousness.pdf.

10. JLL, "Global Real Estate Perspective Q2 2020 Report," *The Investor,* https:// www.theinvestor.jll/global-capital-flows-q2-2020-report/.

11. Bas Verplanken & Henk Aarts, "Habit, Attitude, and Planned Behaviour: Is Habit an Empty Construct or an Interesting Case of Goal-Directed Automaticity," *European Review of Social Psychology* 10, no. 1 (April 15, 2011): 101–134, https://doi.org/10.1080/14792779943000035.

12. Kristine Dery and Ina Sebastian, "Building Business Value With Employee Experience," *MIT Center for Information Systems Research,* June 15, 2017, https:// cisr.mit.edu/publication/2017_0601_EmployeeExperience_DerySebastian.

13. P. Kirk Visscher, "How Self-Organization Evolves," *Nature* 421 (February 23, 2003), https://doi.org/10.1038/421799a.

Chapter 5

1. Carl Zimmer, "100 Trillion Connections: New Efforts Probe and Map the Brain's Detailed Architecture," *Scientific American,* January 2011, https://www .scientificamerican.com/article/100-trillion-connections/.

2. Suzana Herculano-Houzel, Christine E. Collins, Peiyan Wong, and Jon H. Kaas, "Cellular Scaling Rules for Primate Brains, *Proceedings of the National Academy of Sciences of the United States of America* 104, no. 9 (February 27, 2007): 3562–3567. https://doi.org/10.1073/pnas.0611396104.

3. Kenneth L. Beals, Courtland L. Smith, Stephen M. Dodd, J. Lawrence Angel, Este Armstrong, Bennett Blumenberg, Fakhry G. Girgis, et al., "Brain Size, Cranial Morphology, Climate, and Time Machines," *Current Anthropology* 25, no. 3 (June 1984), https://doi.org/10.1086/203138.

4. Michael P. Muehlenbein, *Basics in Human Evolution* (New York: Elsevier, 2015), https://doi.org/10.1016/C2014-0-02208-3.

5. "22 Facts About the Brain: World Brain Day," DENT Neurologic Institute, last modified July 22, 2019, https://www.dentinstitute.com/posts/lifestyle-tips /22-facts-about-the-brain-world-brain-day/.

6. Anders S. G. Andrae, "Total Consumer Power Consumption Forecast," *Nordic Digital Business Summit* (2017), https://www.researchgate.net /publication/320225452_Total_Consumer_Power_Consumption_Forecast.

7. DENT Neurologic Institute, "22 Facts."

8. "The Knowledge," London Taxi, accessed September 30, 2020, http://www .the-london-taxi.com/london_taxi_knowledge.

9. Ferris Jabr, "Cache Cab: Taxi Drivers' Brains Grow to Navigate London's Streets," *Scientific American*, December 8, 2011, https://www .scientificamerican.com/article/london-taxi-memory/.

10. "Naive Bayes Classifiers," Geeks for Geeks, last modified May 15, 2020, https://www.geeksforgeeks.org/naive-bayes-classifiers/.

11. Rohith Gandhi, "Support Vector Machine—Introduction to Machine Learning Algorithms," Towards Data Science, June 7, 2018, https:// towardsdatascience.com/support-vector-machine-introduction-to-machine -learning-algorithms-934a444fca47.

12. Tony Yiu, "Understanding Random Forest," Towards Data Science, June 12, 2019, https://towardsdatascience.com/understanding-random-forest -58381e0602d2.

13. "Every Day Big Data Statistics—2.5 Quintillion Bytes of Data Created Daily," Dihuni: Digital Transformation Simplified, April 10, 2020, https:// www.dihuni.com/2020/04/10/every-day-big-data-statistics-2-5-quintillion -bytes-of-data-created-daily/.

14. "Herbert A. Simon," UBS Nobel Perspectives, accessed September 30, 2020, https://www.ubs.com/microsites/nobel-perspectives/en/laureates/herbert -simon.html.

15. Sam Anderson, "In Defense of Distraction," *New York,* May 15, 2009, https:// nymag.com/news/features/56793/.

16. "What is hyper-personalization?" HGS Digital, accessed September 30, 2020, https://www.hgsdigital.com/blogs/what-is-hyper-personalization.

17. Nick Edouard, "The Attention Economy: The Impact of Attention Scarcity on Modern Marketing," November 14, 2016, https://business.linkedin.com /marketing-solutions/blog/content-marketing-thought-leaders/2016/the -attention-economy---the-impact-of-attention-scarcity-on-mode.

18. Timothy Egan, "The Eight-Second Attention Span," *New York Times,* January 22, 2016, https://www.nytimes.com/2016/01/22/opinion/the-eight-second -attention-span.html.

19. "Think With Google," Google, accessed September 30, 2020, https://www
.thinkwithgoogle.com/feature/mobile-search-behavior/#/.

20. "Case Study: Of Innovation and a Brand New Revenue Stream," Infosys,
2018, https://www.infosys.com/navigate-your-next/digital-capabilities
/accelerate/revenue-stream.html.

21. "AlphaGo," DeepMind, accessed September 30, 2020, https://deepmind.com
/research/case-studies/alphago-the-story-so-far.

22. Jakob Uszkoreit,"Transformer: A Novel Neural Network Architecture for
Language Understanding," Google AI Blog, August 31, 2017, https://ai
.googleblog.com/2017/08/transformer-novel-neural-network.html.

23. "PWC's Global Artificial Intelligence Study: Sizing the Prize," PWC, 2017,
https://www.pwc.com/gx/en/issues/data-and-analytics/publications/artificial
-intelligence-study.html.

24. "General Data Protection Regulation," Regulation (EU) 2016/679 of the
European Parliament and of the Council, April 27, 2016, *Official Journal of
the European Union*, https://eur-lex.europa.eu/legal-content/EN/TXT/PDF/
?uri=CELEX:32016R0679.

25. Jeffrey Dastin, "Insight—Amazon Scraps Secret AI Recruiting Tool That
Showed Bias Against Women," Reuters, October 9, 2018, https://in.reuters
.com/article/amazon-com-jobs-automation/insight-amazon-scraps-secret-ai
-recruiting-tool-that-showed-bias-against-women-idINKCN1MK0AH.

Chapter 6

1. Walter Salzburger, "Understanding Explosive Diversifications Through
Cichlid Fish Genomics," *Nature Reviews Genetics,* no. 19 (2018): 705–717,
https://doi.org/10.1038/s41576-018-0043-9.

2. "The 17 Goals," Sustainable Development, Department of Economic and
Social Affairs, United Nations, accessed September 29, 2020, https://sdgs.un
.org/goals.

3. "Education: From Disruption to Recovery," UNESCO, accessed September
29, 2020, https://en.unesco.org/covid19/educationresponse.

4. "Malcolm Knowles, Informal Adult Education, Self-Direction, and
Andragogy," Infed.org, last modified April 4, 2013, https://infed.org/mobi
/malcolm-knowles-informal-adult-education-self-direction-and-andragogy/.

5. Jackson Nickerson, C. James Yen, and Josepht T. Mahoney, "Exploring
the Problem-Finding and Problem-Solving Approach for Designing
Organizations," *Academy of Management Perspective,* no. 1 (2012): 52–72,
http://dx.doi.org/10.5465/amp.2011.0106.

6. "Social Learning Theory (Albert Bandura)," InstructionalDesign.org, accessed September 20, 2020, http://www.instructionaldesign.org/theories/social -learning/.

7. "Operant Conditioning (B. F. Skinner)," InstructionalDesign.org, accessed September 20, 2020, http://www.instructionaldesign.org/theories/operant -conditioning/.

Chapter 7

1. Anne Casselman, "Strange but True: The Largest Organism on Earth Is a Fungus," *Scientific American,* October 4, 2007, https://www.scientificamerican .com/article/strange-but-true-largest-organism-is-fungus/.

2. Sabine C. Jung, Ainhoa Martinez-Medina, Juan A. Lopez-Raez, and Maria J. Pozo, "Mycorrhiza-Induced Resistance and Priming of Plant Defenses," *Journal of Chemical Ecology* 38 (May 24, 2012): 651–664, https://doi.org/10 .1007/s10886-012-0134-6.

3. Maria Popova, "The Secret Life of Trees: The Astonishing Science of What Trees Feel and How They Communicate," accessed September 30, 2020, https://www.brainpickings.org/2016/09/26/the-hidden-life-of-trees-peter -wohlleben/.

4. "What Is India Stack," About Indiastack.org, accessed September 27, 2020, https://www.indiastack.org/about/.

5. Jeff Kavanaugh and Chad Watt, "Infosys Digital Radar 2020: From Digital Maturity to Living Enterprise," Infosys, January 2020, https://www.infosys .com/navigate-your-next/research/digital-radar-report.html.

6. "Lens of Time: Huddle Masters," biographic, April 24, 2018, https://www .biographic.com/lens-of-time-huddle-masters/.

7. "Gartner Survey Reveals 82% of Company Leaders Plan to Allow Employees to Work Remotely Some of the Time," Gartner press release, July 14, 2020, https://www.gartner.com/en/newsroom/press-releases/2020-07-14-gartner -survey-reveals-82-percent-of-company-leaders-plan-to-allow-employees-to -work-remotely-some-of-the-time.

Chapter 8

1. Rebecca J. Rosen, "6 Animals That Can See or Glow in Ultraviolet Light," *The Atlantic,* August 15, 2011, https://www.theatlantic.com/technology /archive/2011/08/6-animals-that-can-see-or-glow-in-ultraviolet-light/243634/.

2. Sharla Riddle, "How Bees See and Why It Matters," *Bee Culture: The Magazine of American Beekeeping,* May 20, 2016, https://www.beeculture.com /bees-see-matters/.

3. Owen Gaffney, "11 Reasons Bees Matter," World Economic Forum, February 20, 2016, https://www.weforum.org/agenda/2016/02/to-bee-or-not-to-bee-11 -reasons-pollinators-matter/.

4. George A. Miller, "The Magical Number Seven, Plus or Minus Two: Some Limits on Our Capacity for Processing Information, *Psychological Review* 63, no. 2 (1956): 81–97. https://doi.org/10.1037/h0043158.

Chapter 9

1. Michael J. Behe, *The Edge of Evolution* (New York: The Free Press, 2007).

2. "What Is India Stack," About Indiastack.org, accessed September 27, 2020, https://www.indiastack.org/about/.

3. Ed Pegg, Jr., "Lebombo Bone," MathWorld, accessed September 30, 2020, from https://mathworld.wolfram.com/LebomboBone.html.

4. Bruce McClure, "How Often Do We Have a Blue Moon," EarthSky, January 31, 2015, https://earthsky.org/sky-archive/july-2015-blue-moon-and-the-19 -year-metonic-cycle.

5. Chenhao Tan, Vlad Niculae, Cristian Danescu-Niculescu-Mizil, and Lillian Lee, "Winning Arguments: Interaction Dynamics and Persuasion Strategies in Good-Faith Online Discussions," *International World Wide Web Conference Committee,* April 2016, http://dx.doi.org/10.1145/2872427.2883081.

6. Richard H. Thaler and Cass R. Sunstein, *Nudge: Improving Decisions About Health, Wealth, and Happiness* (New York: Penguin, 2016).

Chapter 10

1. Heather Scoville, "The 5 Major Mass Extinctions," ThoughtCo, last modified January 8, 2020, https://www.thoughtco.com/the-5-major-mass-extinctions -4018102.

2. Jon Tennant, "Toothy, Rodent-Like Reptile Is Our Ancient Forebear," *Discover,* October 5, 2016, https://www.discovermagazine.com/planet-earth /toothy-rodent-like-reptile-is-our-ancient-forebear.

3. Charles Darwin, *The Origin of Species by Means of Natural Selection*, 1859, online version accessed September 29, 2002, Darwin Online, http://darwin -online.org.uk/Variorum/1866/1866-412-c-1859.html.

4. Joseph Schumpeter, *Capitalism, Socialism and Democracy* (London: Routledge, 1942/1994), 82–83.

5. Janine Benyus, *Biomimicry: Innovation Inspired by Nature* (New York: William Morrow, 1997).

6. DXC Technology, "Digital Transformation Is Racing Ahead and No Industry Is Immune, *Harvard Business Review* (July 19, 2017), https://hbr.org/sponsored/2017/07/digital-transformation-is-racing-ahead-and-no-industry-is-immune-2.

7. Kiran Bhageshpur, "Data Is the New Oil—and That's a Good Thing," *Forbes*, November 15, 2019, https://www.forbes.com/sites/forbestechcouncil/2019/11/15/data-is-the-new-oil-and-thats-a-good-thing/#4be8a8a87304.

8. Tom Siebel, "Surviving 'A Mass Extinction Event in the Corporate World,'" podcast interview with Saikat Chaudhuri, William and Phillis Mack Institute for Innovation Management, Wharton School of Business, University of Pennsylvania, last modified August 15, 2019, https://mackinstitute.wharton.upenn.edu/2019/surviving-a-mass-extinction-event-corporate-world/

9. "Ambassador from the Future," John Elkington, accessed September 29, 2020, https://johnelkington.com/.

10. Gordon L. Clark, Andreas Feiner, and Michael Viehs, "From the Stockholder to the Stakeholder: How Sustainability Can Drive Financial Outperformance" (March 5, 2015), SSRN, http://dx.doi.org/10.2139/ssrn.2508281.

11. John Elkington, "25 Years Ago I Coined the Phrase 'Triple Bottom Line': Here's Why It's Time to Rethink It," *Harvard Business Review* (June 25, 2018), https://hbr.org/2018/06/25-years-ago-i-coined-the-phrase-triple-bottom-line-heres-why-im-giving-up-on-it.

12. Michael E. Porter, George Serafeim, and Mark Kramer, "Where ESG Fails," *Institutional Investor* (October 16, 2019), https://www.institutionalinvestor.com/article/b1hm5ghqtxj9s7/Where-ESG-Fails.

13. Klaus Schwab, "Davos Manifesto 2020: The Universal Purpose of a Company in the Fourth Industrial Revolution," World Economic Forum, December 2, 2019, https://www.weforum.org/agenda/2019/12/davos-manifesto-2020-the-universal-purpose-of-a-company-in-the-fourth-industrial-revolution/.

14. Klaus Schwab, "Why We Need the 'Davos Manifesto' for a Better Kind of Capitalism," World Economic Forum, December 1, 2019, https://www.weforum.org/agenda/2019/12/why-we-need-the-davos-manifesto-for-better-kind-of-capitalism/.

15. Jeff Kavanaugh, Kerry Taylor, and Nikki Seifert, "CMO and C-Suite: The DNA of Partnership" (in press; publication expected November 2020), Infosys Knowledge Institute.

16. James H. Stock and Mark W. Watson, "Has the Business Cycle Changed and Why?," *NBER Macroeconomics Annual*, no. 17 (January 2003): 159–230, https://www.nber.org/chapters/c11075.pdf.

17. "The Great Reset," World Economic Forum, accessed September 29, 2020, https://www.weforum.org/great-reset/.

18. Warren Buffet, "Berkshire Hathaway Letter to Shareholders," 2001.

19. Jenn-Hui Tan and Benjamin Moshinsky, "Outrunning a Crisis: Sustainability and Market Outperformance," *Fidelity International,* April 16, 2020, https://www.fidelityinternational.com/editorial/article/outrunning-a-crisis-sustainability-and-market-outperformance-2ce135-en5/.

20. Black Rock Investment Institute, *Sustainable Investing: Resilience and Uncertainty,* accessed September 29, 2020, https://www.blackrock.com/corporate/literature/investor-education/sustainable-investing-resilience.pdf.

21. Alex Cheema-Fox, Bridget R. LaPerla, George Serafeim, and Hui (Stacie) Wang, *Corporate Resilience and Response During COVID-19* (Working Paper 2018), https://www.hbs.edu/faculty/Publication%20Files/20-108_6f241583-89ac-4d2f-b5ba-a78a4a17babb.pdf.

22. Business Roundtable, *Statement on the Purpose of a Corporation,* August 2019, https://opportunity.businessroundtable.org/wp-content/uploads/2020/09/BRT-Statement-on-the-Purpose-of-a-Corporation-September-2020.pdf.

23. BlackRock, "Sustainability as BlackRock's New Standard for Investing," accessed September 2020, https://www.blackrock.com/corporate/investor-relations/blackrock-client-letter.

24. Nassim Taleb, *The Black Swan: The Impact of the Highly Improbable* (New York: Random House, 2007).

25. John Elkington, *Green Swans: The Coming Boom in Regenerative Capitalism* (New York: Fast Company Press, 2020).

26. "Jay Coen Gilbert, Bart Houlahan, and Andrew Kassoy—B-Lab Founders: Heroes of Conscious Capitalism," Conscious Capitalism, accessed September 29, 2020, https://www.consciouscapitalism.org/heroes/b-lab-founders.

27. "B Lab Honored as a 2020 World's Most Innovative Company by Fast Company," March 10, 2020, https://bcorporation.net/news/worlds-most-innovative-company-fast-company-2020.

28. Christopher Marquis, *Better Business: How the B Corp Movement Is Remaking Capitalism* (New Haven: Yale University Press, 2020).

29. "Pristine Seas," National Geographic, accessed September 29, 2020, https://www.nationalgeographic.org/projects/pristine-seas/.

30. Enric Sala, *The Nature of Nature: Why We Need the Wild* (Washington, DC: National Geographic, 2020).

31. World Wildlife Fund, "Living Planet Index," accessed September 29, 2020, https://livingplanetindex.org/home/index.

32. World Economic Forum, "Measuring Stakeholder Capitalism: Towards Common Metrics and Consistent Reporting of Sustainable Value Creation," September 2020, http://www3.weforum.org/docs/WEF_IBC_Measuring_Stakeholder_Capitalism_Report_2020.pdf.

33. "Non-Financial Reporting," European Commission, accessed September 29, 2020, https://ec.europa.eu/info/business-economy-euro/company-reporting-and-auditing/company-reporting/non-financial-reporting_en.

34. "Bretton Woords Monetary Conference, July 1–22, 1944," The World Bank, accessed September 29, 2020, https://www.worldbank.org/en/about/archives /history/exhibits/bretton-woods-monetary-conference.

35. Steve Denning, "The Origin of 'The World's Dumbest Idea': Milton Friedman," *Forbes,* June 26, 2013, https://www.forbes.com/sites/stevedenning /2013/06/26/the-origin-of-the-worlds-dumbest-idea-milton-friedman/.

36. Jamie Metzl, "Declaration of Global Interdependence," March 21, 2020, https://jamiemetzl.com/declaration-of-global-interdependence/.

37. "Our Strategy," OneSharedWorld, accessed September 29, 2020, https:// oneshared.world/strategy/.

38. "Text of President John Kennedy's Rice Stadium Moon Speech," US National Aeronautics and Space Administration, accessed September 29, 2020, https:// er.jsc.nasa.gov/seh/ricetalk.htm.

39. William Harwood, "Apollo 11: How Much Did It Cost to Land Astronauts on the Moon?" CBS News, July 16, 2019, https://www.cbsnews.com/news /apollo-11-moon-landing-how-much-did-it-cost/.

Epilogue

1. Carl Sagan, *Pale Blue Dot: A Vision of the Human Future in Space* (New York: Random House, 1994).

INDEX

Page numbers followed by *f* and *t* refer to figures and tables, respectively.

ABOUT THE AUTHORS

Jeff Kavanaugh is vice president and global head of the Infosys Knowledge Institute, the research and thought leadership arm of tech services leader Infosys. Over a 30-year career that has spanned industry, consulting, and tech, Jeff has worked with dozens of companies around the world to improve their competitiveness and accelerate growth. He has served clients across a variety of industries, with a focus on manufacturing and high-tech.

He also serves as an adjunct professor at the Jindal School of Management at the University of Texas at Dallas. He has trained thousands of business consultants and students in areas ranging from foundational critical thinking and communication to strategic frameworks and analytical reasoning. Jeff is the author of *Consulting Essentials: The Art & Science of People, Facts, and Frameworks*, a guide to core professional skills for the digital age.

He has been published in *Harvard Business Review* and other leading periodicals. Jeff has spoken at the World Economic Forum in Davos, the United Nations, and is a regular speaker and chair at conferences in the US and Europe. He also serves as an advisor to the United Nations, universities, and early stage companies. He lives in the Dallas/Ft. Worth area. (https://jeffkavanaugh.net)

Rafee Tarafdar is a senior vice president and chief technology officer of the Strategic Technology Group at Infosys. Rafee leads the company's unit of technology strategists who define and drive large transformational programs and platforms; power programmers who work as full stack developers on complex engineering projects for clients; and expert trackers who bring in deep technical expertise in emerging technology areas while building platforms and solutions for Infosys.

With over twenty years of IT experience, from coding and developing products for the manufacturing and banking industries, to consulting on transformational solutions for retail, consumer goods and logistics clients. Currently he builds deep architecture, technology and programming capabilities, develops new go-to market solutions, and builds platforms for Infosys and their clients. He is based in Bangalore, India.